Word Order in the
Biblical Hebrew Finite Clause

Linguistic Studies in Ancient West Semitic

edited by

M. O'Connor† and Cynthia L. Miller

The series Linguistic Studies in Ancient West Semitic is devoted to the ancient West Semitic languages, including Hebrew, Aramaic, Ugaritic, and their near congeners. It includes monographs, collections of essays, and text editions informed by the approaches of linguistic science. The material studied will span from the earliest texts to the rise of Islam.

Word Order in the Biblical Hebrew Finite Clause

A Syntactic and Pragmatic Analysis of Preposing

ADINA MOSHAVI

Winona Lake, Indiana
EISENBRAUNS
2010

www.eisenbrauns.com

Library of Congress Cataloging-in-Publication Data

Moshavi, A. Mosak (Adina Mosak)
    Word order in the biblical Hebrew finite clause : a syntactic and
pragmatic analysis of preposing / Adina Moshavi.
        p.   cm. — (Linguistic studies in ancient West Semitic ; 4)
    Includes bibliographical references and indexes.
    ISBN 978-1-57506-191-7 (hardback : alk. paper)
    1. Hebrew language—Clauses.   2. Hebrew language—Word
order.   3. Bible. O.T.—Language, style.   I. Title.
    PJ4717.M67   2010
    492.4′5—dc22
                                                                2010013367

To my parents,
Dr. Richard and Orah Mosak

and to my husband,
Shimon

Contents

List of Tables

Abbreviations

General

BH	Biblical Hebrew
NAB	New American Bible
NJB	New Jerusalem Bible
NJPSV	New Jewish Publication Society Version
NP	noun phrase
NRSV	New Revised Standard Version
O	object
RSV	Revised Standard Version
S	subject
V	verb
VP	verb phrase

Reference Works

AfroLing	*Afroasiatic Linguistics*
BDB	Brown, Francis; Driver, S. R.; and Briggs, Charles A. *A Hebrew and English Lexicon of the Old Testament*. Oxford: Clarendon, 1907
BHS	Elliger, K., and Rudolph, W., editors. *Biblia Hebraica Stuttgartensia*. Stuttgart: Deutsche Bibelgesellschaft, 1984
BI	*Balšanut Ivrit*
Bib	*Biblica*
BibOr	*Bibliotheca Orientalis*
BN	*Biblische Notizen*
BSOAS	*Bulletin of the School of Oriental and African Studies*
DiscProc	*Discourse Processes*
FolOr	*Folia Orientalia*
GKC	*Gesenius' Hebrew Grammar*, ed. E. Kautzsch, rev. A. E. Cowley. 2nd ed. Oxford: Clarendon, 1910
HALOT	Köhler, Ludwig and Baumgartner, Walter. *The Hebrew and Aramaic Lexicon of the Old Testament,* rev. Walter Baumgartner et al. 1st English ed. 5 vols. Leiden: Brill, 1994-2000
HAR	*Hebrew Annual Review*
HS	*Hebrew Studies*
HUCA	*Hebrew Union College Annual*
IOS	*Israel Oriental Studies*
JANES	*Journal of the Ancient Near Eastern Society*

JAOS	*Journal of the American Oriental Society*
JBL	*Journal of Biblical Literature*
JLing	*Journal of Linguistics*
JNSL	*Journal of Northwest Semitic Langagues*
Joüon-Muraoka	Joüon, Paul. *A Grammar of Biblical Hebrew*, trans. and rev. T. Muraoka. Subsidia Biblica 14. 2 vols. Rome: Pontifical Biblical Institute, 1991
JPrag	*Journal of Pragmatics*
JQR	*Jewish Quarterly Review*
JSem	*Journal for Semitics*
JSOT	*Journal for the Study of the Old Testament*
JSOTSup	Journal for the Study of the Old Testament Supplement Series
JSS	*Journal of Semitic Studies*
JTT	*Journal of Translation and Textlinguistics*
KUSATU	*Kleine Untersuchungen zur Sprache des Alten Testaments und seiner Umwelt*
Lang	*Language*
LingBer	*Linguistische Berichte*
Leš	*Lešonénu*
LešLaᶜam	*Lešonénu Laᶜam*
Ling	*Linguistics*
LingInq	*Linguistic Inquiry*
Or	*Orientalia*
OTS	*Oudtestamentische Studiën*
Philos	*Philosophica*
Prag	*Pragmatics*
RB	*Revue Biblique*
SBLSemeiaSt	Society of Biblical Literature Semeia Studies
SBLMS	Society of Biblical Literature Monograph Series
ScrHier	*Scripta Hierosolymitana*
Sem	*Semitics*
SIL	Summer Institute of Linguistics
SIGLA	Studies in Generative Linguistic Analysis
SJOT	*Scandinavian Journal of the Old Testament*
SSLL	Studies in Semitic Languages and Linguistics
SSN	Studia Semitica Neerlandica
TheorLing	*Theoretical Linguistics*
TSL	Typological Studies in Language
VT	*Vetus Testamentum*
VTSup	Vetus Testamentum Supplements
ZAH	*Zeitschrift für Althebraistik*
ZAW	*Zeitschrift für die alttestamentliche Wissenschaft*

Technical Notes

The translations of the biblical citations in this work are my own, in consultation primarily with the NJPSV, RSV, and NRSV. An attempt is made to render the syntactic structure of the Hebrew as literally as possible, for the purposes of illustrating the syntactic analyses presented in the text. The results are at times far from idiomatic.

Preposed clauses in the citations are generally marked by underlining when the citation contains more than one clause. Citations consisting of a single preposed clause are not underlined.

The symbol * is used to mark an ungrammatical sentence, and # marks a sentence that is pragmatically unacceptable, being inappropriate in the given context.

Preface

This book has its origins in my 2000 dissertation, *The Pragmatics of Word Order in Biblical Hebrew: A Statistical Analysis*, completed at Yeshiva University under the direction of Richard C. Steiner. I submitted the dissertation to Eisenbrauns that same year, intending to publish it with minor revisions. Continuing to study pragmatic and syntactic issues related to word order over the next six years, I worked on what turned out to be, essentially, an entirely new book on Biblical Hebrew word order. The completed manuscript was submitted to Eisenbrauns in November 2006 and accepted for publication in May 2007.

My dissertation dealt with the pragmatics of inverted (XV) word order in declarative nonsubordinate finite clauses in Genesis and showed by means of multivariate statistical analysis that focus-background structure (including focusing and topicalization, as defined there) and nonsequentiality are associated with word order inversion. In preparing the book, I broadened the scope of the project by including all nonsubordinate finite clauses and analyzed a much larger corpus, Genesis–2 Kings, with the help of electronic searches for various syntactic constructions. The result of the syntactic analysis, presented in chapter 5, is a taxonomy of marked and unmarked word-order constructions in the finite clause. I also gave further attention to the fundamental question whether VSO or SVO is the basic word order in Biblical Hebrew; the conclusions are presented in chapter 2.

On reflection, it became clear that the pragmatic categories used in the dissertation, based as they were to a large degree on discussions in the general linguistic literature, artificially excluded many biblical clauses that intuitively appear to belong to the same categories. A key insight was realizing that focusing and topicalization are fundamentally different kinds of pragmatic functions, not two variations of focus-background structure, as is often claimed (see §6.2 below). In this book, focusing and topicalization have been reconceptualized, using insights from psycholinguistic research on text comprehension and from linguistic research on discourse connectives. The newly defined concepts, I believe, are more intuitively satisfying and represent a significant advance in the understanding of marked word-order function in Biblical Hebrew and, potentially, in other languages as well.

In writing this book, I made considerable effort to present linguistic concepts in clear language and keep cumbersome theoretical apparatuses to a minimum. Multivariate statistical analysis has been omitted on the grounds that it is unnecessary for the purposes of the analysis here. The discussion of the literature has been completely reorganized, with the various approaches categorized under three general models and related to the theoretical linguistic theories that inform them.

An earlier formulation of part of chapter 7 appeared in "The Discourse Functions of Object/Adverbial-Fronting in Biblical Hebrew," in *Biblical Hebrew in Its Northwest Semitic Setting: Typological and Historical Perspectives* (ed. Steven E. Fassberg and Avi Hurvitz; Publication of the Institute for Advanced Studies 1; Jerusalem: Magnes / Winona Lake, IN: Eisenbrauns, 2006), 231–45. An abbreviated version of chapter 8 appeared as "Focus Preposing in Biblical Hebrew" in *Leš* 71 (2009): 35–55 (in Hebrew), and an abbreviated version of chapter 9 appeared as "Topicalization in Biblical Hebrew" in *Leš* 69 (2007): 7–30 (in Hebrew).

The literature on word order in linguistic theory and word order in Biblical Hebrew, already quite considerable at the time of the completion of the manuscript in 2006, has continued to grow. Studies appearing in late 2006 and onward were available too late to be treated in any depth here. An example is Robert D. Holmstedt's 2009 study ("Word Order and Information Structure in Ruth and Jonah: A Generative-Typological Analysis," *JSS* 54:111–39), which presents a more developed pragmatic framework than his earlier studies of word order (see §§2.2.2–2.2.3 below). Word order in biblical poetry has received a great deal of attention of late, no doubt stimulated in large part by Nicholas P. Lunn's 2006 monograph (*Word-Order Variation in Biblical Hebrew Poetry: Differentiating Pragmatics and Poetics*; Paternoster Biblical Monographs; Milton Keynes: Paternoster). The present work does not address word order in poetry, but the concepts of focusing and topicalization developed here can serve as an alternative to the Lambrechtian framework used by Lunn (see §3.3.7, below).

It is a great pleasure to thank those who helped this project come to completion. I am deeply grateful to Richard C. Steiner, who has been my teacher and mentor since I was an undergraduate. As his student, I discovered my love for Hebrew studies and linguistics. Richard Steiner's rigorous and innovative approach to language and textual study has been the inspiration for my research. He has been a tireless source of support throughout the doctoral years and beyond. I particularly thank him for his comments on the dissertation and on the new manuscript.

I would like to thank the other members of my dissertation committee, Ellen F. Prince and Joshua Blau, for their assistance. Ellen Prince provided useful guidance on linguistic issues, and Joshua Blau offered helpful comments. I am particularly grateful to the editors of this series, the late Michael P. O'Connor and Cynthia L. Miller, for their detailed and extensive comments on the dissertation. I would like to thank Amy Becker at Eisenbrauns for her careful copyediting and proofreading of the final manuscript.

I had the opportunity to present some of my work to the international research group on the subject of Biblical Hebrew in its northwest Semitic setting at the Institute for Advanced Study at Hebrew University in 2001–2. I am grateful to many members of the research group, including Steven E. Fassberg, W. Randall Garr, Edward L. Greenstein, Jo Ann Hackett, John Huehnergard, Avi Hurvitz, Jan Joosten, and Elisha Qimron, for their valuable comments. In addition, I thank Elitzur Bar-Asher, Yochanan Breuer, Randall Buth, Vincent DeCaen, Robert D. Holmstedt, Uri Mor, and Yael Ziv for their very helpful comments on various drafts of my work. I also thank Moshe Bar-Asher and my colleagues at the Hebrew University of Jerusalem and Bar Ilan University for their encouragement and support.

Financial assistance came from several sources. I would like to thank the Bernard Revel Graduate School of Yeshiva University for its generous assistance. I am grateful for a doctoral scholarship from the Memorial Foundation for Jewish Culture and for a doctoral dissertation fellowship from the National Foundation for Jewish Culture. I would also like to thank the staff at the Yeshiva University libraries for their research assistance.

This book is dedicated to my beloved parents, Richard and Orah Mosak, to whom I owe everything. They instilled in me a love of learning and encouraged me to follow my ambitions. The ideals they imbued in me have guided me in every area of my life. I also dedicate this work to my husband and soul-mate, Shimon, who has provided unflagging support for all my endeavors. Without his help, it would have been unfeasible to immerse myself in academic pursuits while simultaneously raising five young children. I am also grateful to Shimon for proofreading and commenting on large portions of the manuscript.

My paternal grandparents, Jacob and Pearl Mosak, have been a source of inspiration for me in so many ways. I am grateful to them for their love and support. My late maternal grandparents, Abraham and Shalva Eliezri, were also a source of much love and encouragement. Their passion for their ideals made an indelible impression on me and helped to shape the course of my life. I am grateful to my father- and mother-in-law, Baruch and Ettie Moshavi, for their love and encouragement. Finally, I thank my children, Elisheva, Chaviva, Tziona, Gavriel, and Zecharya, for tolerating the many hours I spent completing this work and, more importantly, for bringing me so much happiness.

Chapter 1

Introduction

1.1. The pragmatics of preposing

Over the last 40 years, the study of word-order variation has become a prominent and fruitful field of research. Researchers of linguistic typology have found that every language permits a variety of word-order constructions, with subject, verb, and objects occupying varying positions relative to each other.[1] It is frequently possible to classify one of the word orders as the *basic* or *unmarked* order, and the others as *marked*.[2] Converting a sentence from an unmarked to a marked construction does not affect the semantic content of the sentence; it does, however, restrict the conditions under which the sentence could serve as an appropriate uterance. Marked syntactic constructions have pragmatic meaning, that is, they encode aspects of meaning which are not semantic but concern the relation of an utterance to its context.[3] Put another way, marked constructions provide an instruction to the addressee regarding the interpretation of the utterance in its context. Marked syntactic constructions are part of a larger group of linguistic forms with a pragmatic contribution to the meaning of an utterance. The strides that have been made in understanding the functions of these forms have highlighted the extent of the interaction between pragmatics and language structure and have shown the importance of studying language as a communicative system.

This work investigates word order in the finite non-subordinate clause[4] in classical BH. A common marked construction in this type of clause is the *preposing* construction, in which a subject, object, or adverbial is placed before the verb. In this work, preposing is formally distinguished from other marked

---

1. The term *typology* has several uses in linguistics; the intended meaning here is the classification of structural language types and the study of language universals, that is, systematically occurring language patterns (Croft 2003: 1). Greenberg's (1966a, 1966b) seminal works form the foundation of this field. For a discussion of research on word order universals and their application to the Semitic language group, see O'Connor (1980: 115–18).

2. On the concept of markedness, see chap. 2, pp. 7ff.

3. For a discussion of pragmatics and its relation to semantics, see Levinson (1983: 1–35).

4. See chap. 4, pp. 48ff., for definitions of these and other syntactic terms relating to the BH clause.

1

and unmarked constructions, and the distribution of these constructions in BH is explored. A contextual analysis of a sample of preposed clauses is carried out in order to determine the pragmatic functions that preposing may express. My thesis is that the majority of preposed clauses can be classified as one of two syntactic-pragmatic constructions: *focusing* or *topicalization*.

In studying the preposing construction, I hope to further our understanding of the BH language system in use. I also hope that this study will contribute indirectly to the cross-linguistic investigation of the relation between linguistic form and pragmatic meaning.

1.2. The corpus for the study

The corpus for a linguistic study should be of a relatively homogeneous nature and should be large enough to yield statistically significant results. The criterion of homogeneity poses a challenge for the study of the Bible, which contains books of various literary genres written over a long period of time. The prose and poetic genres in the Bible have been shown to differ in various linguistic characteristics. For example, the definite article ה, the relative particle אשר, and the object marker את are often lacking in poetry (Freedman 1977; Andersen and Forbes 1983). According to O'Connor (1980: 401), verb gapping occurs in biblical poetry but not in prose.[5] More to the point, poetry appears to exhibit a greater degree of word-order variation than does poetry. For example, clauses with two constituents preceding the verb are rare in prose. In poetry, this pattern occurs with greater frequency (Bloch 1946: 39; O'Connor 1980: 334–35, 342–44).[6]

The present work is limited to the analysis of word order in prose, because, as Joosten (2002) writes, "it is a general rule in research in morphosyntax to take on poetic texts only when the prose rules have been approximately established," a rule equally apt with respect to syntactic-pragmatic research. The exact border between prose and poetry is difficult to determine. Poetry is usually identified based on an accumulation of poetic criteria, none of which is exclusive to poetic texts (Freedman 1977: 6; Watson 1984: 46–57). The identification of isolated poetic segments within a prose text is particularly hazardous, because prose too may make use of poetic devices such as parallelism and chiasmus.[7] In this study, I follow *BHS* in categorizing passages as

---

5. On this point, however, see §9.3 n. 19 (p. 152 below). For a comprehensive study of the syntactic characteristics of biblical poetry, see Sappan (1981). Syntactic studies that are specifically limited to prose texts include Hoftijzer (1981, 1985), de Regt (1988), and Miller (2003).

6. On word-order patterns in poetry, see O'Connor (1980: 297–355), Floor (2005), Rosenbaum (1997), and Lunn (2006).

7. Berlin (1985: 4–16) writes that, though the essential feature of poetry is parallelism, parallelism is also found in prose. The difference is that, in poetry, parallelism is the constructive principle of the text, while in prose it is not used systematically. A similar idea is

prose or poetry, while recognizing that differences of opinion exist regarding specific passages.

Another source of linguistic heterogeneity in the Bible is the diachronic dimension. Scholars distinguish three historical stages of BH: the archaic phase, exhibited in certain poetic passages; the classical phase, dating from the Preexilic Period; and the late phase, dating from the Exilic and Postexilic Period.[8] The classical BH prose corpus consists of the five books of the Pentateuch and the Former Prophets (Joshua–Kings). Late BH texts, such as Ezra–Nehemiah, Chronicles, and Esther, betray the influence of Aramaic and other languages and differ from classical texts in vocabulary, idiomatic constructions, and syntax.[9] The present work is restricted to word order in the classical dialect of BH, that is, word order as manifested in the Genesis–2 Kings corpus.[10] Although source criticism assigns the origins of these books to sources dating from different historical periods, the language of this corpus "presents an astonishing degree of uniformity," particularly in the area of syntax (Joüon-Muraoka §3a).[11]

The conclusions reached in this study are based on two corpuses, one contained within the other. The syntactic analysis of finite non-subordinate word order constructions, presented in chap. 5, is based on computerized searches of the classical BH prose corpus, that is, the prose portions of Genesis–2 Kings.[12] In addition, a statistical analysis of the word order constructions in the prose portions of Genesis (henceforth referred to as the Genesis corpus) was

---

expressed in Jakobsen (1967). Greenstein (2000) notes that parallelism is often found in direct speech in prose passages in the Bible and suggests that this preserves an ancient literary convention. Kugel (1981) takes the radical view that the frequent presence of parallelism in prose texts makes the prose/poetry dichotomy inaccurate and misleading as applied to Biblical Hebrew. For further discussion of the use of poetic devices in prose, see §8.5.

8. On this classification of the stages of BH, see, e.g., Hurvitz (1972, 1982); Kutscher (1982: 12); Joüon-Muraoka (§3b); Rendsburg (1991); Steiner (1997: 146).

9. On late BH syntax, see, e.g., Kropat (1909); Hurvitz (1972, 1982); Polzin (1976); Rooker (1990a, 1990b).

10. This corpus is the basis of linguistic studies such as van der Merwe (1990) and Miller (2003). It might argue against the linguistic unity of this corpus that the traditional dating of the Priestly source (P) in source criticism is in the Postexilic Period. Linguistic evidence shows, however, that this dating of P is mistaken. Hurvitz (1982) finds that the linguistic features of the texts assigned to P are compatible with those of classical prose texts, and exclusively late features do not occur at all in P. According to Hurvitz, P predates Ezekiel, which he views as the transition between classical and late BH. See also Rendsburg (1980). Literary evidence for the preexilic dating of P is presented in Zevit (1982) and Friedman (1997).

11. Despite an overall picture of uniformity, some degree of variation is present in the corpus. Variation is not always attributable to diachronic factors and sometimes can be given a sociological interpretation, as Labov (1972) and others have shown. In addition, as noted by Miller (2003: 27), a certain degree of variation is present even in a homogeneous speech community.

12. The searches were carried out using the Bibloi 8.0 software package, published by Silver Mountain Software.

performed (see §5.6). The selection of Genesis for the statistical analysis was motivated by the fact that this book is a long classical work consisting almost entirely of prose. Because the overwhelming majority of finite clauses in BH prose are unmarked, a long text must be analyzed to yield a sufficient number of marked clauses. The pragmatic analysis of the preposing construction, presented in chaps. 7–9, is based on a contextual examination of all of the finite nonsubordinate preposed clauses in the prose portions of Genesis.

The assumption is made here that the present form of Genesis constitutes a coherent text, regardless of its prehistory. Although Genesis is considered by source critics to have been composed from more than one source, it is widely recognized that the book, as it stands, is a unified literary work. Driver (1913: 8) writes of a "unity of plan" in Genesis that "has long been recognized by critics." Skinner (1930: ii, lxv) considers Genesis to be a "complete and well rounded whole," despite its composite origin as he sees it. In his view, the final redactor of Genesis combined several sources in a purposeful design, giving the work a unity that is "the plan of one particular writer."[13]

The text of Genesis is written in two different discourse registers: narrative and direct-speech quotations.[14] Direct-speech quotations in the Bible appear to be written not in the spoken register actually used in the biblical period but rather in a literary dialect (Rendsburg 1990: 19). We do not have a record of the spoken language itself, but it most likely resembled Mishnaic Hebrew, a literary dialect believed to be closely related to the earlier spoken one.[15] Although direct speech in BH does not represent the spoken register, it is nonetheless distinct from the narrative register. Both Macdonald (1975) and Mali (1983) note the greater degree of word order variation in direct speech as compared to narrative, and Macdonald (1975) notes additional syntactic differences of a systematic nature.

Polak (1999, 2001, 2003) identifies a variety of styles of quoted speech in BH, including a conversational style, a formal style, and styles that are combinations of the first two. The conversational style resembles spoken language in having a high number of clauses with at most one verbal complement, a low number of subordinate clauses, and a low number of long noun phrases. The formal style contrasts in each of these features, having more than one verbal

13. Other scholars who find unified literary structures in Genesis include Childs (1979: 145–57), Rendsburg (1986), Sarna (1989: xvi), Fokkelman (1991), and Alter (1996: xlii).

14. On the definition of direct speech and its distinction from indirect speech (categorized as narrative), see Miller (2003). The issue is addressed in the present work in §4.4.3. Heller (2004: 25) also recognizes narrative and direct speech as two primary types in BH prose but does not provide syntactic or other criteria for distinguishing the two. Heller distinguishes five types of direct speech, based in large part on Longacre's (e.g., 1982, 2003) discourse-type typology; these are narrative, predictive, expository, hortatory, and interrogative discourse.

15. See, e.g., Steiner (1992: 21); Sáenz-Badillos (1993: 112–13).

complement, many subordinate clauses, and many long noun phrases. Polak notes (2001: 63; 2003) that some BH narrative is written in a conversational style, which he argues indicates origin from an oral narrative.[16]

In this study, I distinguish only two registers, narrative and direct-speech quotations. Although Polak is undoubtedly right that we should recognize a variety of direct speech (as well as narrative) registers, the Genesis corpus is too small for a statistical comparison of all of the varieties. I will show that even with this oversimplified taxonomy it is possible to identify differences in the frequency and function of preposing in the two registers.

The text utilized in the present work is the Masoretic Text (MT), as exemplified by *BHS*. It is common practice in statistical studies of BH to base the analysis on an attested text, normally the MT, rather than a reconstructed one.[17] Regardless of the merits of textual criticism in any particular instance, it can be argued that including emendations in the data introduces undesirable elements of subjectivity and uncertainty to the statistical analysis. Although the notion of *the* MT is admittedly an oversimplification, differences between Masoretic manuscripts mostly concern vocalization, accentuation, or orthography, and as such are not relevant to syntax or pragmatics.[18] The same is true of the *Qere* and *Ketib* alternations in the Masoretic text of Genesis, with one exception.[19]

1.3. Overview of the chapters

Chapter 2 discusses word-order markedness and justifies the view that the basic word order in BH is verb first. A survey of the previous literature on the pragmatics of preposing is presented in chap. 3. Chapter 4 sets out syntactic definitions necessary for the selection and classification of the data in this

---

16. See also Polak (1999); he argues there that, in comparison to late BH, which is primarily in a written style, classical BH narrative exhibits more of the informal traits characteristic of spoken language.

17. Hurvitz's (1982: 19) comments on this procedure are instructive:

This procedure is not followed out of an axiomatic belief in the supremacy of MT, nor does it imply that it has reached us in exactly the same form in which it left the hands of the ancient writers. . . . However, at the same time it seems to us that a linguistic study whose central purpose is to seek facts and avoid conjectures, should base itself on *actual* texts—difficult though they might be—rather than depend on *reconstructed* texts. These latter are indeed free of difficulties and easy to work with; but we can never be absolutely certain that they ever existed in reality.

See also Rendsburg (1990: 31–32); Miller (2003: 18).

18. More substantive differences can be found in some medieval manuscripts; e.g., the word אחר 'after' in Gen 22:13 has the variant אחד 'one' in several manuscripts, a variant also reflected in the versions. The significance of medieval variants is a matter of debate. Many argue that these variants mostly originate in the medieval period and only coincidentally reflect ancient variants; see discussion in Tov (1992: 37–39) and Revell (1992: 598).

19. The exception is Gen 30:10 *Ketib* בגד *Qere* בא גד. The *Ketib* is probably a prepositional phrase meaning 'with luck'; the *Qere* is a complete clause meaning 'luck has come'.

study. Chapter 5 describes the syntactic varieties of the preposing construction and distinguishes preposing from other similar word-order constructions. A statistical analysis of word order in Genesis is also presented. Chapter 6 explores the concepts of focusing and topicalization and develops definitions to be applied to the biblical corpus. Chapter 7 examines the various pragmatic functions of the preposed clauses in Genesis and determines the frequency of focusing and topicalization. Chapter 8 presents a comprehensive syntactic and pragmatic analysis of focusing in BH. A comprehensive analysis of topicalization is presented in chap. 9. Conclusions are presented in chap. 10.

Chapter 2

Word-Order Markedness
in Biblical Hebrew

The present work proceeds on the principle that verb-subject-object (VSO) is the basic or unmarked order in BH. Marked constructions in which the subject, object, or adjunct precedes the verb are termed *preposed*. I use terms such as *preposing*, *moving*, and the like as a convenient way of describing the correspondence between marked and unmarked constructions, without specifically implying a transformational analysis.[1]

The VSO language group makes up about 10% of the languages in the world (Carnie and Guilfoyle 2000: 3), including most of the West Semitic languages, Egyptian, Berber, Celtic, and other languages (O'Connor 1980: 118).[2] Because the classification of BH as a VSO language is not entirely uncontroversial, it deserves explicit justification. The present chapter examines the arguments for and against basic VSO word order in BH. In §2.1, I examine the concept of basic word order. In §2.2, I examine previous studies of basic word order in BH. Conclusions are presented in §2.3.

2.1. Basic word order: Typological and generative perspectives

As noted in chap. 1,[3] language typology involves, among other things, the classification of languages according to their structural types (Croft 2003: 1). One of the parameters by which languages can be classified is basic word order. "Basic" is often understood to mean the pragmatically unmarked or neutral word order.[4] Of the several orders allowed by a particular language,

1. On the theory-neutral use of transformational terminology, see Birner and Ward (1998: 3); Huddleston and Pullum (2002: 48).
2. Modern Hebrew, however, is an SVO language; see, e.g., Ravid (1977: 23, 38); Berman (1980: 759–60 n. 1; 1997: 323–25).
3. See §1.1 n. 1 (p. 1).
4. The concept of markedness was first developed in the Prague school of linguistics and referred to the member of a pair of contrasting phonemes that is found in neutral contexts. Markedness was subsequently extended in a variety of ways to include disparate notions not exactly comparable to each other. Various criteria are said to be evidence of markedness in phonology, morphology, and syntax (Greenberg 1966b; Croft 2003: 87). The concept of markedness is examined in depth in Battistella (1996).

usually one order occurs in a wide variety of discourse contexts, whereas the others have more restricted uses. The word order with a broader contextual distribution is the unmarked or basic order. Dryer (1995: 112) defines the concept of pragmatic markedness as follows: "a construction is pragmatically marked relative to another if the range of contexts in which it is appropriate is a proper subset of the set of contexts in which the unmarked construction is used."[5] Because the unmarked order is pragmatically acceptable in all contexts, the use of the marked word order is always optional.

Basic word order is sometimes used to mean the statistically dominant order, the one that is most frequent in spoken or written texts.[6] There is a widespread assumption that the pragmatically neutral word order is also the most frequent. According to Greenberg (1966b: 67), textual frequency is the only criterion by which basic word order can be established. "Statistically dominant" is clearly a less meaningful definition of basic word order than "pragmatically neutral," because frequency is a feature of language use rather than language structure. In practice, however, researchers usually rely on textual frequency in establishing basic word order, because proving that a particular order is pragmatically neutral is an extremely involved procedure, requiring the identification and classification of all discourse contexts in which each word order occurs.

Dryer (1995) notes several potential difficulties with relying on textual frequency to determine basic word order. Word order frequency may vary in different text types, raising the question of which text types most accurately represent the frequencies of the various constructions. Longacre (1995: 333) states that narrative texts are the most reliable, while Downing (1995: 20) states that conversational texts are to be preferred. Others claim that conversation and narrative are both suitable as source data as long as the discourse is oral, rather than written (Croft 2003: 111–12). The best approach would appear to be to include a variety of text types in the analysis. A more serious problem is that it is theoretically possible that a word order might be pragmatically neutral yet not the most frequently occurring one; however, this appears to be an atypical situation (Dryer 1995). Dryer concludes that "frequency may be a useful *diagnostic* for pragmatic markedness, even if ultimately it is not a defining characteristic (1995: 116).

---

5. The concept of pragmatic markedness is a "privative" concept, as defined in O'Connor (2002). O'Connor writes (2002:32–33) that "where a linguistic phenomenon is associated with a privative opposition, the unmarked form is acceptable for the whole range of the phenomenon," and the "marked form is acceptable for a subset of the phenomenon."

6. For discussion of textual frequency and other criteria used in determining basic word order, see Brody (1984); Mithun (1992); Dryer (1995). Ziv (1988) examines a variety of criteria for determining basic word order in the register of Modern Hebrew found in children's literature.

It is claimed that there are "free word-order" languages that do not have a basic word order (Thompson 1978; Brody 1984; Comrie 1989: 88; Mithun 1992). In these languages, there is no one order that is statistically dominant and pragmatically neutral as compared to other orders. In languages of this sort, the word order in every sentence appears to be pragmatically motivated (Thompson 1978, Mithun 1992).

A different approach to basic order defines the concept according to the *basic-sentence* criterion. Siewierska (1988: 8) writes that "the term 'basic order' is typically identified with the order that occurs in stylistically neutral, independent, indicative clauses with full noun phrase (NP) participants, where the subject is definite, agentive and human, the object is a definite semantic patient, and the verb represents an action, not a state or event."[7] Because sentences satisfying all these requirements are uncommon, the basic-sentence criterion results in the vast majority of naturally occurring sentences being removed from consideration in determining unmarked word order. It is very possible, therefore, that the basic-sentence criterion and the statistical criterion will yield different unmarked word orders for a particular language.

An important point to be noted is the dependence of the basic-sentence criterion on the criterion of pragmatic neutrality. Basic sentences may exhibit more than one word order. To deal with this problem, Siewierska's criterion specifies that the unmarked order is the one found in "stylistically neutral" sentences. In effect, then, the basic sentence criterion is essentially the pragmatic criterion applied to a small subset of sentence types.

The typological conception of basic word order, whether based on pragmatic neutrality, statistical dominance, basic sentences, or a combination of the above, pertains to the surface structure of sentences. Generative grammarians often use "basic word order" in an entirely different sense, meaning the order that permits the simplest syntactic description of the language. The basic word order is the structure from which all other structures are considered to be derived. For example, McCawley (1970) argues that English is a VSO language because this is its underlying word order: SVO sentences are the product of a transformation inverting subject and verb in the underlying VSO clause. It should be understood that this argument is irrelevant to the *typological* characterization of English word order. The underlying word order in a language is not necessarily the same as the pragmatically neutral / statistically dominant order.

Subsequent works on word order by generative grammarians distinguish between the underlying basic word order from a generative perspective and the pragmatically neutral word order in surface structures. It is widely believed that all VSO languages have an underlying SVO word order, with the verb-first

---

7. A similar definition can be found in Mallinson and Blake (1981: 125).

order produced by movement rules (Carnie and Guilfoyle 2000). This position has not broken down the typological distinction between VSO and SVO languages; on the contrary, current research seeks to explain why the underlying SVO is transformed to VSO in neutral sentences in VSO languages. Both typological and generative conceptions of basic word order have been invoked in discussions of BH, as will be shown in §2.2.

2.2. Basic word order in Biblical Hebrew

Biblical scholars have long been aware that finite clauses in BH are most frequently verb-first.[8] This fact was noted by the 19th-century biblical exegete Malbim (Rabbi Meir Loeb ben Jeḥiel Michael, 1809–79). Malbim (1973: §111) states that the general rule is that the sentence begins with the verb. In his commentary on 1 Kgs 20:18, Malbim (1964: 209) explains this rule as deriving from the principle that the most important item comes first. The verb is generally first because it is usually most important. A noun may be preposed in order to specify something about the noun or in order to express contrast, contradiction, or exclusion (Malbim 1973: §111).[9]

Similar statements regarding word order can be found in the works of scholars such as Ewald (1879: §306b), Müller (1888: §§130–31), König (1897: §339a–e), Davidson (1901: §105), and GKC (§142a, f). In the view of these scholars, word order is motivated by emphasis. The first element in every clause is emphasized, being the newest or most important part of the sentence. In the ordinary verb-first clause, the emphasis is on the action expressed by the verb; if a different element, such as the subject, is emphasized, it will precede the verb. Recent works such as Revell (1989a) and Shimasaki (2002) closely resemble this approach; in their formulations, the element which is the focus of attention is the one that occurs first (see §3.3.4 and §3.3.7).

Viewed from the perspective of language typology, the view of BH described here comes very close to the modern concept of the free word-order language, in which the order of every clause is pragmatically motivated. In modern typology, however, languages are viewed as having free word order

8. The ensuing discussion concerns word order in the nonsubordinate clause. Word order in subordinate clauses is investigated by de Regt (1991), although his definition of the subordinate clause differs from the one followed in this work (see §2.3). According to de Regt, the percentage of verb-first subordinate clauses is even higher than verb-first nonsubordinate clauses. Peretz (1967: 94) states that word order in the relative clause is usually verb-first, as it is in the subordinate clause.

9. I am indebted to Richard Steiner for drawing my attention to the Malbim references. Steiner (1998) notes that the medieval Jewish exegetes are divided on the significance of word-order variation. Baḥye ben Asher (13th century), for example, argues that word order can affect meaning (1966: 2:415), while Abraham ibn Ezra (1089–164) states that word order variation is meaningless (commentary to Qoh 5:1).

only when they do not exhibit a statistically dominant word order—a situation not applicable to BH, as we will see.

Most twentieth-century scholars believe that BH does have a basic word order and that a pragmatic explanation should be sought only for marked word orders. According to the mainstream view, the basic order is VSO. Exponents of basic VSO include Brockelmann (1956: §48), Meyer (1972: §91.2), Lambert (1972: §1277), Givón (1977),[10] Bandstra (1982), Muraoka (1985), Waltke and O'Connor (1990: §8.3), Jongeling (1991), Buth (1995) and de Regt (1991, 2006), among others. Dissenting from this camp and arguing that basic word order is SVO are several researchers such as Joüon (1947)[11] and Schlesinger (1953) and, more recently, DeCaen (1995, 1999) and Holmstedt (2002). In §§2.2.1–2.2.3, I attempt to clarify the points of debate between the VSO and SVO camps and justify the VSO view. In §2.2.4, I address whether word order in BH varies according to discourse type, and in §2.2.5, I discuss word order in the nonverbal and the participial clause.

2.2.1. The statistical dominance of VSO in Biblical Hebrew

Although not every scholar explains how he or she defines basic word order, textual frequency is most frequently cited as evidence for basic VSO word order. Some scholars, such as Meyer and Lambert, do not use terms such as *basic* or *unmarked*, writing simply that BH word order is "mostly" or "habitually" verb first. In his revision of Joüon (1947), Muraoka explicitly links markedness and frequency, writing that "the statistically dominant and unmarked word order in the verbal clause is: Verb-Subject" (Joüon-Muraoka §155k).

According to Jongeling (1991), a statistical analysis of the book of Ruth shows that the verb precedes in 87% of finite clauses (including subordinate ones). In this work, I present a count of nonsubordinate finite clauses in the

---

10. Givón (1977) states that classical BH had a basic word order of VSO and gradually shifted to SVO in the Exilic Period. He compares the classical texts of Genesis and 2 Kings to four books usually held to be late, namely, Esther, Lamentations, Ecclesiastes, and the Song of Songs. These texts, as Givón admits, differ greatly from the classical texts as well as from each other in terms of discourse genre and content. Esther is prose narrative, like Genesis and 2 Kings, while Ecclesiastes belongs to the wisdom-literature genre, and Lamentations and the Song of Songs are poetry. As discussed in §1.2, poetic texts often exhibit a higher frequency of marked word order than prose. Givón's selection of these four texts as representative of late BH is particularly puzzling considering the existence of demonstrably late texts of a much more similar genre to Genesis and Kings, that is, Ezra–Nehemiah and Chronicles. Contrary to Givón's conclusion, these books appear to exhibit unmarked VSO word order, as noted by Buth (1995: 91 n. 11). Additional arguments against Givón's posip tion can be found in Buth (1995: 91).

11. In the revised edition of Joüon by Muraoka (Joüon-Muraoka §155k), Joüon's (1947: §155k) original statement, "L'ordre des mots dans la proposition verbale . . . est normalee ment: Suject-Verbe" is revised to reflect Muraoka's support for the standard VSO view (see §2.2.1.).

book of Genesis, a much larger corpus. The results are similar to Jongeling's, with 84% of verbal clauses having nonpreposed word order (see chap. 5). It is sometimes claimed that figures such as these are misleading because many of the clauses involved lack an explicit subject and are not really VSO. However, because BH drops pronominal subjects unless they precede the verb (see §5.1), one can argue that VO clauses can be classified together with VSO clauses. The case for this position is particularly strong for consecutive forms, where the pronoun can only have been dropped from the postverbal position.

In any case, even if only clauses with subjects are included, the evidence still seems to point to VSO. Jongeling finds that when an explicit subject is present, the subject precedes the verb in only 20% of the clauses. Hornkohl's (2003: 7) M.A. thesis on Genesis reaches a similar conclusion, also including subordinate clauses in the data: 79% of verbal clauses with an explicit subject are verb first.[12] The natural conclusion is that the unmarked position for both subject and object is after the verb.

Some scholars (e.g., Schlesinger 1953; Muraoka 1985: 29; Regt 1991: 160) are of the opinion that sentences with a *waw*-consecutive verb form (*wayyiqtol/ weqatal*) should not be considered in determining basic word order. A reason given for excluding this type of clause is that the subject necessarily follows the verb in these clauses (Muraoka 1985: 28).[13] Fleshing this statement out, the argument would seem to go something like this: the consecutive form is not just a "positional variant" (Revell 1989b: 32) of the simple form but has semantic or pragmatic significance of its own. A sentence involving this semantic/pragmatic factor (let us call it *x*) necessarily contains a consecutive form and, ipso facto, verb-first word order; only clauses lacking this factor exhibit word-order variation. According to this logic, including consecutive forms in the data inappropriately skews the results in favor of VSO word order.

What exactly *x* represents is unclear; but it certainly is not the most obvious candidate, temporal sequentiality. As will be discussed in §3.2, "consecutive" forms are not always sequential, nor must a clause relating a sequential event contain a consecutive form. A simpler explanation of the consecutive/simple-verb distribution is that verb form is conditioned on word order. The consecutive form is a positional variant of the simple form that is used whenever the verb immediately follows a conjunction. If any element intervenes between conjunction and verb, whether a negative particle, clausal adverb, or preposed constituent, a simple form is selected. As Blau (1993: §60) writes,[14]

---

12. This figure was obtained by combining the figures for verb-first order in narrative and direct speech, calculated separately by Hornkohl.

13. DeCaen (1995, 1999) and Holmstedt (2002, 2005) argue for the omission of consecutive forms on other grounds; for discussion, see §2.2.2.

14. See also Bergsträsser (1962: §6c); Revell (1989b: 3).

> The tenses with consecutive *waw* (*wayyqtl, weqtl*) are used whenever the syntac-
> tic environment permits the use of *waw copulative*; otherwise the simple tenses
> (*qtl, yqtl*) [are used].

It follows from this that eliminating consecutive forms from a text count is statistically invalid, skewing the results in favor of SVO by eliminating many VSO clauses from the data. Most clauses in BH start with the conjunction, particularly in narrative texts, but to a lesser extent in direct speech as well. I found that in Genesis more than 99% of clauses in narrative have a conjunc-tion, and 65% in direct speech. The vast majority of VSO clauses (excluding those containing preverbal particles), then, will necessarily have a consecutive form and would not be counted.

In his examination of word order, Muraoka (1985: 30–31) excludes consec-utive forms and restricts his count to a sample of conversational texts, in which the frequency of SVO word order is significantly higher than in narrative texts. Although he concludes that VSO order is nonetheless statistically dominant, this result is not directly relevant to the present study because in Muraoka's study all orders in which the verb precedes the subject, including object-first (OVS) and adjunct-first (AVS) orders, are counted as having "normal" (that is, relative-VS) order. Hornkohl (2003: 8–10) examines the issue from a different angle, reasoning that, if BH is in fact an SVO language and the predominance of VSO is only due to the widespread use of consecutive forms, one would expect to find SVO as the dominant order in clauses in which consecutive forms are grammatically constrained from appearing due to the presence of an initial particle or subordinating conjunction at the head of the clause. Hornkohl counts all of these clauses in Genesis and shows that, contrary to the SVO hy-pothesis, VSO is the most frequent word order: 76% of narrative clauses and 58% of direct-speech clauses are verb-first, with an overall frequency of 66% verb-first word order.[15] It can be concluded that the textual-frequency criterion, however it is defined, leads to the firm conclusion that basic word order in the BH finite clause is VSO.[16]

2.2.2. Word order in the basic sentence

DeCaen (1995, 1999) has adopted Siewierska's basic-sentence criterion for the typological classification of BH, arguing the statistical-dominance criterion leads to a "naïve and theoretically uninteresting" conception of basic word order (1999: 118 n. 22).[17] According to DeCaen (1995: 137; 1999: 118 n. 22)

---

15. I have calculated these percentages using Hornkohl's raw statistics. The percentages given by Hornkohl (2003: 8) differ somewhat because he eliminates clauses without an overt subject.

16. On word order in the nonverbal and participial clause, see §2.2.4.

17. DeCaen's main interest, however, is in basic word order from the generative per-spective, as will be discussed in §2.2.3.

the basic-sentence criterion leads to the rejection of VSO as the basic order for BH. Coordinated clauses are not basic sentences and are excluded from consideration; thus, clauses with consecutive forms, the most common VSO type, are not considered in determining basic word order. An additional category that is omitted in the basic-sentence criterion is the modal clause. Citing Niccacci (1987) and Revell (1989b), DeCaen (1995: 24) asserts that clauses with modal imperfects, jussives, or imperatives have VSO order, whereas clauses with indicative imperfects have SVO order.[18] Because only indicative clauses are basic sentences, it follows that SVO is the basic word order. More precisely, DeCaen's conclusion is that BH is a verb-second (V2) language, like German, which requires the verb to be in second place in the clause, whether the first element is the subject or a different element (DeCaen 1995: 24).[19]

DeCaen explains the verb-initial (V1) order characteristic of modal clauses by noting that the modal category is marked relative to the indicative category. According to DeCaen (1995: 111–22), the verb form found in *wayyiqtol* is actually a modal form; in addition, he posits that the doubling of the initial prefix represents a complementizer signifying modality (1995: 128–229, 296). The modal nature of *wayyiqtol* explains why these forms always have V1 order. Although this interpretation of the consecutive form is certainly open to challenge, the more fundamental point for present purposes is the connection drawn between modality and marked word order. Modality is a semantic feature of the verb that does not vary with discourse context and is independent of pragmatic neutrality. Although modal verbs are marked in comparison to indcative verbs, this has nothing to do with whether clauses with modal verbs are pragmatically marked. In other words, the fact that modal clauses are generally VSO is perfectly compatible with the VSO basic word-order hypothesis. What is more critical to the V2 argument is whether indicative clauses are in fact always or most often SVO.

The latter issue is addressed by Holmstedt (2002). Holmstedt's (2002: 139) count of indicative clauses in Genesis (including subordinate clauses but excluding clauses without overt subjects and excluding *wayyiqtol* clauses)[20] shows that a slim majority actually have VSO order, with 303 out of 554 clauses (55%) being VSO. Holmstedt, however, argues that many of these clauses, such as the subordinate ones, should not be counted because they do not sat-

---

18. The claim regarding indicative clauses, of course, does not include the most common indicative clause type, the clause with a consecutive form. For further discussion of this view, see §3.3.4.

19. According to DeCaen, BH is V1 in subordinate clauses, which typically have verb-first order.

20. Holmstedt excludes clauses with *wayyiqtol* due to their "unique morphological characteristics" (2002: 133); see §2.2.3 for his explanation of why clauses with *wayyiqtol* always have VSO order.

isfy the basic-sentence criterion.[21] Holmstedt proposes that negative clauses should be omitted as well because, he asserts, they are closely related to modal clauses (2005: 147 n. 36). The basic sentence criterion also excludes sentences that are not stylistically neutral, as Holmstedt points out. But how does one go about deciding which clauses are neutral, if it is not already known which order is marked? Holmstedt (2005: 148–49) points out that clauses occurring in certain contexts, specifically contrastive ones, are likely to be pragmatically marked;[22] these clauses are therefore not taken into account. Omitting all of these categories yields a majority of SVO, albeit from a much smaller group of data (175 clauses in all).

A difficulty with these results lies in the procedure used to weed out the pragmatically marked clauses. Although contrast is one kind of context likely to contain a pragmatically marked clause, there are many types of pragmatic functions that do not involve contrast, including the noncontrastive varieties of focusing and topicalization (see chaps. 8, pp. 121ff., and 9, pp. 144ff.), as well as other less-common functions such as marking simultaneity and anteriority or marking the onset of a new narrative unit (see chaps. 3, pp. 18ff., and 7, pp. 104ff.). If clauses appearing to have any of these functions are omitted as well, the total number of clauses in the data is drastically reduced, leaving only 65 clauses by my estimate.[23] While it appears that SVO is still the majority word order among the remaining clauses, there is no way to know whether more clauses need to be omitted.

Holmstedt's statistics highlight the drastic effect of the basic sentence criterion on text counts. Out of thousands of finite nonsubordinate clauses with overt subjects in Genesis (including *wayyiqtol*), only 175 remain according to Holmstedt's calculations, and considerably less once more potentially marked clauses are omitted. Determining the word order of a language on the basis of such a small sample seems somewhat precarious. More importantly, basic word order in this approach bears little resemblance to the way the language is most frequently used.

---

21. In the following summary I rely on Holmstedt (2005), which is the clearest presentation of his methodology, although the corpus analyzed there is Proverbs.

22. It can be objected that clauses in a contrastive context need not be marked, even if BH uses word order to mark contrast: the use of a marked construction is always optional, because the neutral word order is always available. It is not known how often pragmatically marked constructions are used in contexts that permit these constructions.

23. The effect is particularly extreme on narrative indicative clauses, where 84 out of the 103 must be omitted. When an additional clause in the data is omitted for technical reasons, the result is 15 SV clauses out of 18 (83%). In direct speech, omitting the potentially marked clauses as well as a few found in poetic passages and several others disqualified on syntactic grounds yields 28 SV clauses out of 47, or 60%.

2.2.3. The generative perspective on basic word order in Biblical Hebrew

DeCaen (1995, 1999) argues that the basic word order in BH from the generative perspective is SVO. Working within the framework of the widely accepted generative-grammar theory known as Government-Binding (GB) theory, De-Caen (1999: 118 n. 2) finds that GB "virtually dictates an underlying SVO for Hebrew."[24] This analysis of BH fits the current consensus, mentioned above, that all languages have SVO basic word order from the generative perspective. In DeCaen's view, this underlying SVO order in BH becomes typological V2 on the level of surface structure. Although DeCaen rejects the majority VSO view in his typological classification of BH, this position is not the logical consequence of assuming SVO underlying word order; rather, it results from his utilization of the basic sentence criterion. In other words, DeCaen's findings regarding the generative analysis of BH do not inherently contradict the majority view that BH belongs *typologically* to the VSO language group.

Holmstedt's (2002, 2005) work is set in a "generative-typological" framework, which starts with the generative premise that the underlying structure in every language is SVO. The main focus of his approach, however, is the investigation of the basic order of surface structures, that is, in the typological classification of BH as an SVO language. Holmstedt accounts for the statistical dominance of VSO by a generative concept known as "triggered inversion." He hypothesizes that inversion to VSO occurs when a subordinating or function particle, negative particle, or interrogative particle precedes the subject and verb. He further posits that inversion is also triggered by modality, accounting for the majority of modal clauses with VSO order. The VSO order in *wayyiqtol* clauses is explained as triggered by a historical "complementizer" form contained within the consecutive verb and preserved as the doubling of the verbal prefix. Pragmatically motivated preposing rules are also recognized. It should be noted that the concept of triggered inversion does not serve as *evidence* for typologically basic SVO; rather, it is a mechanism that accounts for the existence of VSO clauses in Holmstedt's SVO typological scheme. A similar mechanism can be invoked by the majority view taking BH to be VSO: the basic word order of surface structures can be accounted for by a mandatory (rather than a triggered) inversion rule to VSO, and SVO clauses can be explained as the product of pragmatically motivated preposing rules.

---

24. Buth (1995: 80–81) argues against an underlying SVO, pointing out that SVO languages such as English typically have OSV as the marked construction, derived by moving the object to initial position. In BH, OSV word order is almost unheard of; the orders that appear are SVO and OVS. Although this argument seems highly attractive, the generative grammarian can account for the discrepancy between English and BH by positing minor differences in the underlying SVO structure of the two languages.

2.2.4. Word order and discourse type

Studies of word order typology generally characterize languages as having a single basic word order. Longacre (1982), however, has claimed that verb-first languages such as BH typically exhibit different unmarked orders in certain discourse types. In BH, he claims, expository discourse exhibits basic SVO word order. What Longacre actually means by this, as he explains there, is that nonverbal clauses predominate in expository discourse, and these clauses most typically have subject-predicate word order, which he takes to be *comparable* to SVO (Longacre 1982: 472; 1989a: 111). Thus, it is not actually claimed that there is a discourse type in which SVO is the unmarked order for *finite* clauses. Word order in the nonverbal clause is addressed in the next section.

2.2.5. Word order in the nonverbal and the participial clause

The basic word order in BH nonverbal clauses appears to be subject-predicate (e.g., Davidson 1901: §103; GKC §141l), in contrast to basic VSO in finite clauses. Muraoka (1985: 8–9) shows that subject-predicate word order is the most common one, based on a statistical analysis of representative samples of conversational, narrative, and legal texts. According to Andersen (1970), the word order depends on whether the clause is "identifying" or "classifying": identifying clauses are usually subject-predicate, while classifying clauses usually have the reverse order. An entirely different approach is taken by Joosten (1989), who argues that the SP/PS opposition is one of aspect rather than pragmatic function. Further discussion of nonverbal clause word order can be found in Rosén (1965); Blau's (1973b) review of Andersen (1970); Hoftijzer's (1973) review essay on Andersen (1970); Revell (1989a, 1999); Muraoka (1990, 1991); Zewi (1992, 1994); Buth (1999); and DeCaen (1999), among other studies.

It appears that participial predicates in BH are like nonverbal predicates, generally occurring after the subject (see, e.g., Andersen 1970; Muraoka 1985; Joosten 1989; Buth 1999). The present study is restricted to finite clauses, so I will not explore word order in nonverbal and participial clauses further.

2.3. Conclusion

In conclusion, basic word order in the typological sense is the pragmatically unmarked order. Basic word order is usually established by the criterion of statistical dominance. The mainstream view that BH is typologically VSO is strongly supported by the statistical evidence. BH, like other VSO languages, has an underlying SVO word order from the generative perspective, but this fact does not affect the typological classification of the language. Basic word order in BH does not vary according to discourse genre.

Chapter 3

Previous Studies of the Functions of Preposing in Biblical Hebrew

This chapter reviews prior studies of the function of preposing in BH. Given that VSO is the unmarked word order in BH, preposed word orders such as SVO and OVS can be assumed to have pragmatic functions. The pragmatic significance of postverbal word order is outside the scope of this study and is not addressed here.[1]

Three general models of preposing can be identified in the literature, each involving a central concept that motivates all or most preposing: *emphasis*, *backgrounding*, and *information structure*. The three concepts do not all have the same scope. Emphasis is not thought to explain all preposed clauses, while universal scope is sometimes claimed for backgrounding. There is a multitude of variations of each model, and the approaches of some researchers do not fit neatly into a single model. Nevertheless, I believe that grouping all of the approaches into three categories is helpful in making sense of the bewildering variety of explanations that have been offered for preposing.

3.1. The emphasis-centered model

As discussed in §2.2, according to one school of thought, the first element in every clause is emphasized, being the newest or most important part of the sentence (Ewald 1879: §306b; Müller 1888: §§130–31; König 1897: §339a–e; Davidson 1901: §105; GKC §142a, f; Revell 1989a; Shimasaki 2002). For these scholars, BH is essentially a free word-order language. A different school of thought takes VSO as the basic word order, with preposing motivated by emphasis. Adherents of the latter view include Brockelmann (1956: §48), Lambert (1972: §1277), Meyer (1972: §91.2), and Muraoka (1985). Thus, Muraoka (1985: 30) writes that in the unmarked VSO word order "neither S nor V receives special emphasis."

The concept of emphasis has been criticized as overly subjective and vague. It is difficult to say whether an emphasis on the preposed element was really

---

1. Studies discussing postverbal word order in BH include Lode (1984, 1988); Rosenbaum (1997); Heimerdinger (1999).

intended or whether the researcher is simply assuming it to exist because of that element's position at the head of the clause. In addition, the notion of emphasis in and of itself does not explain why and for what purposes the speaker wishes to emphasize something. Muraoka (1985: i) writes that the term *emphasis* is often used "without much thought being given to precisely what is meant by the term, nor, more importantly, to the question why the writer or speaker possibly felt the need for an emphatic form or construction."[2] Muraoka attempts to clarify the concept of emphasis, stating that it is a psychological function that is often accompanied by "intensified emotion" (1985: xiv).

Most scholars who discuss emphasis view it as the dominant but not the only function of preposing. Muraoka (1985: 32) writes that emphasis is "what seems to lead to the reverse order in a good number of places, but there remain many others where one can hardly perceive any emphasis." For Niccacci (1990: 20), emphasis (under the name "foregrounding") constitutes only one of three axes influencing word order, as explained further in §3.2.

In §§3.1.1–3.1.7, I examine additional functions that have been cited to explain preposing in the emphasis-centered model. As discussed in these sections, there is an effort made by certain scholars to link some of these functions, specifically, contrast and circumstantiality, to the concept of emphasis.

3.1.1. Contrast and contrastive structures

Contrast is widely cited as a function of preposing. The exact meaning of this concept is a difficult problem. Andersen distinguishes between "contrast," which compares "the participants in two parallel but in some ways different activities" (1974: 150), and "antithesis," which involves not only contrast but also "contradiction or opposition" (1974: 179).[3] Muraoka (1985: 54, 59) posits two apparently identical categories, substituting the term *juxtaposition* for *contrast*.[4] I adopt the terms *juxtaposition* and *antithesis* in the ensuing discussion, with *contrast* used as an umbrella term encompassing both.

Several scholars note that two distinctive structures are used to achieve contrast: "chiastic" structures involving a normal clause followed by a preposed one and "parallel" structures involving a pair of preposed clauses.[5] The two patterns are illustrated in (1) and (2), respectively.

2. See also Bandstra (1982: 79), van der Merwe (1989).

3. See also Myhill and Xing (1993), who define contrast as a pair of sentences whose predicates have opposite meanings and whose contrasted nouns are members of a set. Contrast in this sense corresponds to Andersen's antithesis.

4. The use of preposing for contrast is also discussed in Steiner (1997: 166; 2000: 259–60).

5. See also Steiner (1997: 166). More than one scholar has noted a resemblance between contrastive chiastic structures and poetic chiasmus; see, e.g., Sappan (1976); Khan (1988: 89); Muraoka (1985: 36). It should be noted, however, that prose chiasmus is more restricted in form than the poetic type. Poetry exhibits a wide variety of chiastic patterns (O'Connor

(1) Gen 4:4–5

וישע י׳ אל הבל ואל מנחתו: ואל קין ואל מנחתו לא שעה

And the LORD paid heed to Abel and his offering; <u>and for Cain and his offering</u> He paid no heed.

(2) Gen 41:13

ויהי כאשר פתר לנו כן היה אתי השיב על כני ואתו תלה:

And as he interpreted to us, so it came to pass; <u>me he restored to my office, and him he hanged.</u>

According to Andersen (1974), the parallel structure is used for juxtaposition, and the chiastic structure may express antithesis. A separate use of the chiastic structure according to Andersen is to stress the similarity between two situations. According to Khan (1988: 88–90), both parallel and chiastic structures may set up a relation of contrast or similarity.

Contrastive chiastic structures often involve the same verb in both clauses, as in (1). The connection between repeated verbs and chiasm is discussed by Driver (1913: 130), Ginsberg (1942: 230), Gordis (1944: 150), Cassuto (1961a: 27; 1961b: 91–92), Ben David (1971: 856), McEvenue (1971:43; 1974), Blau (1972), Andersen (1974: 46), and Paran (1989). Paran considers chiastic structures with repeated verbs to be a stylistic device, not necessarily contrastive, which he calls the "circular inclusio."[6]

There is some disagreement as to whether contrast is a separate category from emphasis. Ewald (1879: §309a) refers to emphasis and contrast as two separate functions of preposing,[7] while Davidson (1901: §105) states that emphasis usually involves "some degree of antithesis, latent or expressed." Muraoka (1985: 54) speaks of preposing as expressing emphasis or contrast but also refers to contrast as "one aspect" of emphasis.

3.1.2. Circumstantiality, anteriority, and simultaneity

Circumstantiality is another concept frequently mentioned alongside emphasis in connection with preposing. According to GKC (§156a), the circumstantial clause concerns "the particular circumstances under which a subject appears as performing some action, or under which an action . . . is accomplished."[8] The circumstantial clause is most frequently a participial or nonverbal clause with subject-predicate word order:[9]

1980: 391–400), while prose chiasmus is restricted to the VSO-SVO/OVS type. On the use of stylistic devices such as chiasmus in prose, see §8.5.

6. See §8.5 for further discussion of repeated-verb structures.

7. See also Malbim (1973: §§111–14).

8. See also GKC (§§141e, 142a); Ewald (1879: §306c); Müller (1888: §§131, 151); Driver (1892: §156); Davidson (1901: §150).

9. According to Joosten (2002), there are more than 170 examples of circumstantial clauses with a predicative participle in Genesis, Josh 1–10, Judges, 1–2 Samuel, and 1–2

(3) Gen 18:1

וירא אליו י׳ באלני ממרא **והוא ישב פתח האהל כחם היום**:

And the LORD appeared to him by the oaks of Mamre, **and (= while) he was sitting at the entrance of the tent in the heat of the day**.

In the finite circumstantial clause, the subject precedes the verb, mimicking the subject-predicate order found in the nonfinite circumstantial clause.

Several scholars, including Ewald (1879: §306c), Müller (1888: §§130–31), and Davidson (1901: §105), link word order in the finite circumstantial clause to the emphasis principle. Because the circumstantial clause describes a state rather than an action, the verb is de-emphasized relative to the subject and hence follows it. S. R. Driver (1892: §160 obs.) and Muraoka (1985: 33), however, see emphasis and circumstantiality as separate categories. Driver (1892: §157) and GKC (§141e) link circumstantiality to contrast.

In the classic sense, the circumstantial clause is one that refers to a *concomitant* state or event, that is, an accompanying state or event simultaneous with the previous clause. The circumstantial clause is viewed as semantically subordinate to the preceding clause, despite being coordinate on the grammatical level. A nonfinite example is (3), above, which can be rendered by a subordinate clause, 'while he was sitting'.[10] Oddly, though, it is hard to find finite clauses of this type. Joosten (2002) points out that a finite clause describing a concomitant event should contain an imperfect verb; as he shows, there are hardly any clauses of this type. Although a number of concomitant finite clauses with perfects are cited in the literature, most of these are not found in a narrative context but occur in direct speech, following a rhetorical question or a request:[11]

(4) Gen 18:13

למה זה צחקה שרה לאמר האף אמנם אלד <u>ואני זקנתי</u>:

Why did Sarah laugh, saying, "Shall I indeed bear a child, <u>and I am old</u>?"

I will argue in §7.3.2.1 that this type of preposing does not mark circumstantiality but is a special construction that marks the justification for a preceding utterance. All in all, it would appear that the finite circumstantial clause in the classic sense is something of a phantom.[12]

Kings; see there for further citations.

10. See Müller (1888: §151); Driver (1892: §156); Davidson (1901: §137). Eskhult (1990: 31), who is an advocate of the backgrounding approach (see §3.2), compares the circumstantial clause to the Arabic *ḥal* clause, which describes a circumstance under which a subject performs an action.

11. Other examples of this type cited in the literature are Gen 24:31 and 26:27.

12. See further on in this section (p. 23) for discussion of supposed circumstantial clauses that precede rather than follow the main clause.

A number of cited examples of finite circumstantial clauses describe events *anterior* to the main clause event; for example, 1 Kgs 1:41 and Judg 16:31. In order to view examples such as these as circumstantial, it is necessary to broaden the circumstantiality category to include anterior events as well as the classical simultaneous type. Considering that finite simultaneous circumstantial clauses are hardly to be found, however, this sort of definition seems artificial. Andersen (1974) and Muraoka (1985) broaden the concept of circumstantiality even further to include parenthetical comments and clauses that interrupt the chain of the narrative. This conception comes very close to the idea of "backgrounding," as discussed in §3.2, below. Kotzé (1989) finds the concept of circumstantiality generally wanting, showing that the category is not consistently understood in the literature and cannot be characterized in terms of particular syntactic features. He concludes that it is used as a catch-all term.

A more plausible approach is to abandon circumstantiality as a function of preposing in the finite clause and to view *anteriority* as the relevant pragmatic function. The use of preposing to mark anteriority is an unmistakable phenomenon, recognized as early as the Jewish exegete Rashi (Rabbi Solomon ben Isaac, 1040–1105 c.e.). Rashi comments on והאדם ידע את חוה אשתו 'And the man knew Eve his wife' (Gen 4:1):[13]

כבר קודם העניין של מעלה קודם שחטא ונטרד מגן עדן, וכן ההריון והלדה, שאם כתב
"וידע אדם" נשמע שלאחר שנטרד היו לו בנים

Already before the above matter, before he sinned and was banished from the garden of Eden, and so too the pregnancy and birth. For if it had written "וידע אדם" it would have meant that after he was banished he had children.

Malbim (1973: §117) formulates Rashi's observation as a general rule: "When [the text] speaks about a matter that already took place prior to that time, it always advances the subject ahead of the verb." Several scholars (e.g., König 1897: §§115–17; GKC §106f; Bergsträsser 1962: §6d) mention anteriority as one of the uses of the perfect verb form. According to some (Müller 1882: §152; Driver 1892: §§76 obs., 160 obs.; GKC §142b), it is the preposing of the subject that conveys anteriority; the anterior clause has a perfect verb as a result of its SV word order. More recent discussions of preposing to mark anteriority include the works of Williams (1976: §573), Givón (1977, 1983), Kutscher (1982: §66),[14] Fox (1983), and Zevit (1998).[15]

___

13. Text from Chavel (1983).

14. Zevit (1998: 13 n. 18) cites Shraga Assif as stating that Kutscher was teaching this theory to students as early as the late 1960s; in addition, he cites a personal communication from Menaḥem Z. Kaddari that in the 1940s Neḥama Leibowitz was circulating collections of examples of this phenomenon discussed by the medieval Jewish exegetes.

15. Zevit (1998: 15) has an unusual understanding of anteriority. He defines anteriority as including the pluperfect (past perfect) as well as the preperfect, which refers to an event that had "commenced but not necessarily terminated in the past prior to the beginning of

A separate phenomenon is the use of a pair of preposed clauses to mark *simultaneity*. Davidson (1901: §141) and GKC (§141e) note the use of preposing in clauses such as (5):

(5) Gen 19:23

השמש יצא על הארץ ולוט בא צערה:

The sun rose upon the earth, and Lot came to Zoar.

Davidson and GKC explain this as an atypical kind of "circumstantial" clause that precedes the main clause; thus, (5) can be rendered 'As the sun rose, Lot came to Zoar'. Given the arguments already presented against circumstantiality as a function of preposing, a different explanation of such examples is desirable. A notable feature is the use of preposing in the "main" clause as well as the "circumstantial" clause, something not seen with the classic circumstantial clause. In addition, in some cases it is not clear that one event is subordinate to the other, as in (6):

(6) 1 Sam 9:17

ושמואל ראה את שאול וי' ענהו הנה האיש אשר אמרתי אליך זה יעצר בעמי:

And Samuel saw Saul, and God told him, "Here is the man that I told you, "This one will govern my people."

In Joüon's (1947: §166) view, preposing in these cases marks a temporal relation of simultaneity between two clauses, rather than a relation of semantic subordination.[16] The structures of both clauses contribute to specifying the type of simultaneity involved. A sequence of two preposed clauses with perfects, such as (5) and (6), indicates two simultaneous instantaneous actions. A subject-first participial clause followed by a preposed clause with the perfect, such as (7), indicates a durative action and a simultaneous instantaneous action.

(7) Gen 38:25

הוא מוצאת והיא שלחה אל חמיה לאמר לאיש אשר אלה לו אנכי הרה

She was being brought out, and she sent to her father-in-law, saying, "By the man to whom these belong, I am with child."

When two instantaneous events are concerned, it may be difficult to determine from the context whether the events are truly simultaneous or one immediately follows the other.[17] It is plausible, however, that simultaneity and near-simultaneity constitute a single category from the pragmatic perspective.

---

another action." The preperfect category includes many clauses that are more commonly considered simultaneous.

16. See also Williams (1976: §573).

17. According to GKC (§164), a sequence of perfects refers to a rapid sequence of events, citing as evidence many of the same verses as does Joüon. See also König (1897: §119).

3.1.3. Narrative-unit demarcation

Driver (1892: 201) notes that subject-first clauses sometimes mark the "commencement of a new thread" in the narrative:

(8) Gen 16:1

וְשָׂרַי אֵשֶׁת אַבְרָם לֹא יָלְדָה לוֹ

And Sarai, Abram's wife, had born him no children.

Similar observations are made by Brockelmann (1956: §48), Jongeling (1980), Khan (1988: 86–88), and Lambdin (1971: §132), among others. Lambdin and Khan note that preposed temporal adverbials as well as preposed subjects occur at the beginning of an episode. Paragraph-marking is a central theme in Heller (2004)'s study of the function of clause types in BH. According to Heller (2004: 56), "isolated and independent *QATAL* clauses consistently mark paragraph boundaries." Although most *qatal* clauses are preposed, Heller does not make reference to word order in his study.

The kind of narrative unit marked by preposing is a matter of debate. Eskhult (1990: 33, 40, 50) writes that preposing may mark a new episode or paragraph. Khan (1988: 86) states that subject-preposed clauses "typically occur at span boundaries" (for definition of the span, see the next paragraph). The notion of the boundary is conceived rather broadly by Khan to include circumstantial or background information, which many would consider to be internal to the span. For Khan, Lambdin, and Heller, preposing may mark the end as well as the beginning of a unit; however, evidence for the marking of unit endings is more tenuous than for the unit-onset marking function.[18]

The nature and definition of units such as the episode, the paragraph, and the span are subject to various interpretations. The episode is a narrative unit, whereas the paragraph is variously viewed as a literary, thematic, or even a grammatical unit.[19] Longacre (1979) conceives of the paragraph as a unit ex-

---

18. See also Mirsky (1977; 1999: 11–36), who states that the ends of verses and larger thematic units are often marked by change of word order. By this, Mirsky means not necessarily preposing but inversion of whatever word order is exhibited in previous clauses within the unit. Although in most of Mirsky's examples the unit ends with a preposed clause, in two cases the clauses within the unit exhibit preposed order, and the last clause exhibits verb-first order (Pss 22:24, 23:2–3). Many of his examples are from poetry or nonverbal clauses, although he does cite several cases involving preposed nonsubordinate finite clauses in the classical BH prose corpus, including Gen 19:3, 23:15; Deut 17:17; Josh 16:8; 2 Kgs 4:4. It should be noted that several of these can be alternately explained as topicalized or focused clauses, as defined in the present work. I am indebted to Uri Mor for the Mirsky reference.

19. Givón (1983: 8) attempts to quantify the description of the paragraph, stating that the thematic paragraph is linked "in a statistically significant but not absolute fashion" to the quantitative concept of "topic continuity." Every noun phrase is considered by Givón to be a topic. Continuity and discontinuity are coded by a number of means including word order, morphology, and phonology. Discontinuous topics are generally coded by full noun phrases

hibiting thematic unity and marked by special grammatical structures. Paragraphs according to Longacre encode notions such as conjoining, temporal relations, logical relations, elaborative devices, and reportative devices. Exter Blokland (1995) criticizes Longacre's model of the paragraph as essentially literary and semantic and puts forth a different grammatical model based on syntactic criteria. Khan's span is a semantic/pragmatic concept, referring to a textual unit "in which there is some kind of uniformity" (1988: xxxv). He distinguishes between the topic span, a unit that is "about" a single referent, and the theme span, which he defines as a unit concerning a single "semantic domain."

Any theory of textual units in the Bible should certainly take into account the traditional Jewish text division, the system of פרשה פתוחה 'open portion' and פרשה סתומה 'closed portion'.[20] The biblical text is divided into sections, marked by a space extending to the end of the line (the open portion) or by a space within the line (the closed portion). The open portion seems to mark a major division and the closed portion a minor division (Tov 1992: 50). However, the correspondence between these two division types and narrative units such as episodes and paragraphs remains to be clarified. The traditional portions mark many kinds of divisions, including divisions between different stories, between major episodes or scenes in a story, between component sections of an episode, between paragraphs, and between speeches in a dialogue (Ulrich 2003: 303).

3.1.4. Attraction

Several scholars claim that preposing may result from a process of "attraction." According to Malbim (1973: §115), when an object at the end of one clause is the same as the subject in the next clause, preposed word order may result:

(9) Gen 25:33–34

וימכר את בכרתו ליעקב: ויעקב נתן לעשו לחם ונזיד עדשים

And he sold his birthright to Jacob. And Jacob gave Esau bread and lentil stew.

Joüon-Muraoka (§155oa) makes a similar statement regarding a final object and states that "it is difficult to say whether the resultant chiasmus is by design

---

or accented independent pronouns, whereas continuous topics are coded by unaccented independent pronouns, clitic pronouns, verb agreement, or zero anaphora (1983: 31–32). In verb-first languages, preposing is also used to code discontinuity (1983: 33). Paragraphs generally open with a discontinuous topic and generally exhibit continuity of the main topic within the paragraph (1983: 9). For a study of topic continuity in BH, see Fox (1983).

20. See, e.g., Lundbom (1999: 74); Tov (2001: 50–51); Hoop (2003: 3–4). I am indebted to Richard Steiner for the Lundbom reference.

or not"; in other words, preposing from attraction may be an unconscious process without pragmatic significance.[21] König (1897: §339f) states that similar syntactic categories are apt to go together; thus when a clause ends with the subject, the next clause may also start with the subject.

3.1.5. Miscellaneous factors

Muraoka (1985: 34–44, 169) identifies a number of miscellaneous factors associated with a tendency for subject preposing.[22] Sentences having איש in the sense 'someone/everyone' as the subject[23] or having God as the subject are frequently preposed. Preposing is also common in sentences at the beginning of a statement and in sentences occurring in legal texts. Muraoka states furthermore that certain adverbs and adverbial expressions, particularly anaphoric ones, are normally clause-initial; examples are מחר, לכן, כדבר הזה כה, כה, כן, and עתה. The implication is that clauses beginning with these words or phrases are pragmatically unmarked.

3.1.6. Preposing in direct speech

Several scholars note that preposing in direct speech is more frequent than in narrative and often unexplainable by any of the factors discussed above. Bloch (1946) notes that speech occupies an intermediate point between narrative and poetry with respect to degree of word order variation. Macdonald (1975) finds that preposing ("inversion") is much more common in direct speech than in narrative, and emphasis, which is largely responsible for preposing in narrative, is far less important in direct speech. He goes so far as to claim that "in Spoken [Hebrew] Inverted Word Order *appears to be the norm*" (1975: 163; capitalization and emphasis original). Mali (1983) finds that direct speech in the Former Prophets exhibits a greater degree of deviation from VSO word order than narrative; he asserts, further, that in some syntactic structures in direct speech the order of verb and subject is free.

3.1.7. Conclusion

Emphasis is widely viewed nowadays as a frustratingly subjective concept, despite Muraoka's efforts to give the concept a modern linguistic interpretation. Perhaps the main contribution of the emphasis-centered model is the categorization and description of cases in which preposing is *not* directly motivated by emphasis. Many of the functional categories described above, such as anteriority, simultaneity, and the marking of a new narrative unit, are significant categories that must be addressed in any comprehensive treatment

21. A more probable explanation of clauses such as these involves the concept of topicalization (see §3.3.1.2).

22. These factors are also discussed by Muraoka in his revised version of Joüon's grammar (Joüon-Muraoka §155).

23. This was noticed earlier by Bloch (1946: 37), as Muraoka notes.

of word order. As we will see, the achievement of contemporary work on word order lies not so much in the discovery of new types of preposing but rather in the formulation of conceptual frameworks that yield a more systematic and economical account of the types already observed.

3.2. The backgrounding and temporal-sequencing models

A contemporary alternative to the emphasis-centered model is the *backgrounding* model, which explains preposing on the basis of the *foreground-background* distinction. The *temporal-sequencing* model is closely related to the backgrounding model, and is treated together with it in the ensuing discussion.

According to Grimes (1975), narrative can be divided into "foreground," which relates events, and "background," which presents explanatory material, introduction of participants, and setting. Hopper (1979: 213) develops this distinction further in an influential article, defining foreground as "the actual story line," or "the parts of the narrative which relate events belonging to the skeletal structure of the discourse"; background consists of supportive material that does not itself narrate the main events.[24]

Longacre (1994, 2003: 62–118) applies the concepts of foreground and background to BH, applying these first to verb form and only secondarily to word order. In narrative, the foreground, which designates sequential events, is characterized by the *wayyiqtol* form; *qatal* designates the background ("offline"), which describes secondary, usually nonsequential events.[25] Because *wayyiqtol* clauses are always verb-first and *qatal* clauses are usually preposed, this is roughly equivalent to a VSO-foreground, SVO-background scheme.[26]

24. Hopper (1979) supplies a list of criteria differentiating foreground and background: e.g., the foreground is frequently characterized by temporal succession, perfective verb forms (not to be confused with the BH perfect), and subject continuity, while the background is characterized by simultaneity, imperfective verb forms, and changes of subject. Givón (1987) argues that the foreground/background distinction is conceptually a graded rather than a binary distinction.

25. According to Longacre, (1982: 459–60; 2003: 57–58), each discourse type, including the narrative, predictive/procedural, hortatory, and expository types, has its own scheme of marking foreground and background. The link between *qatal* and backgrounding is characteristic of narrative; in predictive discourse the background is marked by *yiqtol* (1982: 468; 2003: 106). Longacre's conception of narrative is not in opposition to direct speech; thus, direct speech in Longacre's scheme is also classified as belonging to any of the above types, including narrative (see also Heller 2004: 23). As mentioned in §2.2.4, Longacre (1982: 472) views the expository discourse type as having a different basic word order than narrative, based on the fact that expository discourse consists mainly of nominal clauses with subject-predicate word order.

26. Longacre, however, views *qatal* as marking background whether the clause has verb-first or preposed word order. *Qatal* with a preposed noun is used to "introduce or feature a participant or prop" (2003: 71), whereas *qatal* with verb-first word order is used "to present a preliminary action." Longacre's theory also distinguishes between different degrees

Other scholars with a similar paradigm include Eskhult (1990), Dawson (1994), Niccacci (e.g., 1990, 1994, 1997), and van Wolde (1997). Niccacci bases his theory on the linguistic model of H. Weinrich and its application to BH by W. Schneider. Niccacci (e.g., 1990: 19–21; 1997), distinguishes two levels of "linguistic attitude": "narrative" (i.e., foreground) and "commentary" (i.e., background).[27] Payne's (1991) analysis also bears a strong similarity to the backgrounding approach, although he does not use these terms. He explains preposing as side-stepping the event line for various purposes. Heller (2004: 431) views foreground and background as important for understanding the choice between *wayyiqtol* and other verb forms, but does not address word order at all.[28] Buth combines the foreground-background framework with an information-structure approach, as described in §3.3.5.

The nature of the foreground-background distinction is open to various interpretations. For Longacre, foreground and background relate to the way in which discourse is structured. Reinhart (1984) understands the concepts as cognitive in nature, relating to the way information is organized and processed by the human mind.[29] Although foreground is usually sequential and background nonsequential, the foreground/background concepts are inherently independent from temporal sequencing, because a speaker can choose to represent sequential events as background.

In the temporal-sequencing model, the somewhat elusive foreground-background concepts are replaced by the more concrete notions of sequentiality and nonsequentiality. Givón (1977) finds that the BH imperfect, occurring mostly in VS clauses, marks temporal continuity (i.e., sequentiality), while the perfect, generally occurring in SV clauses, marks an anterior or unsequenced

---

of backgrounding: the "secondary storyline," which relates secondary, off-line events, is marked by *qatal*, whereas more backgrounded activities are marked by participial and non-verbal clauses, among other constructions (2003: 79). For a critique of Longacre's theory, see Heimerdinger (1999); some of Heimerdinger's criticisms are discussed further in this section.

27. The "narrative-commentary" axis is only one level of Niccacci's analysis, which also includes two other axes, the "foreground-background" axis (actually referring to emphasis rather than foreground-background in the previously discussed sense) and a temporal "linguistic-perspective" axis.

28. Heller's model is considerably more complex than Longacre's. According to Heller, foreground-background is only one of two main functions of non-*wayyiqtol* clauses; the other function is marking initial and final paragraph boundaries (see §3.1.3 above). Multiple non-*wayyiqtol* clauses are said to mark background information, while isolated non-*wayyiqtol* clauses mark paragraph boundaries (2004: 431). As far as *wayyiqtol*, uninterrupted *wayyiqtol* chains in narrative are said to mark main-line events, while isolated *wayyiqtol* clauses are claimed to mark backgrounded, rather than foregrounded, information (2004: 430–31). For a review of Heller, see Zewi (2004).

29. A similar approach is adopted Hatav (1985).

event.[30] According to Myhill (1992a; 1992b: 172–77; 1995), BH and other VSO languages use the unmarked word order for sequential past events and marked word order for nonsequential events.[31] More recently, Goldfajn (1998) writes that SV word order signifies an event that is anterior, simultaneous, or posterior.

There is some disagreement over the intended scope of the backgrounding/ temporal-sequencing models. Longacre would like his backgrounding model to pertain to all preposed clauses with *qatal*, and Myhill (1995) makes a similar claim with regard to the temporal-sequencing model. Other scholars such as Givón, Buth, and Goldfajn assume that the marking of background/nonsequentiality is restricted to *qatal* clauses with a preposed subject; the preposing of complements or adjuncts is assumed to be motivated by other factors.

The model presented by Longacre, as described above, centers on the assertion that *wayyiqtol* always marks foreground and *qatal* background. This assertion has been challenged by Heimerdinger, who points out that "an evaluative comment, a descriptive detail, a summary, an enumeration," as well as "explanatory information such as flashbacks" may all be marked by *wayyiqtol* (1999: 261).[32] Furthermore, *qatal* clauses are not always backgrounded (Heimerdinger 1999: 93–98).[33] Cook (2004: 264) asserts that, though foregrounding and backgrounding are pragmatically marked by *wayyiqtol* and *qatal*, respectively, there are "any number" of other pragmatic factors that affect the choice of verb form as well.

Givón's assertion of a clear-cut correspondence between temporal sequencing and verb form is also open to challenge. Although most consecutive forms do refer to sequential events, this is not always the case, as pointed out by Buth (1995: 86–87) and Cook (2004: 257–61). A review of the first 10 chapters of

30. By "imperfect," Givón means both the consecutive and the simple imperfect. See also Dempster (1985).

31. Myhill (1995) presents an unconventional description of preposing in clauses with future time reference: in modal clauses, preposing is used in commands with third-person animate subjects. In non-modal clauses, preposing marks unilateral good prophecies, neutral prophecies, bad prophecies, unilateral promises, hopes, hostile intentions, bad self-prophecies, and guesses. Not surprisingly, Myhill (1995: 113) comments: "I cannot say with absolute certainty that the categories in table 3 [i.e., the nonmodal categories described above] represent the best possible analysis of these data."

32. Heimerdinger's own understanding of the foregrounding concept is different from the one discussed in this section; a foregrounded element for him is one that is "thrown into relief by the writer or speaker and is perceived as such by the reader or hearer" (1999: 222). Thus, clauses in the storyline are not considered foregrounded unless they are specially highlighted. According to Heimerdinger, foregrounding in this sense is marked not by specific clause structures (1999: 239) but by other devices such as repetition and evaluation.

33. Longacre (1989, 1992) addresses this argument by introducing a distinction between primary and secondary storylines. Perfect clauses carry the secondary storyline, which is normally background but can be promoted to foreground under certain circumstances.

Genesis turns up seven clear instances of *wayyiqtol* marking a nonsequential event or state: Gen 2:25 (ויהיו); 3:24 (ויגרש); 5:4 (ויולד); 7:17 (וירבו); 7:23 (וימח); 9:20 (ויחל); 10:30 (ויהי). In addition, although Driver (1892: 84–88) is doubtful that *wayyiqtol* can indicate the pluperfect (anterior) within a narrative, Martin (1968–69), Buth (1994a, 1995), Collins (1995), and Cook (2004) cite a number of convincing examples, including Judg 11:1 (ויולד) and 2 Sam 12:27 (וישלח).[34]

A different way of evaluating the backgrounding and temporal-sequencing models is examining how they account for the various categories of preposing discussed in §3.1 above. Preposed clauses traditionally viewed as expressing emphasis do not fit naturally in either model. The background category includes anterior clauses as well as parenthetical comments. Pairs of simultaneous preposed clauses do not fit the background concept as well, because the second clause in the pair, if not the first, is usually a "main" event (see §3.1.2). As far as preposing to mark a new textual unit, this may at times coincide with backgrounding, as in (8), above, but it is hard to see why this should always be the case. The backgrounding explanation is particularly inapt for chiastic contrastive structures such as (10), as Bailey and Levinsohn (1992) have pointed out.

(10) Gen 41:51–52

ויקרא יוסף את שם הבכור מנשה כי נשני אלהים את כל עמלי ואת כל בית אבי:
ואת שם השני קרא אפרים כי הפרני אלהים בארץ עניי

And Joseph called the name of the firstborn Manasseh, "For God has made me forget all my hardship and my father's entire house." And the name of the second he called Ephraim, "For God has made me fruitful in the land of my affliction."

The backgrounding model assigns the naming of the firstborn child to the foreground and the naming of the second (with *qatal*) to the background, although the second child turns out to be at least as central to the storyline as the first.

The temporal-sequencing model succeeds in accounting for anterior and simultaneous clauses, as well as many parenthetical clauses. It is also able to incorporate many contrastive clause pairs, which frequently involve simultaneous events. However, the claim that preposing always marks nonsequenti-

---

34. See also the discussion and further references in Waltke and O'Connor (1990: §33.2.3). Hatav (1997: 57) has defended the link between *wayyiqtol* and sequentiality, stating that her study of *wayyiqtol* forms in classical Hebrew prose shows that only 6% of 2,445 *wayyiqtol* clauses are clearly nonsequential (see also Hatav 2000b). Heller (2004: 430) also believes there is a consistent link between *wayyiqtol* and sequentiality. According to Cook (2004: 264), the high degree of correlation between *wayyiqtol* and sequentiality is due to the fact that *wayyiqtol* is a narrative verb and the fact that temporal succession is the natural order in narrative.

ality is easily refutable; many preposed clauses, including some contrastive clauses such as (10), are clearly sequential.[35]

In conclusion, the backgrounding model and temporal-sequencing models are not applicable to all preposed clauses. The most plausible formulations of the theory apply exclusively to subject-preposed clauses; thus, object-preposing and adjunct-preposing are not afforded an explanation. Furthermore, many subject-preposed clauses do not describe backgrounded or nonsequential events and cannot be accounted for within these models.

A noteworthy aspect of both models is that they view the function of preposing as relating to the clause as a whole. The preposed subject is not significant in and of itself; it is preposed merely in order to create a marked structure. The perspective is radically different in the model we turn to next, the information-structure model. In this model, the function of preposing is understood as relating specifically to the preposed element; it is this element, therefore, that is the object of attention.

3.3. The information-structure model

A number of scholars have recently adopted an information-structure model of BH word order. The field of information structure has its origin in work by H. Weil in the 19th century, was developed further by linguists of the Prague school, and was subsequently taken in various directions by European scholars such as Halliday and American scholars such as Chafe. Information structure concerns the ways in which sentence structures convey a message to the addressee regarding the interpretation of the sentence in its context.[36]

In §3.3.1, I survey information-structure concepts as they are described in the general linguistic literature. In §§3.3.2–3.3.7, I describe various models of BH word order that are based on information-structure concepts.[37] The models are categorized according to the scholar most responsible for their development.

---

35. Representative examples from Genesis are Gen 4:18; 10:24, 25, 26–29; 11:27; 14:4; 15:17; 18:7; 19:6, 10.

36. The term "information structure" was introduced by Halliday (1967). Syntactic and prosodic structures that mark information structure are sometimes known as *information-packaging* devices because they organize the informational content of the sentence in a manner appropriate to the context. For this term, see, e.g., Chafe (1976); Valldují (1992); McNally (1998).

37. Information structure has also been applied to the study of Modern Hebrew word order; see, e.g., Bendavid (1958); Ben-Horin (1976); Rosén (1977: 322–24; 1982); Giora (1982); Nir and Roeh (1984); Ziv (1988); Glinert (1989: §37); Kuzar (1989, 2002); Azar (1993).

3.3.1. Introduction to information-structure concepts

3.3.1.1. Theme-rheme/topic-comment

In work on information structure by linguists from the Prague school, it is frequently asserted that sentences divide into "theme" and "rheme." Mathesius states that the theme is "what is given by the context," "what is being commented upon";[38] the new part of the sentence is the rheme. Theme and rheme are also known as "psychological subject" and "psychological predicate," respectively. According to the principle of "functional sentence perspective" (Firbas 1966b, 1992), the normal position for the theme is at the beginning of the sentence. Sentences beginning with the rheme are marked as emotive. The terms *topic* and *comment*, introduced by Hockett (1958: 201), are generally taken to be synonymous with *theme* and *rheme*.[39] In the ensuing discussion, the terms are used interchangeably.

There have been many attempts to define rigorously the concept of theme or topic. Gómez-González (2001) describes three approaches to the concept: the "aboutness" approach, in which the topic is what the sentence is about; the "informational" approach, in which the topic is the "given" (i.e., known) part of the clause, and the "syntactic" approach, in which the topic is the first element of the clause.[40] The most widely accepted approach is the "aboutness" approach. For some, the topic is what the discourse, rather than the sentence, is about.[41] Discourse topic and sentence topic can be viewed as interrelated; van Oosten (1985: 23), for example, sees the sentence topic as "a constituent inside

38. See, e.g., Mathesius (1975: 156).
39. Others distinguish between topic-comment and theme-rheme. For Halliday (2004: 65), for example, topic is a particular type of theme.
40. According to Reinhart (1981), a sentence is "about" an entity if it is intended to increase our knowledge about that entity. The topic is the referential entry under which the proposition expressed by the sentence is stored in the addressee's knowledge (1981: 80). A similar definition can be found in Gundel (1985: 86; 1988: 210). Lambrecht's (1994: 131) definition of topic is also similar, except that he allows a clause to have more than one topic (1994: 147). Vallduví (1992) understands topic (which he terms "link") using a "filing" metaphor similar to Reinhart's description: the topic represents the address of the file card in which the information provided by the sentence is stored (see also Vallduví and Engdahl 1996). The "backward-looking center" of Centering Theory is viewed by some as a model for topic in the sense of aboutness (Walker, Joshi, and Prince 1998a).
Another variety of the informational approach is Firbas's (e.g., 1966a, 1966b, 1992) theory of "communicative dynamism": the topic is the element that advances the communication the least. For Givón (1983), topicality is a scalar notion depending on the degree of continuity with the previous discourse.
For the "syntactic approach," see, e.g., Halliday (1967). Firbas (1966a) rejects this approach on the grounds that in emotive sentences the rheme is first, as mentioned above.
41. See, e.g., Keenan and Schieffelin (1976); Van Dijk (1977: 132–40). In Dik's 1989 version of Functional Grammar, the pragmatic function of Topic refers to the discourse topic, with four subtypes being distinguished: New Topic, Given Topic, Resumed Topic, and Sub-Topic (1989: 267). See Bolkestein (1998) for a detailed critique of how the term Topic is used

a sentence which most directly evokes the discourse topic which is relevant in the current sentence."[42]

The various definitions of topic remain problematic. The most accepted conception of topic, the notion of "aboutness," has thus far resisted objective formulation, despite valiant efforts on the part of many researchers. Gómez-González (2001: 31) sums up the state of the field as follows: "the intricacies raised by the numerous and heterogeneous variations of the semantic interpretation have led many scholars to conclude that Theme/Topic in terms of aboutness cannot be regarded as an objectively identifiable unique category, but as a clearly intuitive, and therefore subjective concept."

3.3.1.2. Topicalization

The term *topicalization* first appears in Ross (1967: 115) as the name for the English preposing transformation.[43] This transformation moves a noninitial expression to the head of the clause, yielding a structure such as *Cake, I eat with a spoon.*[44] The term *topicalization* is also used to refer to the structure produced by the topicalization transformation. It was noticed later by Gundel (1977: 134–35; 1985: 88 n. 10) and others that the topicalization construction exhibits two distinct accentuation patterns.[45] The first has the primary accent on an element other than the preposed constituent, for example, *Cake, I eat with a **spoon**.*[46] A second pattern, restricted to the casual register, has the primary accent on the preposed element: ***Cake** I asked for, not pie.* This type of sentence marks the preposed constituent as the focus, that is, the new information in the clause (see §3.3.1.3). It has become customary to reserve the term *topicalization* for the former syntactic-prosodic pattern; the latter pattern is termed *focus-movement* or *focusing* (see §3.3.1.3).[47]

---

in Functional Grammar research. Critical analyses of the concept of discourse topic can be found in Brown and Yule (1983: 68–124) and Gómez-González (2001: 25–31).

42. Further exploration of the relation between sentence topic and discourse topic can be found in Goutsos (1997) and in Floor's (2004) dissertation on BH.

43. Postal (1971: 142) calls this transformation "*Y*-Movement," on the grounds that the resulting sentences are similar to those found in Yiddish. Further discussion of the transformation and its syntactic constraints can be found in Chomsky (1977).

44. Although Ross's topicalization includes only preposed NPs, this definition was later broadened by some to include preposed adverbs and prepositional phrases as well. See Prince (1986: 210, example 3).

45. See also Creider (1979: 4 n. 1) and Prince (1986: 209); Ben-Horin (1976) describes corresponding constructions in Modern Hebrew.

46. There is typically a secondary accent on the preposed "cake" as well.

47. Prince distinguishes a third preposing construction in English that she calls "Yiddish-Movement"; for example, "*Can you imagine? Such a rich woman and after all I've done for her, a **shirt** she gave my Harry when he was bar mitsved.*" Yiddish-movement is syntactically and prosodically identical to focus-movement but is dialectically restricted with different pragmatic characteristics (see §6.1.2 n. 9).

As their names suggest, topicalization in the narrow sense and focus-movement appear to have distinct pragmatic functions. This has led to a third use of the term *topicalization*, to denote a syntactic-pragmatic concept, that is, a certain "pragmatically defined type of preposing" (Birner and Ward 1998: 38 n. 9).[48] The latter conception is useful for the cross-linguistic investigation of topicalization, because other languages may not have prosodic patterns identical to English, and in some cases (as in BH) prosodic data may not be available. In other words, topicalization denotes a preposing construction that has the same pragmatic function as the English topicalization (as opposed to focus-movement) construction.

What, however, *is* the pragmatic function of English topicalization? A widespread theory is that topicalization marks the preposed constituent as the topic of the sentence. This idea has its origin in the Firbas's principle of "functional sentence perspective," referred to above (p. 32). According to functional sentence perspective, the subject is most frequently the theme and naturally comes first in the normal clause. When an object or adverbial is the theme, it is placed in the usual place for the theme at the head of the clause, producing a topicalized structure.[49] This hypothesis is inapplicable to verb-first languages such as BH, because the functional-sentence perspective principle does not operate in these languages;[50] in other words; "theme-rheme" is not the operative organizational principle in the normal BH clause. Because the initial element in the BH clause is not ordinarily the theme, there is no reason to expect that a preposed object or adverbial is the theme. In fact, the notion of theme or topic marking is problematic even for subject-first languages such as English. If the concept of topic has no clearly defined meaning (see §3.3.1.1), the idea of topicalization as topic marking is similarly opaque.

A different theory points to the frequently contrastive contexts in which topicalized clauses are found, for example, *I ate an apple and a pear. I liked the pear; **the apple I detested*** (Ben-Horin 1976: 194; Creider 1979: 5 n. 2). The topicalized clause in this example can be said to have the function of contrasting what is said about the apple with what was previously said about the pear. Givón (2001: 2:225) explains that the contrast in topicalization involves the breaking of expectations regarding "various members of a group (type, genus) whose members are expected to display similar behavior, or receive similar treatment." The type of contrast involved in topicalization may involve jux-

---

48. See also Myhill (1985: 181) and Bailey and Levinsohn (1992).

49. See Halliday (1967: 211–23), who terms this function "thematization." A similar view can be found in Lambrecht (1994: 147; see also p. 161). For a review of Lambrecht's work, including his views on topic, see Ziv (1996b).

50. Verbs are in all but exceptional circumstances part of the rheme, irrespective of the language involved; hence, unmarked clauses in verb-first languages begin with a component of the rheme and not the theme.

taposition or antithesis, to use Muraoka's terms: the contrasted items may be simply different or sharply antithetical.

Not all topicalized clauses are contrastive, however. A continuative use of topicalization has also been identified, in which the preposed object refers to an element mentioned just prior to the clause. Mathesius (1975: 158–59) gives as an example of this type: *In returning he met on the plain of Caraci a scholar on a bay mule coming from Bologna, and **him** he questioned about Tuscany.* As we will see in §3.3.3, the contrastive and continuative uses of topicalization have given rise to some uncertainty as to whether topicalization has the core function of expressing "discontinuity," "continuity," or both.

Some of the most important works on English topicalization have not thus far had a significant influence on the study of BH. These works, including Prince (e.g., 1985, 1986, 1988, 1998), Ward and Prince (1991), and Birner and Ward (1998), are discussed in detail in chap. 6 (pp. 90ff.).

3.3.1.3. Focus and focusing

Gundel (1999) identifies three general uses of the term *focus* in the linguistic literature: *informational*,[51] *contrastive*, and *psychological*. There seems to be a fourth use as well, which I term *attentional. Focusing* is the marking of a focus by formal means, whether by prosody, syntax, or both.

Informational focus denotes the new information contained in an utterance. This is the part of the proposition expressed by the sentence that is assumed by the speaker not to be *given*, that is, shared by him and the addressee.[52] The focus supplies the value for an unknown item in the given proposition. In English, an informational focus may be marked by sentence accent, as in ***Bill** ate the doughnuts.* The accenting of *Bill* indicates that the proposition "Someone (X) ate the doughnuts" is given information in the context of utterance. The focus represents a new value for X; that is, "X = Bill."[53] Informational focus answers a *wh*-question that could be appropriately asked at the time of utterance (Lambrecht 1994: 223; Gundel 1999: 295). In the above example, *Bill* is the answer to the contextually appropriate question *Who ate the doughnuts?*

---

51. Gundel uses the term *semantic* focus instead of informational focus.

52. The term *focus* denoting new information was introduced by Halliday (1967) and further developed by Chomsky (1970), Jackendoff (1972), Rochemont (1986), and others. The given information is often termed the "presupposition." I will not use this term due to the possibility of confusion with the concept of pragmatic presupposition (see chap. 4, pp. 48ff.). Focus is related to rheme, if rheme is defined in informational terms (see §3.3.1.1); focus, however, is usually understood as comprising only part of the rheme.

53. For the sake of convenience, the term *focus* is used in this work to denote both the new value for X ("Bill"), as well as the linguistic expression in the sentence that represents this new value (*Bill*). Propositions and the values of the variables they contain are marked by double quotation marks, and linguistic expressions are in italic type.

Informational focus may be marked by devices other than accenting. One such device is the cleft construction, as in *It's **coffee** that I want*. As mentioned above, in the casual register of English, focus may also be marked by preposing, for example, ***Coffee** I want*. In both the cleft and the preposing constructions, the focus is accented in addition to being marked syntactically.

Contrastive focus is a broad concept including, among other things, informational focuses that are contrary to expectation and contrasted topics. One definition of contrastive focus is a focus that is selected from a set of possible candidates (Chafe 1976). For Givón (2001: 225), contrastive focus always includes some degree of contrary belief on the part of the hearer. The wide variety of phenomena included here makes it difficult to define the concept precisely, as noted by Vallduví and Vilkuna (1998: 83). In addition, the term *contrastive focus* is confusing, because it includes topics and focuses. Vallduví and Vilkuna (1998: 85) argue against the merging of focus and contrast, arguing that the two concepts are independent of each other.

Psychological focus is the entity that is currently the center of attention. This concept involves previously mentioned entities, frequently referred to by zero or unaccented pronouns.[54] The term *psychological focus* is somewhat confusing, because this concept is in a sense the opposite of information focus and is much closer to the notion of topic.

Attentional focus is the entity to which the speaker wishes to direct the attention of the addressee.[55] There are many reasons that a speaker might draw attention to a particular clause element; thus, attentional focus is a general concept with a variety of applications. Attentional focus resembles the classic concept of emphasis and suffers from the same deficiency as that concept, notably, the nonspecific nature of the definition.

An influential theory incorporating both topic and focus has been developed by Lambrecht (1994); this theory is discussed in §3.3.7.

The following sections discuss models of word order developed by scholars of BH that are based on the information-structure concepts discussed above.

3.3.2. Bendavid: Psychological subject and predicate

Bendavid devotes a chapter to BH word order in his work comparing Biblical and Mishnaic Hebrew (1971: 785–855). Bendavid is clearly influenced by the Prague school work on information structure, invoking the concepts of psychological subject and psychological predicate. He classifies word orders based on the placement of the new information, i.e., the psychological predicate. Bendavid describes BH as having a kind of reverse functional sentence perspective. In the "calm" sequence, the new information is at the end. An

---

54. See Gundel, Hedberg, and Zacharski (1993).
55. See, e.g., Taglicht (1984: 1, 7) and Erteschik-Shir (1997: 11; 1998). According to Taglicht, a focus is an element that is marked for prominence for various pragmatic purposes.

alternative is the "strong" sequence, in which the new information is at the beginning. The strong sequence is used in answering questions and in order to express contrast and emphasis. There is also a third order in which the new information is in the middle.

3.3.3. Bandstra

Bandstra's dissertation on כי (1982: 72–88) appears to be the first work to present a systematic model of BH preposing based on the concepts of topicalization and focusing.[56] Bandstra writes that the topic is the given part of the clause, "that part of the clause that represents the writer's thematic choice, that about which he will say something new" (1982: 74). According to Bandstra, the topicalization construction marks a topic mentioned in the preceding material in order to maintain continuity in the text. This category accounts for preposing traditionally attributed to attraction. Focusing, according to Bandstra, involves new, unexpected information, or a change in topic (1982: 78). Focusing in this conception subsumes the traditional "emphasis" and "contrast" categories.

Bandstra's conception of focus is closest to contrastive focus (see §3.3.1.3): any preposed constituent that is not continuous with the preceding material is termed a focus, including contrastive topics. Topicalization is restricted to the continuative type of preposing (see §3.3.1.2). In a later article (1992), Bandstra expands the concept of topicalization to include focusing as well. Topicalization is described as the placing of new information in the initial slot, which signals discontinuity or transition; it also is said to include cases in which the topicalized element is not new, but is fronted in order to provide continuity. It is not clear how the apparently contradictory categories of continuity and discontinuity are unified under a single heading.

3.3.4. Revell

Revell (1989a: 2) invokes the concept of attentional focus in his explanation of BH word order, although he does not refer specifically to the linguistic literature on focusing. As mentioned in §2.2, Revell believes that word order in every clause, not just in preposed clauses, is pragmatically motivated; in other words, BH is apparently viewed as a free word-order language. He states that "the constituent placed first in the clause is that which the author wishes to be the primary focus of the reader's attention." He lists various types of elements to which the author might choose to draw attention, including a new subject, the time or place of the action at the beginning of a narrative, information

---

56. Bandstra was not, however, the first to invoke the concepts of topicalization and focusing in reference to BH, contrary to van der Merwe (1990: 42). O'Connor (1980: 81, 306–7) discusses the concepts of "focus-marking" and "topicalization" but does not explore the ramifications for preposing.

significant to the story, the answer to a question, a contrastive element, and an anaphoric pronoun or adverb that refers to the preceding context.

In Revell (1989b: 21), the principle governing word order is termed "thematization" and is defined as the arrangement of the components of the clause "in the order of their significance for the speaker or narrator." Revell states that imperfect verb forms are modal when clause-initial and indicative when clause-medial; this assertion is adopted by a number of other scholars including Cook (2001, 2004), DeCaen (1995), Holmstedt (2002, 2005), Joosten (1992), and Shulman (1996). It should be noted that Revell in no way intended his observation to mean that the word-order system as a whole marks the semantic indicative/modal opposition. A position such as this would contradict Revell's view that the *weqatal* form, which serves as a syntactically conditioned variant of the indicative imperfect, is used whenever a speaker wishes to place an indicative verb in clause-initial position (Revell 1989b: 21). For Revell, the modal/indicative rule is a secondary consequence of the thematization principle: modal verbs tend to be the most significant part of the clause and are therefore usually clause-initial (Revell 1989b: 21).[57] As Shulman points out, modals are occasionally clause-medial when the speaker wishes to place the focus on a different clause component (1996: 241–49).[58]

3.3.5. Buth: A synthesis of information structure and foreground-background

In Buth's (1987) dissertation on Biblical Aramaic and subsequent work on BH, topic and focus are set within the Functional Grammar framework, developed by Dik (1980, 1989).[59] In Functional Grammar, language is viewed primarily as an instrument of communication; as a result, "pragmatics is seen as the all-encompassing framework within which semantics and syntax must be studied" (Dik 1989: 7). It is posited that all languages have an initial preposed position ("P1") that may be used for marking topic and focus. Topic in Functional Grammar denotes what the sentence is about (Dik 1980: 16) or, in a later version of the theory, what the discourse is about (Dik 1989: 266–77).[60] Topics that are continuous or resumed are likely to be marked by being placed in P1. Focus is understood as the most important part of the utterance; this definition

---

57. Cook's statement "word order is grammatically relevant in Biblical Hebrew: it distinguishes between modal and indicative verbs" (2004: 265) is made possible only by his reinterpretation of *weqatal* as a modal form. Even with this adjustment, the most common indicative verb form, *wayyiqtol*, is excluded from the VX-modal/XV-indicative scheme. On the relevance of modality to the question of BH basic word order, see §2.2.

58. For examples of XV clauses containing volitive forms in Genesis, see §5.1, p. 65 nn. 2-4.

59. Rosenbaum (1997) has applied the Functional Grammar framework to BH poetry.

60. In an earlier version of the theory (Dik 1980), topicality is defined as what the sentence is about.

includes informational focus as well as contrastive focus (Dik 1989: 277–85).[61]
A focus may be marked when it fills in a gap in the addressee's information, or
is contrastive. Marked topic and focus are denoted in Functional Grammar by
the capitalized terms *Topic* and *Focus*.

Buth (1987: 50–51) proposes an additional function, *Setting*, which "presents the framework" in which the clause is to be interpreted and usually consists of a spatial or temporal phrase.[62] The implication would appear to be that
temporal phrases can be fronted for no reason other than to provide an orienta-
tion for the clause. In later work, Buth proposes a new definition of Topic that
includes the Setting function. The resulting inclusive category is defined as a
constituent that serves "as a frame of reference for relating a clause to its context" (1994b: 217) and is renamed Contextualizing Constituent (Buth 1994b,
1995, 1999). Buth considers contrastive topics to be simultaneously Topics and
Focuses (1994b: 223).

An innovation of Buth's is the synthesis of the information-structure and
foreground-background models to yield a comprehensive theory of BH preposing.[63] In his 1987 dissertation, Buth writes that backgrounded clauses
may be marked in Biblical Aramaic by putting a "pseudo-topic" in the preposed position. Buth refines this idea in later works (1994b, 1995). Influenced
by Levinsohn (1990),[64] Buth proposes that *wayyiqtol* (VSO) clauses mark
continuity-foreground, and *X-qatal* (SVO/OVS) clauses mark discontinuity-
background.[65] One type of discontinuity concerns a particular constituent in the
clause, which is preposed to mark it as Focus or Contextualizing Constituent. A
different type is temporal discontinuity (i.e., nonsequentiality), which concerns
the clause as a whole. This type of discontinuity may also be marked by preposing, although the discontinuity does not concern the preposed constituent.

61. See also de Jong (1981) and Dik et al. (1981). For critical discussion of Topic and
Focus in Functional Grammar, see, e.g., Siewierska (1991); Bolkestein (1998).

62. On the distinction between Topic and Setting, see Hannay (1991: 146). On Setting in
BH, see also Rosenbaum 1997: 41–44. Winther-Nielsen (1992) cites Gen 1:1 as an example
of preposing to mark Setting in BH.

63. The synthesis of topic and background is most fully explained in Buth's later articles, although it is clearly present as early as his 1987 dissertation.

64. Levinsohn (1990) describes BH topicalization as the marking of discontinuity: the
discontinuity may concern a switch in participants, or a switch in the thematic or temporal
progression of the story. See also Levinsohn's earlier (1987) discussion of word order and
discontinuity in the book of Acts. The debt to Levinsohn is acknowledged in Buth (1995: 97
n. 14). Levinsohn, however, does not feel that background is a useful concept with respect to
preposing. In Bailey and Levinsohn (1992), the thesis is advanced that all preposing is either
focusing or topicalization.

65. A precedent for this paradigm is Lambdin (1971: §132), for whom *we-* + verb (VSO)
signifies a "conjunctive-sequential" clause, and *waw* + nonverb (SVO/OVS) signals a "disjunctive" clause. Disjunctive clauses may be contrastive, circumstantial, explanatory, parenthetical, terminative, or initial (see also Waltke and O'Connor 1990: §§8.3, 39.21–23).

Buth (1994b: 218) writes, "The marked Contextualizing Constituent ('Topic') may not itself be the point of discontinuity. The clause as a whole is the Discontinuity, not the marked term." A further use of preposing is to mark a new paragraph or narrative unit (1995: 89–90). Buth suggests that this too can be viewed as a type of discontinuity, and the preposed element in these cases can be termed a Contextualizing Constituent (1995: 90): "the contextualizing constituent . . . can be said to mark the clause for a wide range of relationships which includes a backgrounding-discontinuity where the discontinuity does not refer to a switch of a 'topic,' but to a higher level of discontinuity." A further extension of the contextualizing constituent concept is to include the preposed constituent that marks a "dramatic pause" within the story (1994b: 226–27). The dramatic pause marks a peak in the story, which is a sequential, foregrounded event. This too, it is proposed, should be viewed as a subtype of discontinuity-background (1995: 92).

An apparent inconsistency in Buth's model regards the claim that Topics are necessarily discontinuous. As noted above, in Functional Grammar continuous topics as well as discontinuous topics are thought to be marked by preposing. Buth's definition of contextualizing constituent should include continuous topics, because these elements certainly orient the clause to its context. If this is the case, not all preposing involves discontinuity.

More fundamentally, it is questionable whether Buth is successful in unifying all the different types of discontinuities. By applying the term *Contextualizing Constituent* to cases in which the preposed item does not actually function as Topic or Setting, Buth is calling very different things by the same name. A similar problem concerns the concept of dramatic pause, which occurs in a foregrounded clause but is nevertheless included in the background category.

3.3.6. Gross: A focus-centered model

Gross has investigated BH word order in a number of articles (e.g., 1987a, 1988a, 1993a, 1993b, 1994, 2001b, 2004), a monograph on BH word order (1996) in collaboration with Disse and Michel, and another monograph on doubly preposed clauses, particularly in poetry (2001a).[66] Disse (1998) also published his 1996 dissertation on information structure, adopting a similar theoretical framework.

Gross uses a syntactic framework developed by W. Richter, with some modifications. He distinguishes a preverbal field ("Vorfeld") and a main field ("Hauptfeld") in the clause (1996: 48, 149). The preverbal field may contain

66. The main conclusions of Gross (1996) are summarized in Gross (1999) and in a review article by van der Merwe (1999c). The monograph on double preposing is examined in a review article by Bailey (2004). The discussion in this section focuses on the conclusions of the 1996 monograph, because the pragmatics of double preposing, as well as the functions of preposing in poetry, are outside the scope of this study (see §§1.2 and 5.4.2).

one or more items. Certain conjunctions, "clause deictics" and "text deictics," and clausal adverbs relate to the entire sentence and always stand at the outer edge of the preverbal field. A number of other syntactic categories are always or usually in the preverbal field, including interrogative particles and deictic particles such as שם, כן, כה, זה, and אז.

Gross (1996: 53–66) discusses the concept of theme (topic) extensively, but does not make use of it in his pragmatic description of preposing. He uses *topicalization* as a purely syntactic term referring to a preposed structure. On the pragmatic level, preposing is analyzed primarily in terms of focus. In defining focus, Gross (1996: 66–72) utilizes J. Jacobs's relational view, in which an element is considered a focus if that element was chosen from a set of potential referents.[67] This conception of focus closely resembles Chafe's (1976) definition of contrastive focus (see §3.3.1.3 above). A sentence is allowed by Gross to have multiple focuses.

Gross (1996; 1999: 40–45) describes a number of other circumstances, aside from focusing, in which preposing occurs. A temporal adjunct may be preposed without being focused. A nonfocused subject may be preposed at the beginning of a narrative or quoted speech,[68] in an answer to a discourse-initial request,[69] in a background description, in "authorial commentary" within a narrative, or in "supplement" information (e.g., an anterior event). Additional reasons for preposing are "connection," in which the preposed item is identical to an item in the previous clause, and "enumeration," which is an "on-the-one-hand/on-the-other" or "neither-nor" construction.[70]

Van der Merwe (1999c: 290) points out that because he omits the notion of topic from his pragmatic analysis of preposing, Gross is unable to provide a comprehensive account of preposing: "the complexity of his findings . . . and the number of cases that he has to leave out of consideration . . . indicate that his notional category of focus can explain only one aspect of his data." This criticism is taken into account in Gross's 2001 monograph, in which the concept of topic is identified as one of the functions of preposing (2001a: 310).

3.3.7. Heimerdinger, van der Merwe, and Shimasaki

Much of the latest research on BH word order is modeled after Lambrecht's (1994) work on information focus.[71] In his revision of his dissertation, Heimerdinger (1999) develops a theory of preverbal and postverbal word order in which Lambrecht's model plays an important role. A similar preposing

---

67. This definition of focus is also adopted by van der Merwe (see §3.3.7). De Regt (2006: 292) writes similarly that preposing occurs with "restrictive" or "contrastive" focuses, which are picked "out of a set of possibilities."

68. See, e.g., 1 Kgs 20:17, 2 Kgs 1:6.

69. See, e.g., Judg 6:18.

70. See, e.g., Deut 7:5, 9:9.

71. For a review of Lambrecht (1994), see Polinsky (1999).

model appears in van der Merwe (1999b) and van der Merwe and Talstra (2002–3: 83).[72] Floor (2003, 2004) follows Lambrecht and Heimerdinger in his overall approach.[73] Another work influenced by Lambrecht is Shimasaki's (2002) revision of his 1999 dissertation.[74] An additional scholar who applies Lambrecht's framework to BH is Bailey (2004), in a review article on Gross (2001). Lunn has applied Lambrecht's model to BH poetry in his (2006) revision of his 2004 dissertation.

Topic for Lambrecht is what the sentence is about. Focus is defined in informational terms as "the element of information whereby the presupposition and the assertion differ from each other" (1994: 207),[75] in other words, focus is the information conveyed by the sentence, minus the portion that the addressee already knows. According to Lambrecht sentences must have a focus, but may have no topic, one topic, or more than one.

Lambrecht combines focus and topic structures into a single prosodic paradigm.[76] Most sentences can be categorized as having one of three focus/topic articulations, each having a characteristic accentuation pattern (the main accent in the clause is marked by bold type):

(11) Lambrecht's topic/focus articulations[77]

a. Predicate focus = Topic-comment   *My car broke **down**.*
    (Answer to *What happened to your car?*)

---

72. Van der Merwe (1999b) cites Heimerdinger as a reference. Van der Merwe's approach to BH word has evolved over the years. In van der Merwe (1989, 1991), preposing is described as marking topic or focus. Like Gross, Van der Merwe defines focus as "a particular item from a number of possible alternatives" (van der Merwe 1989: 128). Topic is "that part of a sentence which determines the frame of interpretation" (1989: 128). Topics are marked by preposing in cases of contrastive topics, new topics, and interruptions of narrative sequences. In van der Merwe et al. (1999: §47), the functions of preposing are described as marking focus, marking a new or reactivated topic, and marking a simultaneous or nearly simultaneous event. Focus is defined there as "the most salient information conveyed by a particular utterance," a definition closest to attentional focus.

73. Floor (2003, 2004) elaborates on the category of topic, distinguishing four subcategories, and shows that marked word-order constructions contribute to the development of discourse themes.

74. For a review of Shimasaki, see Holmstedt (2003).

75. Lambrecht (1994: 52) defines the (pragmatic) presupposition of a sentence as "the set of propositions lexicogrammatically evoked in a sentence which the speaker assumes the addressee already knows or is ready to take for granted at the time the sentence is uttered" (this definition is slightly modified later on in the book). Some problems with Lambrecht's definition of focus are discussed in Dryer (1996: 517).

76. For Lambrecht, focus/presupposition and topic/comment are closely related notions; thus, the predicate-focus clause can also be described as having "topic-comment" structure, where the subject is the topic and the predicate (the focus) is the comment. Sentence-focus structures are those that have a comment and no topic. Further comments on this paradigm appear in §6.1.1.

77. See Lambrecht (1994: 222–23).

    b. Argument focus = Identificational   *My **car** broke down.*
       (Answer to *What broke down?*)
    c. Sentence focus = Event reporting   *My **car** broke down.*
       (Answer to *What happened?*)

Predicate focus is the unmarked articulation, and argument and sentence focus the pragmatically marked types. In predicate focus, the focus is "projected" from a constituent within the verb phrase to include the entire verb phrase.[78] Thus, although only the word *down* is accented in (11a), the focus is the verb phrase *broke down*. The predicate-focus structure is also a topic-comment structure: the subject is the topic and the verb phrase the comment. In the argument-focus articulation, the accent is on the focused argument; in (11b), the focus is the subject *my car*. In sentence focus, the entire sentence is the focus and simultaneously the comment: sentence-focus sentences have no topic. Sentence focus in intransitive clauses is marked by an accent on the subject, as in (11c);[79] the focus is projected from the subject to include the entire sentence. The sentence-focus articulation, as in (11c), is identical to the argument-focus articulation with a focused subject, as in (11b): in both of these articulations, the accent is on the subject.

    According to Lambrecht (1994: 138–40), the sentence-focus category includes two types of sentences: "presentational" and "event-reporting" sentences. Presentational sentences indicate the existence of a referent (e.g., *There was a man*), or the appearance of a new referent in the discourse (e.g., ***John** arrived*). Event-reporting sentences announce an event concerning a referent new to the discourse (Lambrecht 1994: 14), (e.g., *My **car** broke down.*) Lambrecht explains that both of these types are "thetic judgments," that is, sentences that simply recognize a fact, as opposed to the ordinary sentence, which involves both recognizing a subject and recognizing what is expressed about the subject by the predicate.[80]

    The intriguing identity between argument- and sentence-focus articulations[81] in Lambrecht's paradigm leads Heimerdinger, van der Merwe and Shimasaki

---

    78. On focus projection, see Halliday (1967: 208); Chomsky (1970: 92–93); Ladd (1980: 74); Selkirk (1995: 554); Gussenhoven (1999).

    79. On this sentence pattern, see Schmerling (1976: 22).

    80. See Kuroda (1972). Kuno (1972) calls sentence-focus sentences "neutral descriptions."

    81. It should be noted that argument-focus (with a focused subject) and sentence-focus articulations are identical only for intransitive clauses. In transitive sentence-focus sentences, both subject and complement are accented: *The **children** went to **school***. See, e.g., Selkirk (1995: 556) and Lambrecht (1994: 121, example 4.2d). This accentuation pattern is identical with the predicate-focus articulation, rather than the argument-focus articulation. However, in a later work Lambrecht (2000: 620–21) argues that transitive thetic sentences with a lexical subject and object should be excluded from the sentence-focus category, thereby preserving the identity between subject- and sentence-focus articulations.

to hypothesize a comparable phenomenon in BH: "Although we do not have access to the accentuation patterns of BH, I will hypothesize below that also in BH one and the same construction is used in instances of argument and sentence focus, viz. the fronting of nonverbal constituents in verbal clauses" (van der Merwe and Talstra 2002–3: 77). This leads to the following model: unmarked word order, which is verb-first, is typically used for predicate focus, while preposing is used to mark argument and sentence focus. It is noted that not every verb-first clause has predicate focus; the clause may have an argument-focus structure that is marked only by accenting (van der Merwe and Talstra 2002–3: 80).

It is clear that argument and sentence focus, as defined by Lambrecht, are not sufficient to account for all BH preposing. Backgrounded/nonsequential clauses, for one thing, would not seem to fit either category. Van der Merwe and Talstra (2002–3: 83) address this issue by broadening the sentence-focus category to include background clauses. Other preposing types not included in the paradigm, as noted by van der Merwe and Talstra, include preposed topics that are compared, contrasted, or listed (e.g., Deut 4:7–8, 4:13–14, 28:67).[82]

Heimerdinger's model is a combination of Lambrecht's paradigm and a notion he calls the "dominant focal element." The dominant focal element is the part of the focus which is "the informationally pivotal element of the assertion" (1999: 167–68) and is determined by a combination of syntactic and pragmatic factors. Clauses with predicate focus are usually verb-first, unless the choice of the dominant focal element is surprising in some respect (1999: 201–6, 212); in these cases, the dominant focal element is preposed. Another cause of preposing in the predicate-focus clause is the contrastive-topic construction (1999: 183–85). Argument-focus clauses are always preposed, as are sentence-focus clauses. Like van der Merwe and Talstra, Heimerdinger widens the sentence-focus category, this time to include narrative flashbacks.

Shimasaki (2002), who models his theory loosely after Lambrecht, asserts that the focus in BH is always at the head of the clause. BH is thus apparently seen as a free word-order language, in which word order is always pragmatically determined (see §2.2). Shimasaki takes an attentional approach to focus, defining it as a constituent that is marked as a "prominent piece of information" (2002: 42). All preposing can be explained as argument or clause (= sentence) focus. Clause focus for Shimasaki is a clause "marked for a high-cost cognitive effort" (2002: 145). Clause-focus clauses may have "inter-clausal level implications" (2002: 150), including exclamation/proclamation, contrasting the whole proposition, and circumstantiality. The concept of circumstantiality according to Shimasaki "covers a wide range of connotations," including

---

82. It should be noted Lambrecht did not intend his paradigm to cover these pragmatic sentence types. He also recognizes a separate "contrastive topic" accentual pattern; that is, *The **children** went to **school**, and the **parents** went to **bed*** (1994: 124, 291–95).

anteriority, simultaneity, parenthetical or explanatory information, condition, concession, and cause. Alternatively, a clause with clause-focus structure may have a "text-unit level implication" (2002: 163) such as textual-unit onset or closure, topic announcing (which he terms "topicalization"), and topic shifting. According to Shimasaki, clauses with clause-focus structure are typically non-sequential (2002: 148).

The proper definition of the sentence-focus category is an important issue for word-order models based on Lambrecht. Sentence focus in Lambrecht's definition, being restricted to event-reporting and presentational clauses, clearly does not apply to many preposed clauses.[83] Van der Merwe and Talstra's proposal to include backgrounded clauses in the sentence-focus category is problematic, given that a backgrounded clause in an English narrative would not normally be uttered with the articulation used for event reporting. Even more problematic is Shimasaki's catch-all conception of sentence-focus as including a wide variety of pragmatic functions.

An even more fundamental issue, however, is whether the link between preposing and sentence focus, in the strict sense of the term, is valid for classical BH prose in the first place. Lambrecht (2000: 638) notes the use of subject fronting for sentence focus in some verb-initial languages, although he states that it is more typical in these languages for the subject to be placed in the post-verbal object position.[84] The evidence that preposing marks sentence-focus in BH is underwhelming. According to more than one scholar, event-reporting sentences in BH typically have VS, not SV, word order (Joüon-Muraoka §155nd; Qimron 1998).[85] As far as presentational clauses, there is a preposed example of an existential clause in Job (1:1): אִישׁ הָיָה בְאֶרֶץ עוּץ 'There was a man in the land of Uz'. In the classical BH prose corpus, however, this existential structure is extremely rare.[86] The usual formula for an existential clause involves a nonpreposed וַיְהִי form, as shown in (12):[87]

---

83. Lambrecht's characterization of sentence focus in a later work (2000: 620–21) is even narrower, excluding all transitive clauses except for those with pronominal objects (see p. 43 n. 81 above).

84. In SVO languages, preposing is not used to mark subject focus; instead, sentence-focus sentences may be given VS order (Lambrecht 2000: 634).

85. Qimron provides a list of examples, including Gen 27:35, 31:1, 42:29–30, 45:16; Judg 16:23, 16:24; 1 Sam 10:2, 14:29; 2 Sam 3:23, 12:18, 15:10; 1 Kgs 21:13, 14; 2 Kgs 8:7, 9:13. Some of these (Gen 27:35, 2 Sam 3:23, 2 Kgs 8:7) can be categorized as presentational clauses. Genesis contains two counterexamples to Qimron's observation: the direct-speech clauses in Gen 37:20 and 37:33 are event-reporting clauses with SV word order.

86. Two examples that I found in the classical BH prose corpus are 2 Sam 12:1 (in a direct-speech quotation) and 2 Kgs 7:3.

87. Additional examples from the classical BH prose corpus are Num 9:6; Judg 17:1; 1 Sam 1:1, 9:1; and 2 Sam 21:20.

(12) Judg 13:2

ויהי איש אחד מצרעה ממשפחת הדני

There was a man from Zorah from the tribe of the Danites.

The other type of presentational clause, as mentioned above, indicates the appearance of a new referent; in BH, this kind of clause would presumably contain the verb בוא or a synonym. It has already been remarked by Joüon-Muraoka (§155nd n. 2) that clauses with בא typically have VS, not SV, order. A statistical examination of all of the finite nonsubordinate clauses in the classical BH prose corpus containing the verb בוא in the Qal and having a presentational meaning confirms this observation: a total of 36 out of 44 (82%) clauses have VS word order.[88] Although this figure does not prove that preposing does not mark sentence-focus in the eight preposed clauses,[89] the small number of clauses involved does not provide convincing evidence that sentence-focus, as opposed to some other pragmatic category, is the function of preposing in these clauses. In any case, it is evident that presentational preposed clauses are quite rare in classical BH prose.

3.4. Conclusion

As the the emphasis-centered model has largely fallen out of favor, backgrounding/temporal-sequencing and information-structure models dominate the field of contemporary research on BH word order. In the backgrounding model and the temporal-sequencing variation of this model, preposing is seen as marking a characteristic relating to the clause as a whole. These models fall short of a global paradigm for word order but succeed in explaining some types of subject-preposing, including parenthetical remarks, anterior clauses, and (in the case of the temporal-sequencing model) simultaneous clause pairs. The use of preposing to mark a new narrative unit cannot necessarily be incorporated in the background concept; however, this function has in common with backgrounding functions the characteristic that it pertains to the clause as a whole rather than to the preposed constituent.

In the information-structure approach, the function of preposing is seen as relating specifically to the preposed constituent. Focusing and topicalization together account for all of the clauses formerly considered emphatic, contras-

---

88. SV clauses falling into alternate pragmatic categories already identified, such as simultaneous clauses, parenthetical clauses, or topicalization, were eliminated from the count, because the category of sentence focus is not needed to explain the marked word order in these cases. The remaining SV clauses are Gen 46:31, 47:1, 48:2; Josh 2:2; Judg 13:6; 1 Sam 23:27; 1 Kgs 13:1; and 2 Kgs 4:42.

89. As explained in §2.1, marking a pragmatic category by preposing is always a choice made by the speaker/writer; thus, even if preposing could be used to mark sentence-focus, this does not mean that every sentence with a sentence-focus interpretation, or even the majority of these sentences, would necessarily be preposed.

tive, or due to attraction. The division of labor between focusing and topical-ization is a matter of debate among Hebraists, mirroring a variety of opinions found in the general linguistic literature. Scholars disagree as to whether it is informational, contrastive, or attentional focus that is relevant to preposing. An additional point of disagreement is whether topicalization marks continuity, discontinuity, or both.

Like the backgrounding/temporal-sequencing models, the information-structure model cannot serve as a comprehensive framework for BH word order. Preposing to mark anteriority or simultaneity does not fit either the topi-calization or the focusing category, nor does preposing clauses marking the be-ginning of a narrative unit. Although an attempt has been made to integrate the backgrounding and information-structure models in a global "discontinuity" paradigm, the two models seem to concern two fundamentally different types of pragmatic functions. It is likely that both information-structure functions and backgrounding-type functions are involved in the preposing phenomenon. It is not clear, however, which type of function is widespread in the biblical corpus.

The present study explores the significance of information-structure func-tions for preposing in BH. The concepts of focusing and topicalization are clarified and redefined so that they provide insights into when and why prepos-ing occurs. A sample of preposed clauses is examined to determine whether information-structure functions are statistically dominant or whether functions that relate to the clause as a whole, such as simultaneity and anteriority, are the dominant kind. In addition, differences between preposing in narrative and direct speech are explored. In subsequent chapters, focused and topicalized clauses are analyzed in detail from the syntactic and the pragmatic perspectives.

Chapter 4

The Biblical Hebrew Finite Clause
and Its Constituents

This chapter defines syntactic categories relating to the BH verbal clause and its constituents. A structural approach, in which syntactic categories are defined using formal rather than semantic criteria is followed wherever possible. Unfortunately, linguistic categories do not always have neat boundaries even when defined in structural terms (Huddleston and Pullum 2002: 90). A category may have central members that possess all of the characteristics typically associated with the category, as well as peripheral members that have only some of these characteristics. Trying to decide which category to assign to a peripheral item is at times a fruitless and artificial endeavor. My present purpose, however, is not to write a BH grammar but simply to delineate criteria for selecting and categorizing the clauses in the Genesis corpus. The definitions set out here, therefore, are designed to minimize the number of cases viewed as indeterminate.

As noted in chap. 1, the present work analyzes word order in the nonsubordinate finite clause. The terms *clause*, *finite*, and *nonsubordinate* are all given explicit definition here. In §4.1, I discuss the distinction between sentence and clause. In §4.2, I define finite and nonfinite clauses. In §4.3, I address the subordinate clause and its various semantic subtypes. Certain problems in distinguishing subordination from coordination, including the syntactic analysis of direct and indirect speech, are addressed in §4.4. The constituents of the clause and their syntactic classification are discussed in §4.5. I concentrate on issues relevant to the Genesis corpus and do not attempt to provide a comprehensive description of the BH finite clause.

4.1. The clause and the sentence

A clause minimally includes a predicate. In the verbal clause, the predicate is the verb; in the nonverbal clause, the predicate is nonverbal and may be, for example, a noun phrase, prepositional phrase, or subordinate clause. Clauses are either *simple*, containing a single predication and no subordinate clauses, or *complex*, containing a main predication and one or more subordinate clauses. Both simple and complex clauses are included in the present study.

The *sentence* is a syntactic unit consisting of a single clause or a group of coordinated clauses. Although the idea of the sentence is intuitively clear, the formal definition of this concept continues to elude linguists. In spoken language, prosody is used to indicate which clauses go together to constitute a unit, and punctuation serves the same purpose in written language. Yet it is not clear that units so delineated always constitute a syntactic sentence.[1] For example, clauses that most likely constitute two separate sentences may nonetheless appear in a single orthographic sentence, joined by a semicolon or dash:

(13) I saw Marcia yesterday; she looked upset.

In Biblical Hebrew, the quest for the sentence is probably an exercise in futility. The researcher trying to define the sentence in Biblical Hebrew must grapple with texts that appear to be one interminably long sentence, because almost every clause in narrative begins with the coordinator וֹ. Although the traditional verse division groups clauses into units, there is no particular reason to think that verse division corresponds to syntactic sentence boundaries. Given this situation, I ignore the coordination of clauses to form sentences and treat each clause, whether simple or coordinated, separately. The only coordination recognized here is the coordination of subordinate clauses, which generally involves a clear end boundary (see §4.3).

Determining the boundary of the individual clause is also problematic. Because verbs in BH inflect for number, gender, and person, clauses need not contain an explicit subject. If compound verbs are recognized, one faces the problem of deciding whether two successive verbs with the same implicit subject constitute two separate clauses or a single clause. In this study, I make the simplifying assumption that each verb belongs to a separate clause.[2]

---

1. Huddleston and Pullum (2002: 1729) write that the question whether an orthographic unit marked by punctuation is a syntactic sentence "may have no determinate answer."

2. One case that cannot be analyzed in this way is ואת כל חילם ואת כל טפם ואת נשיהם שבו ויבזו ואת כל אשר בבית 'And all of their wealth and all of their children and their wives they took captive and took as booty, and everything in the house' (Gen 34:29). The two verbs are preceded by a sequence of three coordinated noun phrases and followed by a fourth. The first and last of the noun phrases, ואת כל אשר בבית and ואת כל חילם, serve as a discontinuous coordinate complement of the second verb, ויבזו. The intermediate coordinated phrases ואת כל טפם ואת נשיהם relate to the first verb שבו. The sense of the sentence is, roughly, 'they took captive and took as booty respectively their children and wives, and all of their wealth and everything in the house'. The interwoven structure of the Hebrew construction makes it necessary to consider it a single clause with a compound verb phrase rather than two coordinated clauses.

4.2. Finite and nonfinite clauses

The *finite* clause is a clause with a finite verb form as predicate. The BH finite forms are listed in (14).

(14) Finite verb forms
Perfect	כָּתַב
Perfect consecutive	וְכָתַב
Imperfect	יִכְתֹּב
Imperfect consecutive	וַיִּכְתֹּב
Jussive	יִבֶן
Cohortative	נִכְתְּבָה
Imperative	כְּתֹב

Jussive and imperfect forms are distinct only in Hiphil verbs, in certain weak verbs (ע"ו and ע"י) in Qal, and in ל"ה verbs in all binyanim.

The *nonfinite* forms are the infinitive construct (לִכְתֹּב), infinitive absolute (כָּתוֹב), and participle (כּוֹתֵב). Certain forms are ambiguous in theory, capable of being interpreted as a participle or a perfect (e.g., בָּא, קָם), but these can usually be disambiguated in context based on the meaning of the clause in context.

4.3. Subordinate and nonsubordinate clauses

The *subordinate* clause functions as a constituent of the *superordinate* clause that contains it. Clauses that are not subordinate to other clauses are termed *independent* or *nonsubordinate* clauses.[3]

Finite subordinate clauses may or may not be marked as such by a subordinator. The most common subordinators are אשר and כי. The conditional subordinate clause has its own subordinators, as described in §4.3.2.1. Infinitive clauses are always subordinate and are not marked by subordinators. When several subordinate clauses are coordinated, the subordinator is frequently omitted in all but the first clause:

(15) Deut 22:7

שלח תשלח את האם ואת הבנים תקח לך **למען ייטב לך והארכת ימים**:

You shall let the mother go, and the young you may take for yourself, **so that it may go well with you, and [so that] you may live long.**

Although not explicitly marked as such, והארכת ימים is subordinate because it is coordinated with the preceding subordinate clause, למען ייטב לך.

I now discuss the various types of subordinate clauses, including *relative* clauses, *adjunct* clauses, and *content* clauses. The discussion is limited to the

___

3. In this study, I use the term *nonsubordinate*, rather than *independent*, because the latter is sometimes used to refer to a clause that is not coordinated with other clauses. A nonsubordinate clause, in contrast, may be coordinated with another clause.

finite subordinate clause, because nonfinite subordinate clauses are in any case excluded from the data.

4.3.1. The relative clause

The *relative* clause modifies a noun phrase and contains an explicit or implicit anaphoric pronoun referring to that noun phrase. Finite relative clauses in classical BH prose are generally marked by אשר:

(16) Gen 18:8

ויקח חמאה וחלב ובן הבקר **אשר עשה**

And he took curds and milk and the calf **that he had prepared**

A relative clause may occur without an antecedent noun phrase:

(17) Gen 43:16

ויאמר לאשר על ביתו

And he said to **[the person] who was in charge of his house**

4.3.2. The adjunct clause

The *adjunct* clause is a subordinate clause that functions as an adjunct in the superordinate clause (see §4.5 for a definition of the adjunct). The adjunct clause category as understood in the present study is narrower than in some other treatments, because many structures traditionally considered to be adjunct clauses are treated here as prepositional phrases. In the traditional approach, words such as אחרי 'after' and עד 'until' are defined as prepositions when their complements are noun phrases but as subordinators when their complements are clauses. Thus, עד in עד היום הזה 'until this day' (Exod 10:6) is a preposition, whereas in עד יצמח זקנכם 'until your beards grow' (2 Sam 10:5) עד is a subordinator, and the entire structure is an adjunct clause.

According to a prominent school of thought in modern linguistics, however, prepositions can take clauses as complements. Hebraists adopting this approach include Waltke and O'Connor (1990: §§38.3–38.7) and Steiner (1997: 169). According to this approach, both עד היום הזה and עד יצמח זקנכם are prepositional phrases.[4] In the present study, particles that govern noun phrases and clauses are considered prepositions in both cases. The clause governed by a preposition is considered a content clause, as discussed in §4.3.3.2.

---

4. See, e.g., Huddleston and Pullum (2002: 598–601). I differ from Huddleston and Pullum in regarding particles as prepositions only when they have a complement; when they occur alone, I retain the traditional classification as adverbs. Thus, אחר is a preposition in the phrase אחר הדברים האלה 'after these things' but an adverb in the clause ואחר ילדה בת 'and afterwards she bore a daughter' (Gen 30:21).

A finite adjunct clause may express the semantic categories of time, cause, condition, or purpose, as discussed in §§4.3.2.1–4.3.2.4. The various semantic types can in some cases be distinguished by their characteristic subordinators.

4.3.2.1. The conditional adjunct clause

Conditional clauses are marked by the subordinators אם and כי. Hypothetical conditionals are marked by the subordinator לו, and negative hypotheticals by לולי. An example of each subordinator is shown in (18)–(21).

(18) אם

אם אמצא בסדם חמשים צדיקם בתוך העיר ונשאתי לכל המקום בעבורם:

If I find in Sodom fifty righteous ones within the city, I will forgive the whole place for their sake. (Gen 18:26)

(19) כי

וכי יגח שור את איש או את אשה ומת סקול יסקל השור ולא יאכל את בשרו

If an ox gores a man or a woman and s/he dies, the ox shall be stoned, and its flesh shall not be eaten. (Exod 21:28)

(20) לו

לו חפץ י' להמיתנו לא לקח מידנו עלה ומנחה ולא הראנו את כל אלה וכעת לא השמיענו כזאת

If the LORD had meant to kill us, he would not have accepted a burnt offering and a grain offering at our hands, and would not have shown us all these things, and he would not now have announced to us such things as these. (Judg 13:23)

(21) לולא

לולי אלהי אבי אלהי אברהם ופחד יצחק היה לי כי עתה ריקם שלחתני

If the God of my father, the God of Abraham and the Fear of Isaac, had not been with me, you would have sent me away empty-handed. (Gen 31:42)

In oaths, אם may be used without an explicit apodosis:

(22) Gen 14:22–23[5]

הרימתי ידי אל י' אל עליון קנה שמים וארץ: אם מחוט ועד שרוך נעל ואם אקח מכל אשר לך

I swear to the LORD, God Most High, Maker of heaven and earth, **if I take a thread or a sandal-strap or anything that is yours [may I be punished].**

---

5. Additional examples from the Genesis corpus are Gen 21:23, 26:29, 31:52, and 42:15.

According to Richard Steiner (personal communication) "an oath may be formulated as a conditional and a self-imprecation is understood as the apodosis: 'if I do such and such (may God do such and such to me as a punishment)'."[6] The full formula with the apodosis can be found in verses such as 1 Sam 3:17 and 2 Kgs 6:31.

In addition to its use as a conditional subordinator, לו serves as an optative adverb expressing a wish (GKC §151e; Joüon-Muraoka §163):[7]

(23) Gen 17:18

לו ישמעאל יחיה לפניך:

O that Ishmael might live before you!

Optative לו could theoretically be explained as a subordinator marking a conditional clause with a missing apodosis, by analogy to oaths with אם.[8] Because the full formula with the apodosis does not occur in the case of לו, however, it is preferable to view optative לו as an adverb from a synchronic perspective, whether or not it derives historically from the conditional subordinator.

4.3.2.2. The causal adjunct clause

Finite clauses expressing cause are marked in Genesis by the subordinator כי:

(24) Gen 2:5

וכל עשב השדה טרם יצמח **כי לא המטיר י׳ אלהים על הארץ**:

And no grasses of the field had yet sprouted **because the Lord God had not caused it to rain upon the earth**.

4.3.2.3. The temporal adjunct clause

Temporal finite clauses are marked by כי or, rarely, by אם, as shown by the parallel verses in (25) and (26) (Joüon-Muraoka §166p).

(25) Deut 12:20

כי ירחיב י׳ אלהיך את גבולך כאשר דבר לך ואמרת אכלה בשר כי תאוה נפשך לאכל בשר בכל אות נפשך תאכל בשר

When the Lord your God enlarges your border, as He promised you, and you say, "I shall eat meat," because you have the urge to eat meat, you may eat meat whenever you desire.

---

6. According to a different view, אם in oaths should be viewed from a synchronic perspective as a negative asseverative particle meaning 'certainly not' (see, e.g., GKC §150; Joüon-Muraoka §166).

7. See also Gen 30:34.

8. In GKC (§151e n. 1), this is suggested as a historical explanation of the optative use. In Huehnergard's (1983: 575) view, optative לו does not derive from the conditional; rather, לו was historically a particle used to mark hypothetical propositions, including those expressed by unreal conditionals and optative clauses.

(26) Deut 19:8

ואם ירחיב י׳ אלהיך את גבלך כאשר נשבע לאבתיך ונתן לך את כל הארץ אשר
דבר לתת לאבתיך:

And when the LORD your God enlarges your border, as he has sworn to
your fathers, and gives you all the land that he promised to give to your
fathers

4.3.2.4. The purpose adjunct clause

Finite adjunct clauses expressing negative purpose are marked by פן 'lest':

(27) Gen 19:15

קום קח את אשתך ואת שתי בנתיך הנמצאת **פן תספה בעון העיר**:

Arise, take your wife and your two daughters who are here, **lest you be
consumed because of the iniquity of the city**.

Positive purpose adjuncts are usually expressed by content clauses governed by
the prepositions בעבור 'for the sake of' or למען 'for the sake of' (see §4.3.3.3).

4.3.3. The content clause

Content clauses are the default type of subordinate clause, lacking special
features found in other types and being less differentiated syntactically from
main clauses (Huddleston and Pullum 2002: 950).[9] Content clauses are marked
by כי and אשר.

It should be noted that כי is not always a subordinator: it also used as an
adverb marking the apodosis of a conditional clause, in the combination כי עתה
(Joüon-Muraoka §167s):

(28) Gen 43:10

כי לולא התמהמהנו **כי עתה** שבנו זה פעמים

For if we had not delayed, we could have already returned twice.

Another use of כי is as an adverb meaning 'but, rather' (Blau 1993: §104):[10]

---

9. Content clauses are also known as complement clauses.

10. The words כי עתה and כי 'rather' are categorized as *clausal adverbs*; for further
discussion, see §5.2.1. Many also recognize an asseverative adverb כי 'surely, indeed' (Muilenberg 1961; Schoors 1981: 160; Muraoka 1985: 160–61; Waltke and O'Connor 1990:
§39.3.4e; *HALOT* s.v. כי; Follingstad 2001). Bandstra (1982) argues against the existence of
asseverative כי. Claassen (1983) and Aejmelaeus (1986) show that many supposed instances
of the asseverative כי involve the causal particle, which functions on various levels in the
discourse. According to Aejmelaeus the asseverative use is the most probable explanation
of כי in oaths (e.g., Gen 42:16) and in cases in which כי occurs in the middle of the clause,
(e.g., Gen 18:20). Both of these examples from Genesis are in nonverbal clauses. A probable
instance of asseverative כי in Genesis in a verbal clause is Gen 22:17.

(29) Gen 17:15

שרי אשתך לא תקרא את שמה שרי **כי** שרה שמה

Sarai your wife, you shall not call her Sarai; **rather**, her name shall be Sarah.

Content clauses have a variety of syntactic functions, as described in §§4.3.3.1–4.3.3.2.

4.3.3.1. Complement of verb

Finite content clauses are frequently the complements of verbs[11] and as such are usually marked by כי:

(30) Gen 30:1

ותרא רחל **כי לא ילדה ליעקב**

And Rachel saw **that she had borne Jacob no children**.

Less frequently, they are marked by אשר:[12]

(31) 1 Sam 18:15

וירא שאול אשר הוא משכיל מאד

And Saul saw **that he was very successful**

4.3.3.2. Complement of preposition

A finite content clause may be the complement of a preposition. Prepositions governing content clauses include אחרי 'after', כ 'when' or comparative 'as', עד 'until', מאז 'from the time', למען 'for the sake of', בעבור 'for the sake of', and יען 'because of'. Some of these require the content clause to be marked by a subordinator such as אשר or כי. Some prepositions, including יען and בעבור, allow the content clause to be marked or unmarked:

(32) Num 11:20

יען כי מאסתם את י' אשר בקרבכם

Because **you have rejected the L**ORD **who is among you**

(33) Num 20:12

יען לא האמנתם בי להקדישני לעיני בני ישראל

Because **you did not trust me, to sanctify me in the eyes of the people of Israel**

---

11. A content clause that is the complement of a verb is also known as an object clause or an objective complement clause. A content clause can also be the subject of a verb, but finite examples in BH are rare. On verbal complementation and, in particular, indirect speech complements, see Miller (2003: 95–129).

12. Other examples (from Joüon-Muraoka §157c) are Exod 11:7, Deut 1:31, 1 Kgs 22:16.

A prepositional phrase containing a content clause may serve as an adjunct expressing time, purpose, cause, comparison, or another semantic concept. Some common types are:

(34) Temporal adjunct

וישבת עמו ימים אחדים **עד אשר תשוב חמת אחיך**:

And stay with him a while, **until your brother's fury subsides** (Gen 27:44)

(35) Purpose adjunct

אמרי נא אחתי את **למען ייטב לי בעבורך**

Please say that you are my sister **so that it may go well with me because of you**. (Gen 12:13)

(36) Causal adjunct

על כן היתה חברון לכלב בן יפנה הקנזי לנחלה עד היום הזה **יען אשר מלא אחרי י׳ אלהי ישראל**:

So Hebron became the inheritance of Caleb the son of Jephunneh the Kenizzite to this day, **because he wholeheartedly followed the LORD, the God of Israel**. (Josh 14:14)

(37) Comparative adjunct

וכאשר יענו אתו כן ירבה וכן יפרץ

And **as they oppressed them**, so they multiplied. (Exod 1:12)

4.4. Difficult issues in defining subordination

In this section, we discuss certain problematic issues relating to subordination: the seemingly subordinate use of the conjunction ו, the syntax of the והיה/ ויהי construction, and the syntax of direct and indirect speech.

4.4.1. The conjunction ו: Coordinator and subordinator?

A coordinated clause with ו may occasionally substitute for a subordinated clause. Such a clause may be semantically equivalent to a conditional clause (Joüon-Muraoka §167b), a purpose clause (Joüon-Muraoka §168b),[13] a complement clause (Steiner 1997: 169), or a relative clause (Steiner 1997: 169). An example of each type is shown in (38)–(41).

(38) Conditional

ועזב את אביו ומת:

And (= if) he leaves his father, he will die (Gen 44:22)

---

13. In this case, a volitive verb form is usual.

(39) Purpose

והביאה לי **ואכלה**

And bring it to me, **and (= so) I may eat it** (Gen 27:4)

(40) Complement

ואם ידעת **ויש בם אנשי חיל**

And if you know **and (= that) there are capable men among them** (Gen 47:6)

(41) Relative

הבה נבנה לנו עיר ומגדל **וראשו בשמים**

Let us build a city and a tower **and its (= whose) head is in the heavens** (Gen 11:4)

Scholars are divided as to the proper syntactic classification of clauses with a "subordinate" ו. Van der Merwe et al. (1999: §40.8) recognize a separate use of ו as a subordinating conjunction. Waltke and O'Connor (1990: §38.1h), in contrast, write that "the system expressed in the text may skew the unexpressed semantic system"; that is, the formally nonsubordinate ו clause may be used to express a logically subordinate idea. Steiner (1997: 168) takes an intermediate view between these positions, stating that "the boundary between coordination and subordination in BH is not as sharp as in English." He views ו as a universal connector that can be used to connect coordinated or subordinated clauses.

Because no formal means of distinguishing "subordinate" from coordinate ו are available, the two types are not regarded as distinct grammatical categories in the present work. Steiner's fuzzy-boundary solution is undesirable for present purposes because it greatly complicates the classification of the data.

4.4.2. The ויהי construction

The syntactic analysis of the ויהי/והיה construction is a contentious point in BH syntax. Several varieties of this construction are shown in (42)–(44).

(42) Gen 4:8

ויהי בהיותם בשדה ויקם קין אל הבל אחיו ויהרגהו:

And it came to pass when they were in the field, and Cain rose up against his brother Abel, and he killed him.

(43) Gen 8:13

ויהי באחת ושש מאות שנה בראשון באחד לחדש חרבו המים מעל הארץ

And it came to pass in the six hundred and first year, in the first month, on the first of the month, the waters dried up from the earth.

(44) Gen 4:14

והיה כל מצאי יהרגני:

And it will come to pass; anyone who meets me may kill me.

In (42), ויהי is followed by a temporal phrase and then by a finite clause beginning with a coordinator. Example (43) is similar except that the finite clause lacks the coordinator. In (44), ויהי is followed immediately by a finite clause, without a coordinator.

In a common analysis of these constructions, the finite clause is taken to be a subordinate clause functioning as the subject of ויהי.[14] Example (42), in this view, is best rendered 'And it came to pass when they were in the field [that] Cain rose up against his brother'.[15] Alternatively, ויהי can be considered a subjectless predicate and the finite clause nonsubordinate. The latter analysis is supported by the fact that finite clauses following ויהי are never marked with a subordinator such as אשר and frequently begin with the coordinator ו. In keeping with my preference for syntactic classification based on formal criteria, I adopt the latter approach.

The subjectless interpretation of ויהי constructions has the additional advantage of avoiding the problem of determining the end-boundary of the purported subject clause. For example, in Gen 4:8, above, the subject clause would presumably include the two coordinated clauses describing the event that happened while they were in the field: 'And Cain rose up against his brother Abel and killed him'. In some instances an argument could be made that the entire following narrative unit should be considered to be one long coordinated subject clause, as in (45):

(45) Gen 22:1

ויהי אחר הדברים האלה והאלהים נסה את אברהם ויאמר אליו אברהם

And it came to pass after these things, and God tested Abraham, and He said to him, "Abraham!"

---

14. See, e.g., BDB §1961.2; Longacre (1989: 67); Niccacci (1990: 160). For a survey of these and other approaches to the syntactic and pragmatic analysis of ויהי, see van der Merwe (1999a). According to van der Merwe et al. (1999: §44.5), ויהי is a discourse marker that "anchors an event, state of affairs, scene, episode or narrative to the time line." In this analysis, ויהי presumably does not function as a verb.

15. This analysis assumes that the temporal phrase serves as an adjunct in the matrix clause. Another possibility is that the temporal phrase belongs to the following finite clause, as suggested in Steiner (1979: 148). The verse would then be translated 'And it came to pass that when they were in the field Cain rose up'. In this interpretation, בהיותם בשדה ויקם קין is viewed as a clause with a preverbal adjunct connected to its clause by a conjunction (see §5.5.2). The case for taking the temporal phrase as belonging to the following finite clause is stronger in cases such as (43), where the finite clause does not start with a conjunction (Richard Steiner, personal communication).

4.4.3. Direct and indirect speech

BH exhibits two types of reported speech, *direct* and *indirect speech* (or direct and indirect discourse).[16] The two types can be distinguished based on their deixis, that is, the way in which elements in the utterance such as personal and demonstrative pronouns, tense, and temporal and spatial adverbs relate to the spatiotemporal context of the act of utterance (Lyons 1977: 2:636; Levinson 1983: 54). In direct speech, deictic elements are interpreted in relation to the context of the quoted utterance: *I* and *you* refer to the reported speaker and his addressee, rather than to the reporting speaker and addressee. In indirect speech, the deictic elements are interpreted in relation to the context in which the speech is reported. First- and second-person pronouns refer to the reporting speaker and his addressee, while the quoted speaker and addressee are referred to by third-person pronouns. The difference is illustrated by (46) and (47):

(46) Gen 29:25

ויאמר אל לבן מה זאת עשית לי

And he said to Laban, "What is this you have done to me?"

(47) Gen 29:12

ויגד יעקב לרחל כי אחי אביה הוא

And Jacob told Rachel that he was her father's kinsman

The direct speech clause in (46) refers to the speaker by a first-person enclitic pronoun, **לי** 'to **me**'. The addressee is referred to implicitly by means of a verb inflected for second person. The indirect speech clause in (47), in contrast, refers to the speaker by the third-person independent pronoun **הוא** 'he' and to his addressee by a third-person enclitic pronoun, **אביה** '**her** father'.

A complex relationship exists between quotations and speech that is reported. Researchers have found that direct speech and indirect quotations never exactly reproduce the reported utterance (Tannen 1986). Quoters are generally unable to remember precisely what has been said and often deliberatively shorten or otherwise alter utterances in quoting them. Some direct speech quotations relate not to an actual utterance but to an utterance that a person could have said or did not say: *Why didn't you tell me, "Don't go to the beach today!"* Other quotations represent an internal speech: *I said to myself, "I must go to sleep right now."* Tannen concludes that all quoted speech is "constructed dialogue," whether the quotation relates to a real or fictitious event.[17]

16. For a comprehensive discussion of the two types of reported speech and their syntactic and pragmatic characteristics, see Miller (2003).

17. The constructed nature of quotations is reflected in requotations in the Bible. Mali (1983) and Savran (1988) show that when one biblical character's speech is requoted by another, the second quotation nearly always exhibits changes such as shortening, lengthening, or paraphrase.

The syntactic status of indirect speech in BH is fairly clear: the indirect speech quotation serves as the complement of the verb in the reporting clause. Like other complement clauses, indirect speech is usually marked by a subordinator such as כִּי and must consist of a complete clause or clauses rather than a sentence fragment (Miller 2003: 76–77).[18]

Direct speech clauses in BH exhibit signs of syntactic independence.[19] Direct speech is not introduced by the subordinator כִּי[20] and occasionally lacks a reporting clause.[21] Unlike indirect speech, direct speech may contain vocatives and exclamations and may consist of a sentence fragment (Miller 2003: 74–75).[22]

Some direct speech clauses, however, have traits suggesting they are subordinated. For example, the direct speech clause is often obligatory in the reporting clause (Miller 2003: 74–75, 199–220), suggesting that it is in fact a complement clause. It has been claimed that לֵאמֹר functions as a subordinator introducing a certain type of direct speech clause (Miller 2003: 163–212); if this is so, citations following לֵאמֹר are subordinated. We may conclude that direct speech clauses vary in their degree of subordination to or independence from the reporting clause.[23]

18. Miller (2003: 120) notes that when an indirect speech quotation is embedded in direct speech, the subordinator may be omitted; e.g., Gen 12:13.

19. Partee (1973) takes the view that direct speech is syntactically independent in English. See also the discussion in Munro (1982) and Li (1986).

20. It has been claimed that direct speech quotations, like other complement clauses, may be introduced by כִּי (the so-called *kî recitativum*); see, e.g., GKC (§157b); Williams (1976: §452); Joüon-Muraoka (§157c); Goldenberg (1991: 79–96). According to this view, כִּי at the beginning of a direct speech citation belongs to the reporting clause rather than to the quoted utterance. An example is וַיֹּאמֶר כִּי אֶת שֶׁבַע כְּבָשֹׂת תִּקַּח מִיָּדִי (Gen 21:30), which is understood to mean something like "And he said that 'These seven ewes you shall take from my hand.'" Some other supposed instances of this phenomenon are Gen 29:32; Exod 3:12, 4:25; 1 Kgs 21:6; 2 Kgs 8:13. Other scholars strongly object to the *kî recitativum* theory, arguing that כִּי introducing direct speech is best interpreted as belonging to the quoted utterance; see Esh (1957); Schoors (1981: 256–59); Aejmelaeus (1986); Bandstra (1982: 165–66); Miller (2003: 103–15). A look at the conversation preceding the quoted utterance reveals in almost all cases that כִּי is one of the following: a causal subordinator ("because"), a temporal subordinator ("when") (see §4.3.2.3), or a conjunction ("rather") (see §4.3.3). For example, in Gen 21:30, Abraham's utterance is a response to Abimelek's preceding question, "What are these seven ewes. . . ?" Rather than respond to the literal meaning of this question, Abraham answers the implied question "Why did you put aside these seven ewes. . . ?" His response is properly rendered, "And he said, 'Because these seven ewes you will take from my hand.'" Schoors (1981: 258–59) concludes that "the *kî recitativum*, as a specific syntactic category, should be deleted from grammars and dictionaries."

21. An example is 2 Kgs 10:15.

22. An example is Gen 42:7.

23. In a similar vein, Quirk et al. (1985: 1023) write that in English "there is a gradient from direct speech that is clearly independent to direct speech that is clearly integrated into the clause structure."

Hatav (2000a) claims that there is a third type of reported speech, "free direct discourse," which is marked by לאמר. Unlike direct speech, which purports to be an exact rendition of the original utterance, free direct discourse represents "more or less" what the original speaker intended to say and in some cases does not report speech at all.[24] Miller (2003: 199), however, asserts that quotations prefaced by לאמר are direct speech, although they may be condensed, hypothetical, or fabricated (Miller 2003: 351).[25] Miller (2003: 412–18) presents a number of arguments against Hatav's view, pointing out the implausibility of considering divine legislation introduced by לאמר to have been "flagged by the narrator/writer as not necessarily presented accurately" (2003: 417). Considering Tannen's (1986) finding that reported speech is never an exact representation of the original utterance, it would seem that the לאמר quotation simply represent the end of the direct speech spectrum in terms of its distance from the quoted utterances.

Direct speech quotations can be analyzed on two levels: the level of the reported utterance and the level of the reporting clause (Miller 2003: 200–201). A direct speech quotation functions as a nonsubordinate clause on the level of the reported utterance, whether or not it is subordinated to the reporting clause. Due to the uncertainty regarding their syntactic status on the level of the reporting utterance, direct speech clauses are analyzed in this study exclusively on the level of the reported utterance.

4.5. Syntactic classification of the constituents of the clause

Clauses are made up of constituents, groups of words that form a syntactic unit. The main constituents participating in the structure of the verbal clause are subjects, predicates (i.e., verbs), complements, and adjuncts. A difficult question that is not resolved here is whether BH predicates and complements participate directly in clause structure or combine to form a verb phrase. On the surface, BH does not seem to involve a VP, because the subject regularly intervenes between the verb and its complements. However, as discussed in chap. 2 (pp. 9–10), according to generative grammar, VSO languages have a VP constituent in their underlying structure, with the position of the verb resulting from some sort of movement. Despite the theoretical importance of the VP issue, it is not particularly relevant to the surface description of BH preposing. In the present work, complements and adjuncts are referring to as *clause-level constituents*, without intending to reject the possibility of an underlying VP.

---

24. See also Follingstad (2001: 453–555), who considers quotations introduced by לאמר as "semi-direct discourse." The word לאמר according to Follingstad indicates that the original citation "has been paraphrased, summarized, reinterpreted—i.e., recontextualized—by the reporting speaker (or narrator), typically with regards to another context" (2001: 546).

25. Even direct speech quotations without לאמר do not always relate to actual speech situations, as both Miller (2003: 290–96) and Hatav (2000a: 15) note.

A clause-level constituent can be classified according to its syntactic class (e.g., noun phrase, prepositional phrase, verb) as well as its syntactic function (subject, verb, complement, or adjunct.) The subject is the clause constituent that triggers verb agreement: ויכתב האיש 'and the man wrote' versus ויכתבו האנשים 'and the men wrote'. The subject is generally a noun phrase but is on rare occasions a nonfinite clause.[26] Subject pronouns take the form of independent personal pronouns, e.g., אני 'I', אתה 'you'.

Complements are for the most part clearly distinguishable from subjects. Unlike subjects, complements do not trigger verb agreement. Again unlike subjects, complements may consist of a prepositional phrase headed by את (although in rare instances את governs what appears to be the subject of the clause).[27] Complement pronouns may take the form of enclitic pronouns attached to the verb (ראיתיו 'I saw **him**').

The distinction between complement and adjuncts is much less straightforward. Semantically, complements generally correspond to arguments of the semantic predicate, while adjuncts express circumstantial concepts such as cause, time, and purpose. A structural distinction can be made between the most central members of the two categories.[28] The prototypical complement is a noun phrase, whereas the prototypical adjunct is an adverb, adverb phrase, or prepositional phrase. The prototypical complement is a required clause element, while the prototypical adjunct is optional. Prototypical complements may be advanced to subject when the verb is changed to a passive binyan (Piel to Pual, Hiphil to Hophal); adjuncts are not likewise advanced.

Unfortunately, many peripheral types of adjuncts and complements are difficult to categorize. Some complements are optional, resembling adjuncts. Some adjuncts are noun phrases, resembling complements. Another difficult case concerns verbs of motion and location, which may require a constituent expressing source, goal, or location. These constituents are considered by some to be complements because they are required and are restricted to certain classes of verbs; others consider these a separate class of "required adjuncts."

26. See, e.g., Gen 4:26.
27. The particle את may mark what one would expect to be the subject in passive constructions; see also, e.g., Gen 4:18, 21:5, and 27:42. According to Steiner (1997: 160), in constructions containing a certain type of medio-passive verb, the object of the corresponding active sentence regularly remains an object in the passive construction and is not advanced to subject; thus, this is not really a case of את governing the subject. In these constructions, the verb is usually in the third person singular and the object retains the accusative marker. In rare cases, את governs the subject of an intransitive verb; e.g., 1 Sam 17:34, Judg 20:44, 2 Kgs 6:5. Studies of the so-called nominative את are cited in Waltke and O'Connor (1990: §10.3b).
28. On the complement/adjunct distinction in English, see Huddleston (1984: 177–225); Matthews (1981: 121–45); Quirk et al. (1985: 723–38); Andrews (1985: 62–153). On complements versus adjuncts in Biblical and Modern Hebrew, see, e.g., Azar (1972); Blau (1973a); Lerner (1975); Ben-Asher (1973: 54–71); Muraoka (1979).

In addition to the theoretical controversies regarding the definitions of complement and adjunct, formidable difficulties are involved in distinguishing the two types in practice in BH. The optionality of a constituent is a central criterion in the classification. Yet deciding whether a constituent is optional frequently requires an in-depth investigation into the meaning or meanings of the clause verb and the various constructions associated with each meaning. Attempting such an investigation is not practical when analyzing a large textual corpus. Due to the theoretical and practical difficulties involved, I do not systematically differentiate between complements and adjuncts in the present study.

Chapter 5

The Syntax of Preposing and Other Word-Order Constructions

A preposed clause in BH generally corresponds to a semantically equivalent verb-first clause; that is, a systematic correspondence exists between the marked and unmarked constructions. In this chapter, I describe the syntactic varieties of preposing and identify the unmarked constructions to which they correspond. In addition, I distinguish preposing from several similar constructions that are not the subject of the present work.

In §5.1, I describe the basic preposing construction and show that almost any verb-first clause in BH can be altered to produce a grammatical and semantically equivalent preposed clause. Although verb-first word order is unmarked in BH, not every preverbal constituent is considered to be preposed. In §5.2, I discuss constituents that normally precede the verb and are not preposed as such. In some cases, an element is obligatorily preposed, producing an *unmarked* preposed structure. Structures of this type are described in §5.3.

Complex variants of the preposing construction, including preposing with a focus adverb and double preposing, are discussed in §5.4. In §5.5, I describe marked word-order constructions that resemble preposing but are syntactically distinct from it. In §5.6, I present statistical data regarding the distribution of the various word-order constructions in Genesis. Conclusions are summarized in §5.7.

The syntactic generalizations in this chapter apply to the classical BH prose corpus, that is, the prose portions of Genesis through Kings. The book of Genesis was analyzed in its entirety and the conclusions tested with respect to the rest of the corpus by means of computerized searches, as noted in chap. 1.

5.1. Preposing

Virtually every verb-first construction can be converted to a preposed one, although this usually requires alterations beyond a simple word-order change. If the unmarked clause contains a consecutive verb form, this is replaced with a simple perfect or imperfect in the preposed construction. The contrast between the verb forms in unmarked and preposed clauses is illustrated by (48), which has two coordinated clauses, the first unmarked with a consecutive verb and the second preposed with a perfect:

(48) Gen 1:5

ויקרא אלהים לאור יום ולחשך **קרא** לילה

And God **called** the light Day, and the darkness he **called** Night.

Even clauses consisting of a bare finite verbal form can be converted to a preposed structure. This is accomplished by retaining the normally dropped personal pronoun and preposing it, as in (49):[1]

(49) Gen 21:24

אנכי אשבע:

I swear.

Clauses containing volitive verb forms can undergo preposing as well, as shown in the following examples:

(50) Imperative[2]

והרכש **קח** לך

And the possessions **take** for yourself (Gen 14:21)

(51) Jussive[3]

ועינכם אל **תחס** על כליכם

And never **mind** about your belongings (Gen 45:20)

(52) Cohortative[4]

ואני והנער **נלכה** עד כה

And I and the lad **shall go** over there (Gen 22:5)

It is even possible to prepose the ordinarily dropped subject of an imperative:

(53) Imperative[5]

ואתם **האסרו**

And you **be (= remain) confined** (Gen 42:16)

---

1. Preposed personal pronouns are quite common; representative examples from the Genesis corpus include 10:8, 10:9, 14:23, 15:15, and 33:3.

2. Preposing with imperatives is not uncommon; examples from Genesis include 6:21; 8:17; 14:21; 19:12, 17; 20:13, 15; 23:6, 15; 24:60; 31:16, 32; 42:16, 18, 19, 33 (2×); 43:11, 12, 13; 44:17; 45:17, 19; 47:6.

3. Examples from Genesis include 1:22, 37:27, 44:33, and 45:20.

4. Examples from Genesis include 22:5 and 33:14.

5. Other representative examples are Gen 24:60, 42:19, and 44:17.

One construction that cannot be preposed is the ויהי/והיה ('and it came/will come to pass') clause. Because there is no implicit pronominal subject in this structure, a personal pronoun cannot stand in front of the verb. Thus, (54) for example, cannot be changed to הוא היה בנסעם מקדם.

(54) Gen 11:2

ויהי בנסעם מקדם

And it came to pass when they traveled from the East

Although one might expect the temporal phrase following ויהי clause to be preposable, this does not in fact occur; that is, (54) cannot be altered to בנסעם מקדם היה. It seems that היה has the meaning 'come to pass' only in the *waw*-consecutive form (BDB §1961). Note that when the verb has copular meaning, preposing is perfectly appropriate, as in (55).

(55) Gen 29:17

ורחל היתה יפת תאר ויפת מראה:

And Rachel was beautiful in form and beautiful in appearance.

The syntactic function of a preposed constituent may be subject, complement, or adjunct:

(56) Subject

וכוש ילד את נמרד

And **Cush** fathered Nimrod (Gen 10:8)

(57) Complement

ואת הצפר לא בתר

And **the bird** he did not cut in two (Gen 15:10)

(58) Adjunct

בעוד שלשת ימים ישא פרעה את ראשך מעליך

In another three days Pharaoh will lift up your head from you (Gen 40:19)

The syntactic category of the preposed constituent may be noun phrase, prepositional phrase, adverb, or adjective:

(59) Noun phrase

ואביו שמר את הדבר:

And **his father** kept the matter in mind. (Gen 37:11)

(60) Prepositional phrase

ולחשך קרא לילה

And **the darkness** He called Night (Gen 1:5)

(61) Adverb

שמה קבר אברהם ושרה אשתו:

There Abraham and his wife Sarah were buried (Gen 25:10)

(62) Adjective

תמים היה בדרתיו

Blameless was He in his generation (Gen 6:9)

Preposing is normally performed on an entire clause-level constituent. When the constituent involved is a compound phrase, there are several preposing options. In most cases the entire phrase is preposed, even when it is a long coordinated chain: [6]

(63) Gen 47:1

אבי ואחי וצאנם ובקרם וכל אשר להם באו מארץ כנען

My father and my brothers, and their flocks and herds and all that is theirs, have come from the land of Canaan

An alternative is to prepose the first part of the compound phrase and postpose the remainder to the end of the clause.[7] The preposed element may or may not be resumed by a pronoun in the postposed phrase. The resumptive type is shown in (64) and (65) and the nonresumptive type in (66) and (67).[8]

(64) Gen 44:3

והאנשים שלחו המה וחמריהם:

And **the men** were sent away, **they and their asses**

(65) Gen 17:9

ואתה את בריתי תשמר אתה וזרעך אחריך לדרתם:

And **you**, keep my covenant, **you and your offspring after you throughout their generations**.

6. Additional examples of compound noun phrases preposed in their entirety in the Genesis corpus include Gen 9:2; 20:5; 22:5; 27:37; 31:38, 42; 35:11; 46:32; and 47:5.

7. Postposing of part of a compound phrase is common in verb-first clauses as well, particularly when the compound constituent is the subject. Representative examples from the Genesis corpus include Gen 6:18; 33:6; 35:6; and 50:14, 22. For discussion of postponed subjects with resumptive pronouns, see Muraoka (1985: 62–63); Waltke and O'Connor (1990: §16.3.2c); Joüon-Muraoka §146c; Naudé (1999). Naudé (1999: 97) states that clause-final phrases such as המה וחמריהם occupy the same position as right-dislocated constituents.

8. See also Gen 24:38, 43:15.

(66) Gen 26:26

ואבימלך הלך אליו מגרר **ואחזת מרעהו ופיכל שר צבאו:**

And **Abimelech** went to him from Gerar, **and Ahuzzath his adviser
and Phicol the commander of his army**.

(67) Gen 44:2

ואת גביעי גביע הכסף תשים בפי אמתחת הקטן **ואת כסף שברו**

And **my cup, the silver cup**, put in the mouth of the sack of the youngest, **and his money for the grain**

Preposing together with postposing occasionally occurs in clauses containing a
noun phrase modified by a prepositional phrase. An example is (68), where the
phrase את האנשים אשר פתח הבית is preposed, and its modifying phrase מקטן
ועד גדול is postponed to the end of the clause.[9]

(68) Gen 19:11

ואת האנשים אשר פתח הבית הכו בסנורים **מקטן ועד גדול**

And **the men who were at the entrance of the house** they struck with
blindness, **from small to great**

5.2. Nonpreposed preverbal constituents

Some constituents stand before the verb in the unmarked clause and are not
considered preposed in that position. These include clausal adverbs (§5.2.1),
negative particles (§5.2.2), and certain adjunct clauses (§5.2.3).

5.2.1. Clausal adverbs

Although the unmarked position of most adjuncts is postverbal, clausal adverbs[10] such as אולי, לכן, הנה, and others always occur in clause-initial posi-

---

9. See also Gen 19:4, where the posponed modifying prepositional phrase is followed
by an appositive phrase: **ואנשי העיר אנשי סדם** נסבו על הבית **מנער ועד זקן כל העם מקצה**
'And the men of the city, the men of Sodom, surrounded the house, **both young and old,
all the people to the last man**'.

10. Clausal adverbs are also known as sentence adverbs. Blau (1977) discusses sentence
adverbials that are separated from the rest of the clause by a conjunction (see §5.5.2) but does
not discuss the sentence adverb (i.e., a one-word adverbial) specifically. The term *clausal
adverb* appears in Waltke and O'Connor (1990: §39.3.2–5) but is defined more broadly to
include negative and restrictive particles, which have very different syntactic characteristics
than the ones discussed here. According to Gross (1996:138–40), a variety of adverbs and
particles that function on the clause or text level, such as הנה, עתה, and לכן, stand at the
margin of the preverbal field, before preposed constituents (see §3.3.6). According to Gross,
(ו)הנה is a "Satzdeiktikon," (ו)עתה is a "Textdeiktikon," and לכן is a conjunctional adverb
(1996: 129–31). Van der Merwe et al. (2002: §41.3) classify as modal adverbs some words
I consider clausal adverbs, such as אך 'surely'. Others, such as הנה, are classified there as

tion. The clausal-adverb class in BH can be defined in a manner similar to the definition of the parallel category in English. Clausal adverbs in English are syntactically and prosodically detached from the sentence and most frequently occur in initial position.[11] The syntactic detachedness of clausal adverbs in English is demonstrated by the fact they cannot be the focus of a cleft sentence and cannot be the focus of negation or interrogation (Quirk et al. 1985: 612, 631; Huddleston and Pullum 2002: 666–68). From the semantic perspective, clausal adverbs have a semantic scope that extends over the entire clause. Quirk et al. introduce the terms *disjunct* and *conjunct* to describe two types of clausal adverbs.[12] Although disjuncts and conjuncts may not be syntactically distinct, the terms are useful in understanding the different types of pragmatic functions that clausal adverbs may serve. Disjunct adverbs express the speaker's attitude to the content of the clause or the manner in which it is expressed; examples in English include *certainly*, *perhaps*, and *fortunately*. Conjunct adverbs signal relations between clauses or larger discourse segments; examples include *therefore*, *similarly*, and *however*.[13]

In BH, the group of adverbs that correspond semantically to English clausal adverbs constitutes a distinct group on syntactic grounds, occurring exclusively in initial position[14] and being syntactically detached from the clause. Although the detachedness of clausal adverbs in BH cannot be established by the syntactic tests referred to above (i.e., the possibility of focus of a cleft construction and focus of negation), evidence on this point can be inferred from the position of clausal adverbs relative to other preverbal elements, as discussed further on in this section. The following is a list of the clausal adverbs occurring in finite

"discourse markers" that "comment on the content of a sentence and/or sentences from a meta-level" (§44). On discourse markers, see n. 13 below.

11. Quirk et al. (1985: 615). English clausal adverbs can also occur anywhere within the clause, set off by commas. Huddleston and Pullum (2002: 1350–62) view clausal adverbs as belonging to the supplement category, a category that also includes appositional phrases and interpolations.

12. Disjuncts and conjuncts may be phrases as well as single-word adverbs. An example of a disjunct phrase in BH is וּלְיִשְׁמָעֵאל שְׁמַעְתִּיךָ 'As for Ishmael, I have heard you' (Gen 17:20). The disjunct and conjunct classes are distinct from the adjunct class (Quirk et al. 1985).

13. Quirk et al. (1985: 627–28, 642). Conjunct adverbs belong to a larger pragmatic category known as *discourse markers* or *discourse connectives*. Discourse connectives are linguistic elements that mark relations between clauses and may be adverbs, coordinating or subordinating conjunctions, interjections, and perhaps even clauses. A tutorial overview of the literature on discourse markers, accompanied by an extensive bibliography, can be found in Schourup (1999). For further discussion, see chap. 6.

14. Some BH adverbs with semantic scope over the clause have freer positioning within the clause, for example, אֵפוֹא 'therefore'. It would seem that these belong to a different syntactic class from the one described here.

clauses in the Genesis corpus.[15] Examples (69)–(73) are clausal adverbs of the disjunct type.

(69) אולי

אולי יחסרון חמשים הצדיקם חמשה

Perhaps the fifty righteous lack five. (Gen 18:28)

(70) הנה [16]

הנה נתתי לכם את כל עשב זרע זרע אשר על פני כל הארץ

Behold, I give you every seed-bearing plant that is upon the face of all the earth (Gen 1:29)

(71) אך [17]

אך טרף טרף

Surely he has been torn to pieces (Gen 44:28)

Clausal adverbs of the conjunct type are shown in (72)–(83).

(72) הן (expressing justification) [18]

הן גרשת אתי היום מעל פני האדמה

Behold, you have driven me this day away from the soil (Gen 4:14)

(73) הלא (expressing justification) [19]

הלא הוא אמר לי אחתי הוא

Surely he said to me, "She is my sister." (Gen 20:5)

15. Some of the adverbs mentioned have other uses as well, as mentioned in the notes below.

16. The word הנה is a presentative with many shades of use, as discussed in, e.g., Labuschagne (1973); McCarthy (1980); Muraoka (1985: 137–40); Kogut (1986); Waltke and O'Connor (1990: §40.2.1); Zatelli (1994). Often, הנה is a conjunct rather than a disjunct, marking the justification for a following utterance (see §7.3.2.1 n. 21, p. 117). Zewi (1996) states that הנה following the speech verb אמר often functions as a kind of conjunction introducing direct speech, on the analogy of Arabic *inna*. In such cases, in her view, הנה belongs to the reporting clause rather than to the quoted utterance, like the supposed *kî recitativum* (see §4.4.3 n. 20, p. 60).

17. The word אך is also a focusing adverb. On preposing with the focusing adverb אך, see §5.4.1.

18. The word הן has some of the same functions as הנה; see Labuschagne (1973); Muraoka (1985); Zewi (1997); Garr (2004).

19. The clausal adverb הלא is viewed here as distinct from the combination of the interrogative particle ה and the negative particle לא. Steiner (1979: 7) writes that הלא can be used idiomatically to introduce an assertion and in this case is not synchronically analyzable as ה + לא. Historically, the clausal adverb may have a separate origin from the interrogative; see Brown (1987); Sivan and Schniedewind (1993); Ben-Ḥayyim (2000: 320); alternatively, the

(74) אולם

ואולם אחיו הקטן יגדל ממנו

Nevertheless, his younger brother shall be greater than he (Gen 48:19)

(75) עתה (expressing conclusion or consequence)[20]

לגור בארץ באנו כי אין מרעה לצאן אשר לעבדיך כי כבד הרעב בארץ כנען
ועתה ישבו נא עבדיך בארץ גשן:

To sojourn in the land we have come; for there is no pasture for your servants' flocks, for the famine is severe in the land of Canaan; and **now**, pray, let your servants dwell in the land of Goshen. (Gen 47:4)

(76) על כן (expressing consequence)

ויאמרו איש אל אחיו אבל אשמים אנחנו על אחינו אשר ראינו צרת נפשו
בהתחננו אלינו ולא שמענו **על כן** באה אלינו הצרה הזאת:

Then they said to one another, "Truly we are guilty concerning our brother, in that we saw his distress, when he pleaded with us and we would not listen; **therefore** this distress has come upon us." (Gen 42:21)

---

clausal adverb may have developed from the use of לא + ה in negative rhetorical questions. Syntactic evidence for the clausal adverb includes the occurrence of הלא in front of a preposed element, as in הלוא נכריות נחשבנו לו 'Surely as foreigners he regards us' (Gen 31:15; appears as example (89) below). Nonidiomatic interrogative הלא is composed of two separable particles (Richard Steiner, personal communication). As described in §§5.2.2 and 5.3.1 below, when a noun phrase or prepositional phrase precedes the verb, ה occurs in front of the preposed phrase and לא immediately precedes the verb; see, e.g., Gen 18:25; 2 Sam 19:22; Job 11:2. Thus, if הלוא in Gen 31:15 were a combination of the interrogative and the negative, one would expect the order to be הנכריות לא נחשבנו לו. Additional syntactic evidence for the clausal adverb is the occurrence of הלא preceding a conditional clause (e.g., Gen 4:7, 1 Sam 15:17) and preceding a left-dislocated element (e.g., Num 23:12, Judg 11:24). Clausal adverbs occur in these structural positions (see below, p. 73 in this section, and §5.2.3), while interrogative ה, as well as the negative particle, does not. Thus, the position of clausal adverb הלא in הלוא אם תיטיב שאת 'Surely, if you do right, there is uplift' (Gen 4:7) contrasts with the position of interrogative ה in אם יגע טמא נפש בכל אלה היטמא 'If someone defiled by a corpse touches any of these, will it be defiled?' (Hag 2:13; see also Job 14:4). For further discussion, see Moshavi (2007c, forthcoming). Brongers (1981) contains a useful discussion of the asseverative use of הלא, although he does not distinguish it formally from the interrogative. The word הלא can serve as a disjunct or a conjunct and strongly resembles הנה in all of its uses. In its occurrences in Genesis, it is typically a conjunct, marking the justification for an adjacent utterance. Although the clausal adverb הלא is usually understood as an asseverative ('surely'), I argue in a forthcoming article (Moshavi forthcoming) that it is best seen as a presentative, like הנה.

   20. The clausal adverb עתה, as opposed to the temporal adverb עתה 'now', is preceded by ו; see Waltke and O'Connor (1990: §39.3.4f).

(77) לכן (expressing consequence)

לכן ישכב עמך הלילה תחת דודאי בנך:

Then he may lie with you tonight in return for your son's mandrakes. (Gen 30:15)

(78) כי (after negative clause) [21]

ויאמר לא **כי** צחקת:

And he said, "No, **rather**, you did laugh." (Gen 18:15)

(79) כי אם (after negative clause) [22]

לא יירשך זה **כי אם** אשר יצא ממעיך הוא יירשך

This one shall not be your heir; **rather**, your own issue shall be your heir (Gen 15:4)

(80) כי עתה (introducing apodosis after hypothetical conditional) [23]

כי לולא התמהמהנו **כי עתה** שבנו זה פעמים:

For if we had not delayed, we could have already returned twice. (Gen 43:10)

(81) אם לא (after negative clause)

לא תקח אשה לבני מבנות הכנעני אשר אנכי ישב בארצו: **אם לא** אל בית אבי תלך ואל משפחתי ולקחת אשה לבני:

You shall not take a wife for my son from the daughters of the Canaan-ites, in whose land I dwell; **rather** to my father's house you shall go and to my family, and take a wife for my son. (Gen 24:37–38)

(82) גם [24]

לא מצאתיה **וגם** אנשי המקום אמרו לא היתה בזה קדשה

I have not found her; and **furthermore**, the people of the place said, "There has been no prostitute here." (Gen 38:22)

---

21. See also, e.g., Gen 19:2, Josh 5:14, 2 Sam 20:21. Both כי and כי אם (79) are discussed further in the context of the focused clause in §8.3.3. On asseverative כי, see §4.3.3 n. 10 (p. 54).

22. See also, e.g., Gen 35:10, Lev 21:14, Num 10:30, 1 Sam 8:19. A slightly different usage is found in Gen 40:14, which is more similar in meaning to the clausal adverb רק; see example (83).

23. The conjunct is not represented in the translation due to the lack of an appropriate English equivalent. See also, e.g., Gen 31:42, Num 22:29, 1 Sam 14:30.

24. The conjunct גם differs semantically from the more common focus adverb גם 'also' in having scope over the whole clause. The function of the conjunct is to add one utterance to another ('furthermore', 'moreover'). See also, e.g., Exod 3:9, 6:2–5; 1 Sam 4:17. The word

(83) רק [25]

ואם לא תאבה האשה ללכת אחריך ונקית משבעתי זאת **רק** את בני לא תשב
שמה

And if the woman is not willing to follow you, then you will be free from
this oath of mine; **but** do not take my son back there (Gen 24:8)

When a clausal adverb occurs in a clause with a detached element, such as a
left-dislocated element or an element connected to the clause with a conjunction (see §5.5.2), the adverb precedes the detached element, as shown in (84)
and (85). [26] This pattern clearly indicates that the clausal adverb itself occupies
a detached position.

(84) 2 Kgs 1:6, 16

לכן המטה אשר עלית שם לא תרד ממנה

Therefore the bed upon which you have alighted, you shall not come
down from it

(85) 2 Kgs 17:36

כי אם את י׳ אשר העלה אתכם מארץ מצרים בכח גדול ובזרוע נטויה אתו תיראו

Rather, the LORD who brought you out of the land of Egypt with great
power and with an outstretched arm, him you shall worship

Further evidence for the detachedness of clausal adverbs is their position relative to a preposed subject, complement, or ordinary adjunct. The clausal adverb always precedes the preposed element. [27] The following examples include
nearly all the clausal adverbs listed above.

גם as a conjunct may precede the disjunct הנה, as in the nonverbal clauses in Gen 38:24 and
Exod 4:14. According to Labuschagne (1966), גם is at times a purely "emphatic" adverb,
lacking an additive meaning. Muraoka (1985: 146), however, feels that "the particle *gam*
almost always retains its additive force." In his comprehensive study of the particle, van
der Merwe (1990: 198) comes to a similar conclusion, writing that "*Gam* almost always has
an additive, inclusive or at least a connective connotation." On preposing with the focusing
adverb גם, see §5.4.1.

25. See also Gen 19:8, 1 Kgs 11:13. The conjunct רק differs semantically from the focus adverb רק 'only' in having scope over the whole clause. In addition, the conjunct has a
contrastive meaning ('but, however') rather than a restrictive one. On the conjunct use, see
Kogut (1996: 204). According to BDB and Muraoka (1985: 131), רק is an asseverative particle in several cases; e.g., Gen 20:11.

26. For examples of a clausal adverb preceding an element separated from its clause by
a conjunction, see examples (131) and (132). In the nonverbal clause, however, a dislocated
element sometimes precedes a clausal adverb, for example: **ויתר דברי שלמה וכל אשר עשה**
וחכמתו הלוא הם כתבים על ספר דברי שלמה 'And the other events of Solomon's reign, and all
his actions . . . surely they are recorded in the book of the Annals of Solomon' (1 Kgs 11:41).

27. This result agrees with Gross's (1996: 138–40) finding that certain adverbs stand at
the margin of the preverbal field, before preposed constituents (see n. 10, p. 68 above).

(86) Exod 32:34 [28]

הנה מלאכי ילך לפניך

Behold my angel will go before you

(87) Exod 9:16 [29]

ואולם בעבור זאת העמדתיך

But for this purpose I have spared you

(88) Gen 3:22 [30]

הן האדם היה כאחד ממנו

Behold, the man has become like one of us

(89) Gen 31:15

הלוא נכריות נחשבנו לו כי מכרנו

Surely as foreigners he regards us, for he has sold us

(90) 1 Sam 28:18

על כן הדבר הזה עשה לך י׳ היום הזה:

Therefore this thing the LORD has done to you this day.

(91) 1 Sam 28:2

לכן שמר לראשי אשימך כל הימים:

Therefore my bodyguard I will make you for life.

(92) Gen 19:2

לא כי ברחוב נלין:

No, **rather**, in the street we will spend the night.

(93) Gen 21:26

וגם אתה לא הגדת לי וגם אנכי לא שמעתי בלתי היום:

And **furthermore**, you did not tell me. And **furthermore**, I have not heard of it until today.

---

28. The word הנה followed by a preposed element is a particularly common construction, occurring also in Exod 32:34; Num 22:5, 32; Josh 2:2, 24:27; Judg 7:13, 14:16, 19:22; 1 Sam 8:5, 24:10, 28:9; 2 Sam 1:6, 13:35, 19:38; 2 Sam 24:17; 1 Kgs 8:27; 2 Kgs 10:9, 19:11.

29. See also Gen 48:19 (example [74], p. 71 above).

30. See also, e.g., Gen 27:37, 39:8, 44:8; Exod 6:12; Lev 10:19.

(94) Gen 24:8

רק את בני לא תשב שמה:

But my son do not take back there.

(95) Gen 35:10

כי אם ישראל יהיה שמך

Rather, Israel shall be your name

(96) Gen 24:38

אם לא אל בית אבי תלך ואל משפחתי

Rather, to my father's house you shall go and to my family

(97) Gen 48:19

ואולם אחיו הקטן יגדל ממנו

Nevertheless his younger brother shall be greater than he

The fact that the clausal adverb always precedes the other preverbal item supports the conclusion that the clausal adverb is not preposed. If both items were
preposed, we would expect to find variation in the relative order of the two
constituents. Furthermore, although double preposing does occur in classical
BH prose, it is much rarer than single preposing (see §5.4.2).[31] Additional con-
firmation of the detached analysis is a case in Genesis of a clausal adverb followed by double preposing:

(98) Gen 4:15

לכן כל הרג קין שבעתים יקם

Therefore any one who kills Cain, sevenfold vengeance shall be taken
[on him]

Because triple preposing is practically unheard of in classical prose, this construction provides additional support for the position that the clausal adverb is
detached rather than preposed.

In conclusion, clausal adverbs stand in a position more peripheral than either preposed or even left-dislocated elements. A clause that begins with a
clausal adverb and continues with the verb is not considered to be preposed.
Because the preverbal position of the clausal adverb is syntactically obligatory,
clausal adverb-verb is the unmarked word order.

---

31. My count in the Genesis corpus identified 21 occurrences (see table 1, p. 85 below).
Single preposing is far more common; as shown in table 1, there are 402 occurrences of
single preposing in the Genesis corpus.

5.2.2. Negative particles: לא and טרם

The negative particle לא precedes the verb whenever clausal negation, rather than subclausal negation, is involved.[32] The negative temporal adverb טרם 'not yet' also precedes the verb in its unmarked position.[33] These negative particles are tightly bound to the verb. As a result, when clauses with לא or טרם undergo preposing, the preposed element precedes both negative particle and verb:

(99) Gen 16:1[34]

ושרי אשת אברם **לא** ילדה לו

And Sarai, Abram's wife, had **not** borne him children

(100) Gen 24:45[35]

אני **טרם** אכלה לדבר אל לבי

I had **not yet** finished speaking in my heart

In rare instances the preposed item intervenes between the negative particle and the verb:[36]

(101) Gen 45:8

ועתה **לא** אתם שלחתם אתי הנה

And now, it was **not** you who sent me here, but God

The construction exemplified in (101) has a special function that is explored in chap. 8.

5.2.3. Preverbal adjunct clauses

Despite the unmarked postverbal position of adjuncts in general, most types of adjunct *clauses* regularly occur at the head of the main clause and are therefore unmarked in the preverbal position.[37] Preverbal adjunct clauses occupy a

---

32. In clausal negation, the whole clause is treated as negative, whereas in subclausal negation, a word or phrase is negated (Huddleston and Pullum 2002: 789).

33. In some cases (none of which occur in Genesis), טרם is not an adverb but a preposition governing a finite clause, as in וישא העם את בצקו טרם יחמץ 'And the people took their dough before it was leavened' (Exod 12:34). See Waltke and O'Connor (1990: §31.6.3c); *HALOT* s.v. טרם.

34. See also, e.g., Gen 20:4 and 21:26.

35. See also, e.g., Josh 2:8 and 1 Sam 3:7.

36. Goldenberg (1971, 1977, 1998a) views this construction as an "imperfectly-transformed cleft sentence." The completely transformed cleft would have a relative particle, yielding something like לא אתם אשר שלחתם אותי הנה. Goldenberg cites parallels to this construction in Mishnaic Hebrew and various dialects of Aramaic. Given the marginality in BH of cleft constructions and negative clefts (if the latter exist at all), it is doubtful whether the לא + preposing structure is related to clefting.

37. An exception is the causal כי clause, which is normally at the end of the clause. A preverbal causal כי clause would be marked; no clauses of this sort, however, are to be found among the finite clauses in Genesis.

position in the clause that is intermediate between the preposed position and
the clausal-adverb position. Adjunct clauses are more detached from the clause
than preposed constituents. This can be seen from the fact that the adjunct
clause is regularly connected to the rest of the clause by a conjunction, something that does not ordinarily happen with preposed constituents:[38]

(102) Gen 34:17

ואם לא תשמעו אלינו להמול ולקחנו את בתנו

And if you will not listen to us to be circumcised, we will take our
daughter

(103) Gen 32:18–19

כי יפגשך עשו אחי ושאלך לאמר למי אתה ואנה תלך ולמי אלה לפניך:
ואמרת

**When Esau my brother meets you, and asks you, "To whom do you
belong, and where are you going, and whose are these ahead of
you?"** you shall say

A preverbal adjunct clause may be followed by a preposed constituent. In
(104), for example, a conditional clause is followed by a preposed subject.

(104) Gen 42:19

אם כנים אתם אחיכם אחד יאסר בבית משמרכם

If you are honest men, one of your brothers shall be confined in your
place of detention

As compared to the clausal adverb, the adjunct clause is more closely connected to the clause. When a clause contains both a clausal adverb and a preverbal adjunct clause, the clausal adverb precedes the adjunct clause:[39]

(105) Gen 24:49

ועתה אם ישכם עשים חסד ואמת את אדני הגידו לי

And now, **if you will deal loyally and truly with my master,** tell me

(106) Judg 21:21

והנה אם יצאו בנות שילו לחול במחלות ויצאתם מן הכרמים

And behold, **if the daughters of Shiloh come out to dance in the
dances,** come out of the vineyards

---

38. A conjunction sometimes intervenes between an initial element, usually a time adjunct, and the verb; see §5.5.2 for further discussion. I consider this to be a separate construction from preposing.

39. A similar observation is made in Blau (1977: 9) with regard to the relative order
of sentence adverbial and conditional clause. See also, e.g., Exod 19:5, 32:32, 33:13; Num
22:34; Judg 9:16; 1 Sam 20:29.

5.3. Unmarked preposed constituents

Certain grammatical forms, including interrogative pro-forms and a number of time adverbs, are either constrained to or generally appear before the verb.[40] The preverbal position is the unmarked position for these forms. In §§5.3.1 and 5.3.2 it is shown that, unlike clausal adverbs, these forms occupy a preposed position in the clause.

5.3.1. Interrogative pro-forms

Interrogative pro-forms occurring in finite nonsubordinate clauses in Genesis are listed in (107).

(107) Interrogative pro-forms

מה (זה/זאת)	'what'[41]
מי	'who'
מתי	'when'
אנה	'to where'
אי מזה	'from where'
מאין	'from where'
למה (זה)	'why'
מדוע	'why'
איך	'how'

That interrogative forms stand in the same position as preposed constituents can be seen from the fact that preposing does not ordinarily occur in clauses with an interrogative.[42] When interrogative forms occur in left-dislocated constructions, they occur after the dislocated element. Example (108) is an example of a dislocated element followed by an interrogative pronoun.

(108) Gen 31:43

ולבנתי **מה** אעשה לאלה היום או לבניהן אשר ילדו:

And to my daughters, **what** can I do to these today, or to their children whom they have borne?

---

40. Gross (1996: 105–6) lists various forms that are obligatorily or preferably preposed; these include interrogative particles and a variety of deictic particles including demonstrative pronouns and spatial and temporal adverbs (see §3.3.6). His list includes a number of words that are not preposed in the majority of cases, such as מחר 'tomorrow' and היום 'today'. In the present work, the category "unmarked preposed forms" is restricted to forms that are always or nearly always preposed.

41. The particle מה is also used as an exclamatory particle, as in מה נורא המקום הזה 'How awesome is this place!' (Gen 28:17); see also, e.g., Gen 38:29. Exclamatory particles such as מה, like their homonymous interrogative counterparts, are always preposed. Interrogative and exclamatory מה must be distinguished from the indefinite pronoun מה, as in וראיתי **מה** והגדתי לך 'And if I learn **anything**, I will tell you' (1 Sam 19:3). Unlike the interrogative pronoun, the indefinite pronoun need not be preposed. See also, e.g., 2 Sam 18:22, 18:29.

42. One exception is Gen 27:37, in which the interrogative is preceded by a prepositional phrase and an adverb: ולכה אפוא מה אעשה בני 'And for you, then, **what** can I do, my son?' On אפוא, see n. 14 (p. 69).

Although it stands at the head of the clause, interrogative ה is not preposed.[43] Unlike the interrogative pro-forms, interrogative ה can occur with a preposed element. In these cases, interrogative ה precedes the preposed element:[44]

(109) Gen 18:25

השפט כל הארץ לא יעשה משפט:

Shall the Judge of all the earth not deal justly?

(110) Gen 34:31

הכזונה יעשה את אחותנו:

Should he treat our sister as a harlot?

5.3.2. Clause-initial time adverbs and the demonstrative adverb כה

Although time adjuncts are normally postverbal,[45] certain time adverbs, as well as the demonstrative adverb כה, normally or exclusively occur before the verb.[46] The time adverbs occurring in Genesis are listed in (111).

(111) Clause-initial time and כה
        אחר   'afterward'[47]
    אחרי כן   'afterward'[48]
        אז   'then'[49]

---

43. Interrogative ה rarely appears with a coordinating conjunction in the classical prose corpus. An apparent exception, והלוא עמך שם צדוק ואביתר הכהנים 'And surely Zadok and Abiathar the priests will be with you there' (2 Sam 15:35), is not actually the interrogative הלוא. The word הלוא in this clause is the asseverative clausal adverb (see n. 19, pp. 70–71 above). This interpretation is followed by the NJPSV and NRSV, which take the sentence as declarative and omit the adverb. (The RSV, however, which generally does not recognize the clausal adverb הלא, translates the verse with a rhetorical interrogative, 'is it not?').

44. See also, e.g., Gen 3:11, 17:17; Num 11:22; Judg 14:15; 2 Sam 19:22. In Deut 4:32 and 34, ה appears after או.

45. The normal postverbal position for time adjuncts in general is confirmed by a survey of a group of representative time adjuncts in the classical BH prose corpus. All of the occurrences of the following words and phrases were checked: מחר 'tomorrow'; היום 'today'; ביום 'on the . . . day (of)'; בחדש 'in the . . . month (of)'; בשנה/בשנת 'in the . . . year (of)'; all temporal infinitive phrases involving the prepositions ב, כ, or אחרי. The incidence of preposing of these expressions is 27% overall. This result indicates clearly that the normal position for time adjuncts is postverbal, as it is for adjuncts in general. The time adverbs listed in (111) are exceptional in normally preceding the verb.

46. A similar observation is made by Gross (1996: 105–6).

47. Temporal אחר is always clause-initial in the classical BH prose corpus

48. The phrase אחרי כן is almost always clause-initial, except in ויהי clauses, which always begin with the verb (see §5.1), and in Josh 10:26, 1 Sam 24:8, and 2 Sam 21:14.

49. The word אז is always clause-initial in verbal clauses in the classical prose corpus. In the nonverbal clause, it occurs between the subject and predicate, as in Gen 12:6 and 13:7.

עתה 'now' [50]
כה 'thus' [51]

Just like interrogative pro-forms, the adverbs in (111) do not occur in clauses with an additional preverbal constituent. The natural conclusion is that the adverbs stand in the preposed position and are not detached like clausal adverbs. [52]

5.4. Complex variants of the preposing construction

5.4.1. Preposing with a focusing adverb

A constituent that is the focus of a focusing adverb such as גם 'also', אף 'also', רק 'only', or אך 'only' may undergo preposing. [53] Several different structures are possible, corresponding to different unmarked constructions. [54] There are at least two different means of forming a postverbal phrase with a focus particle: [55]

(112) Gen 19:35

ותשקין **גם בלילה ההוא** את אביהן יין

And they made their father drink wine **that night also**

(113) Gen 22:20

הנה ילדה מלכה **גם הוא** בנים לנחור אחיך:

Behold, **Milcah, she also** has born children to your brother Nahor:

In (112), גם precedes the focused expression, whereas in (113) גם focuses a personal pronoun that is coreferential with the immediately preceding expression, מלכה. A structure such as (112) can be converted to a preposed structure by moving the גם phrase to a preverbal position:

(114) Gen 13:5

וגם ללוט ההלך את אברם היה צאן ובקר ואהלים:

And **also Lot, who went with Abram,** had flocks and herds and tents

---

50. The word עתה (without ו, as a time adjunct rather than a clausal adverb) is preverbal in the vast majority of cases. The exceptions are Num 22:38; Judg 8:2, 8:6, 9:38, 11:7; 1 Sam 9:12, 17:29; 1 Kgs 12:4, 21:7.

51. The demonstrative adverb כה 'thus' is almost always preverbal in the classical BH prose corpus, with the exceptions of Exod 5:15 and Num 22:30.

52. In Deut 7:5, כה stands after an initial clausal adverb.

53. The focusing uses of גם and רק are distinct from their uses as conjuncts, as noted above in §5.2.1 (pp. 72–73).

54. For a comprehensive study of constructions with גם, see van der Merwe (1990).

55. In a rare type that does not occur in Genesis, גם precedes a cataphoric pronoun that refers to a following appositive lexical expression, for example, ויעשו גם הם חרטמי מצרים בלהטיהם כן 'And **they also**, the Egyptian magicians, did the same with their spells' (Exod 7:11).

The structure exemplified in (113) may be preposed in one of two ways. First, both the lexical expression and the following גם phrase may be preposed together. An alternative is to prepose the lexical expression, with the גם phrase remaining in its original position. The two options are illustrated by the close-to-minimal pair in (115) and (116).[56]

(115) Gen 4:26

ולשת **גם הוא** ילד בן

And **to Seth, [to] him also** a son was born

(116) Gen 10:21

ולשם ילד **גם הוא**

And **to Shem** were born [sons], **[to] him also**

5.4.2. Double preposing

An unusual variant of preposing is the double preposing construction. In this construction, two clause constituents precede the verb:[57]

(117) Gen 6:16

ופתח התבה בצדה תשים

And **the entrance of the ark in its side** you shall put

(118) Gen 48:5

אפרים ומנשה כראובן ושמעון יהיו לי:

Ephraim and Manasseh, like Reuben and Simeon, shall be mine.

5.5. Other marked word-order constructions

In this section, I discuss marked word-order constructions that resemble preposing but are syntactically distinct from it. These include left-dislocation and the clause in which an initial element is separated from the clause by a conjunction.

5.5.1. Left-dislocation

Left-dislocation, traditionally known by Hebraists as *casus pendens*, bears a close resemblance to preposing but has an entirely different syntactic structure. In both constructions, a constituent stands before the verb. In left-dislocation,

---

56. Representative occurrences of the first pattern from the Genesis corpus include Gen 4:22 and 19:38. A representative example of the second pattern is Gen 4:4.

57. A discussion of the functions of this construction can be found in Disse (1998: 1:190–99). Gross's (2001a) monograph is devoted to the syntactic and pragmatic analysis of double preposing in BH poetry and prose.

the initial element is resumed by a coreferential pronoun within the body of
the clause;[58] no resumption of this sort is found in the preposed clause. The
resumptive element in left-dislocation is usually a pronoun or pro-adverb but
may also be an anaphoric lexical expression such as הנפש ההיא 'that person';
see example (124). In the examples that follow, the left-dislocated element and
the resumptive element are bold.

(119) Gen 26:15

וכל הבארת אשר חפרו עבדי אביו בימי אברהם אביו סתמום פלשתים

And **all the wells which his father's servants had dug in the days of
Abraham his father**, the Philistines had stopped **them** up

(120) Gen 3:12

האשה אשר נתתה עמדי הוא נתנה לי מן העץ

The woman whom you gave to be with me, she gave me from the tree

In (119), the direct object is dislocated, followed later by an enclitic resumptive
pronoun. In (120), the subject is dislocated, followed by a resumptive personal
pronoun.[59]

When a phrase headed by את or another preposition is dislocated, the preposition may be retained, as in (121), or dropped, as in (122).

(121) Gen 35:12

ואת הארץ אשר נתתי לאברהם וליצחק לך **אתננה**

The land which I gave to Abraham and Isaac, to you I will give **it**

(122) Gen 28:13

הארץ אשר אתה שכב עליה לך **אתננה** ולזרעך:

The land upon which you are lying, to you I will give **it** and to your
descendants.

The detachment of the left-dislocated element as compared to the preposed element is evident from several facts. First, the clause following the

---

58. The term *left-dislocation* originates from work in transformational-generative grammar (Ross 1967). As applied to BH, of course, left-dislocation is a misnomer, because the
NP standing at the head of the clause is to the right of the clause, not the left. Left-dislocation is termed "isolation of the natural subject" by Reckendorf (1895–98) and Bravmann
(1953); in Waltke and O'Connor (1990: §4.7), it is called the *nominative absolute*. On left-
dislocation in BH, see further, e.g., Driver (1892: §§193–201); GKC (§143); Brockelmann
(1956: §123a–h); Lambert (1972: §1282); Bloch (1986); Gross (1986, 1987b, 1988b); Khan
(1988); Naudé (1990); Joüon-Muraoka (§156); Zewi (1999). For Gross (1987b: 187–90), the
pendens construction need not involve resumption.

59. Other representative examples from the Genesis corpus include Gen 15:4, 24:7, and
44:17.

left-dislocated element is syntactically complete without it, which is not the case with the preposed clause. Second, as shown in (122), a preposition is often omitted from the dislocated element, something that does not occur in preposed elements. These two characteristics suggest that the left-dislocated element does not have a syntactic function (e.g., subject or complement) with respect to the clause—hence the term *casus pendens*, 'suspended case'. The preposed constituent, in contrast, has the same syntactic function that it would have in its unmarked position.

A third mark of detachment is that the left-dislocated element is often connected to the clause with a conjunction, like the preverbal adjunct clause (see §5.2.3). The left-dislocated element may also be preceded by a second conjunction. In (123), a single conjunction occurs between the dislocated element and the clause; in (124), two conjunctions are present.[60]

(123) Josh 15:16

אשר יכה את קרית ספר ולכדה ונתתי לו את עכסה בתי לאשה:

Whoever attacks Kiriath-sepher and takes it, I will give Achsah my daughter **to him** as wife.

(124) Gen 17:14

וערל זכר אשר לא ימול את בשר ערלתו ונכרתה הנפש ההוא מעמיה

Any uncircumcised male who is not circumcised in the flesh of his foreskin, that person shall be cut off from his people

Although it is detached, the left-dislocated constituent is not entirely external to the clause. As already mentioned in §5.2.1, a clausal adverb precedes a left-dislocated constituent. In (125), for example, the dislocated element stands after the conjunct לכן.[61]

(125) 2 Kgs 1:6, 16

לכן המטה אשר עלית שם לא תרד ממנה

Therefore **the bed upon which you have alighted**, you shall not come down from **it**

The resumptive element in the dislocation construction may appear in the normal postverbal position, as in (119), or may be preposed, as in (120). Resumptive subject pronouns are generally preposed.[62]

---

60. See also, e.g., Lev 26:36; 1 Kgs 12:17, 15:13.

61. This appears as (84), p. 73 above. See also 2 Kgs 17:36, example (85), p. 73 above.

62. See example (120), p. 82; additional representative examples include Gen 14:24, 15:4, 24:7, 44:17; Exod 12:16; Deut 1:30, 38, 39.

5.5.2. The preverbal constituent connected to its clause with a conjunction

In this unusual construction, a normally postverbal constituent is placed in preverbal position and connected to the rest of the clause with a conjunction:[63]

(126) Gen 22:4

בַּיּוֹם הַשְּׁלִישִׁי וַיִּשָּׂא אַבְרָהָם אֶת עֵינָיו

On the third day, Abraham lifted up his eyes

(127) Gen 27:34

כִּשְׁמֹעַ עֵשָׂו אֶת דִּבְרֵי אָבִיו וַיִּצְעַק צְעָקָה גְּדֹלָה וּמָרָה עַד מְאֹד

When Esau heard his father's words, he cried out with an exceedingly great and bitter cry

The intervening conjunction makes this construction resemble left-dislocation more than preposing. As with the left-dislocated element, a preverbal constituent followed by a conjunction may also be preceded by one:

(128) Exod 32:34

וּבְיוֹם פָּקְדִי וּפָקַדְתִּי עֲלֵיהֶם חַטָּאתָם:

And on the day when I make an accounting, I will bring them to account for their sins.

Many cases of preverbal constituents followed by conjunctions involve temporal adjuncts, as in the examples above. In some cases, however, the preverbal constituent is the subject:[64]

(129) Gen 44:9

אֲשֶׁר יִמָּצֵא אִתּוֹ מֵעֲבָדֶיךָ וָמֵת

Whichever of your servants it is found with, [he] shall die

(130) 1 Sam 17:20

וְהַחַיִל הַיֹּצֵא אֶל הַמַּעֲרָכָה וְהֵרֵעוּ בַּמִּלְחָמָה:

And **the army that was going forth to the battle line**, [they] shouted the war cry.

63. Adjunct clauses that are regularly preverbal, as discussed in §5.2.3, are not included in this category. As noted there, an intervening conjunction is quite common in clauses of this type. Blau (1959, 1977) discusses the sentence adverbial separated from its clause by a conjunction in BH and other Semitic languages. In his view, the adverbial typically serves as the psychological subject of the clause, that is, the part that is known from the context. Steiner (1979: 9) rejects this pragmatic interpretation in his review of Blau (1977), stating "it seems to me that sentence-initial temporal adverbials are used in BH to introduce a **new** temporal frame of reference—not to refer to an old one." Driver's (1892: §§123–29) discussion of casus pendens includes many examples of clauses with a preverbal constituent connected to its clause with a conjunction. The corresponding Arabic construction is discussed in Bravmann (1953: 17–21), Blau (1977), and Kinberg (1985).

64. Additional examples are cited in Steiner (1979: 9).

Table 1. Word-order constructions in finite nonsubordinate clauses in Genesis.

	Number	*Percentage*
1. Nonpreposed[65]	2,901	84.0
2. Marked preposing	402	11.6
3. Unmarked preposing[66]	71	2.1
4. Double preposing	21	0.6
5. Preposing with focus adverb	26	0.8
6. Other marked constructions[67]	33	1.0
Total	3,454	

Like the left-dislocated constituent, the initial constituent connected to its clause by a conjunction comes after a clausal adverb:

(131) 1 Sam 25:27

ועתה **הברכה הזאת אשר הביא שפחתך לאדני** ונתנה לנערים המתהלכים
ברגלי אדני:

And now **this present that your maidservant has brought to my lord**, let [it] be given to the young men who follow my lord.

(132) Num 22:11[68]

הנה **העם היצא ממצרים** ויכס את עין הארץ

Behold, **the people that has come out of Egypt**, [it] covers the face of the earth

5.6. A statistical analysis of word-order constructions in Genesis

The Genesis corpus contains 3,454 nonsubordinate finite clauses, according to the definitions established in chap. 4. Table 1[69] categorizes these clauses according to their word-order construction, based on the definitions set forth in this chapter. Table 1 confirms that the nonpreposed construction is

65. This category includes clauses that are not preposed and do not have a marked construction such as left-dislocation. A clausal adverb, negative adverb or particle, or adjunct clause may precede the verb.

66. This category includes clauses with obligatorily preverbal elements.

67. This category includes left-dislocations and clauses with a constituent (other than an adjunct clause) connected to the clause by a conjunction.

68. Although this segment is often rendered as two conjoined clauses (e.g., NRSV: "A people has come out of Egypt and has spread over the face of the earth"), this interpretation requires ignoring the definite articles in העם and היצא.

69. In this and other tables, the percentages do not add up to precisely 100% because of rounding.

the unmarked construction, constituting 84% of all the finite nonsubordinate clauses in Genesis. Preposing is by far the most common marked word-order construction, with a frequency of about 12%. Unmarked preposing constitutes 2% of the clauses, and double preposing and preposing with a focus adverb occur in less than 1% of the clauses each. The other marked constructions together account for 1%.

In the chapters that follow, I explore the pragmatic function of marked preposing, as represented in category 2 in table 1. My purpose is to identify the speaker's/writer's motivation in choosing the more unusual preposed construction over the corresponding unmarked construction. Unmarked preposing, as represented in category 3, has no special pragmatic function, because a nonpreposed option is not available for these clauses. Clauses exhibiting unmarked preposing, therefore, are not addressed further. From this point on, the term *preposing* will be used to denote exclusively the marked type of preposing. The constructions represented in categories 4 and 5 are certainly worthy of pragmatic investigation, but there are too few occurrences of these types in Genesis to allow for a reliable analysis.[70] Left-dislocations and clauses with a constituent connected to the clause by a conjunction (both included in category 6) are also sparsely attested in Genesis. As such, they are not addressed further in this work, despite their undeniable interest from the pragmatic perspective.

Table 2 shows the frequency of preposing as compared to unmarked word order. In this table, the number of preposed clauses is compared with the number of clauses that are unmarked but are hypothetically preposable. In the first row, the nonpreposed clauses (category 1 in table 1) are tallied, subtracting the nonpreposable ויהי/והיה clauses, of which there are 72. The next row tallies the marked preposed clauses from category (2) in table 1. Table 2 shows that preposing occurs in 12.4% of the clauses that theoretically allow this construction.

As discussed in §3.1.6, several researchers have claimed that direct speech exhibits a higher frequency of preposing than does narrative. Table 3, which breaks down the results in table 2 according to discourse register, confirms this claim. The frequency of preposing in narrative is only 7.6%, whereas the frequency in direct speech is considerably higher, at 21.7%. The *chi*-square test shows that the difference between the two frequencies is statistically significant.[71] Despite the higher frequency of preposing in direct speech, however, it

70. Buth (1999: 88) contends that in double fronting the first element is a topic and the second a focus (see §3.3.5 for further discussion). Double preposing in Modern Hebrew is discussed in Ziv (1996a: 179), who states that the principle governing sentences of this sort is that "the initial fronted constituent must be anchored in the discourse, if any fronted entity is."

71. The *chi*-square test is used to determine whether the difference between two population proportions is statistically significant. The *chi*-square value is associated with a probability, *p*. According to standard statistical methodology, *p* must be less than .05 to be considered significant; in this case, *p* is less than or equal to .001.

**Table 2. Frequency of preposing in preposable finite
nonsubordinate clauses in Genesis.**

Word order	Number	Percentage
Nonpreposed	2,829	87.6
Preposed	402	12.4
Total	3,231	

**Table 3. Relation between discourse register and word order
in preposable finite nonsubordinate clauses in Genesis.**

Discourse register		Nonpreposed	Preposed	Total
Narrative	No.	1,964	162	2,126
	%	92.4	7.6	
Direct speech	No.	865	240	1,105
	%	78.3	21.7	
Total	No.	2,829	402	3,231
	%	87.6	12.4	

Chi-square = 131.682
$p \leq .001$

is clear that preposing is still the marked order in this register, since the majority of direct-speech clauses (78.3%) are not preposed.

Table 4 (p. 88) categorizes preposed clauses according to the syntactic
class of the preposed element. Almost all preposed elements are noun phrases
(64.9%) or prepositional phrases (32.8%).[72]

Table 5 (p. 88) shows that preposed clauses are about evenly divided between subject preposing and complement/adverbial preposing.

5.7. Conclusion

The preposed constituent must be carefully distinguished from other elements that precede the verb. Clausal adverbs and most types of adjunct clauses
are unmarked and non-preposed in the preverbal position. There are two types
of preposing: the optional, marked type and the syntactically obligatory and
hence unmarked type (e.g., the preposing of interrogative pro-forms and certain time adverbs).

72. Noun phrases governed by את are considered prepositional phrases.

**Table 4. Syntactic class of the preposed element in
marked preposed clauses.**

Class	Number	Percentage
Noun phrase	261	64.9
Prepositional phrase	132	32.8
Adverb[73]	3	0.7
Adjective[74]	2	0.5
Headless relative clause[75]	3	0.7
Other[76]	1	0.2
Total	402	

**Table 5. Syntactic function of the preposed element in
marked preposed clauses.**

Class	Number	Percentage
Complement or adverbial	204	50.7
Subject	196	48.8
Ambiguous[77]	2	0.5
Total	402	

The various types of preverbal constituents discussed in this chapter differ
in terms of their degree of detachment from the clause. The most detached is
the clausal adverb, which stands as a rule before all other constituents except
for an initial conjunction. In the next place are the preverbal adjunct clause, the

73. These are 18:5 (כן), 25:10 (שמה), and 31:42 (ריקם).
74. These are Gen 6:9 (תמים) and 27:33 (ברוך).
75. These are Gen 34:11, 41:28, and 41:55.
76. The preposed element in Gen 47:9 is a compound phrase consisting of a coordinated
noun and adjective, מעט ורעים 'few and bad' (see *HALOT* s.v. מעט).
77. The ambiguous cases are Gen 36:13, 14. Both clauses contain the copular verb היה,
a demonstrative pronoun and a definite noun phrase. Because both the demonstrative and
the noun phrase are definite, it is unclear which is the subject and which the predicate. According to Dyk and Talstra's (1999) rules for determining subject and predicate in nominal
clauses, however, there is a definitive answer in these cases: in a nominal clause containing a
demonstrative pronoun and a definite noun phrase, the demonstrative pronoun is the subject;
see also Lowery (1999).

left-dislocated constituent, and the element separated from the clause by a conjunction. There are insufficient data to distinguish between the degrees of detachedness of these three types. Next is the preposed element, whether marked or unmarked. Most integrated is the negative particle, which comes after a preposed constituent and is nearly always immediately adjacent to the verb.

Of all of the marked word-order constructions, preposing is by far the most common. In the following chapters, I examine the pragmatic functions of preposing.

Chapter 6
Focusing and Topicalization

This chapter explores the pragmatic concepts of focusing and topicalization and applies these concepts to BH preposing. The approach here draws on previous research on information structure as well as on psycholinguistic research. I will show that, although both focusing and topicalization provide an instruction regarding the interpretation of the clause in its context, the two types differ regarding the context involved. Focusing signals a relation between the clause and the context of the addressee's attention state, whereas topicalization signals a relation between the clause and the linguistic context that accompanies it. As such, topicalization functions in a manner similar to discourse connectives that signal a pragmatic relation between two sentences or text segments. Focusing is discussed in §6.1 and topicalization in §6.2.

6.1. Focusing

As noted in §3.3.1.3, there appear to be four distinct conceptions of focus: informational focus, contrastive focus, psychological focus, and attentional focus. Psychological focus is very similar to the concept of topic, as mentioned in §3.3.1.3. The shortcomings of the contrastive and attentional focus concepts have already been discussed: contrastive focus blurs the distinction between topic and focus, and attentional focus is essentially a modernized version of emphasis.[1] Informational focus, therefore, appears to be the most useful conception of focus for explaining preposing. Informational focus is the part of the proposition expressed by the sentence that is assumed by the speaker/writer to be new, rather than given. The ensuing sections examine the nature of informational focusing in more detail.

6.1.1. Constituent, predicate, and sentence focus

As mentioned in §3.3.7, Lambrecht has advanced the idea that informational focus may be an argument, a predicate, or an entire sentence. For purposes of clarity, I substitute the term *constituent focus* for argument focus, because Lambrecht's "argument focus" may be any clause constituent (other than the predicate) and is not necessarily an argument of the verb. In this section, it is

---

1. The concept of attentional focus may be useful in understanding a "stylistic" use of focusing, discussed in §8.5.

argued that the concepts of predicate focus and sentence focus relate to given information of an entirely different type from constituent focus, and that the concept of informational focus, strictly speaking, applies only to the constituent type.

As discussed in §3.3.1.3, informational focus identifies an unknown element in the given proposition, answering an implicit *wh*-question. An example of constituent focus is the sentence *Bill* *ate the doughnuts*, with the primary accent on *Bill*. This sentence expresses a semantic proposition, represented informally as "Bill ate the doughnuts." The accenting of *Bill* indicates that the proposition "x ate the doughnuts" is given information in the context of the utterance[2] and reflects an assumption that *Who ate the doughnuts?* is a contextually appropriate question. The given proposition is directly related to the semantic content of the sentence and is derived by replacing the focus *Bill* with a variable.

Given this understanding of informational focus, one would expect predicate and sentence focus to reflect given propositions in which the variable x represents the predicate and the entire sentence, respectively. Thus, Lambrecht (1994: 223) writes that a predicate-focus sentence such as *My car broke **down*** could be used appropriately following the question *What happened to your car?*, reflecting the given proposition "My car x"; the sentence-focus sentence such as *My **car** broke down* is said to be appropriately used following a question such as *What happened?* Sentence-focus, then, apparently reflects the given proposition "x happened."

As Lambrecht's further discussion makes clear, however, this description of predicate and sentence focus is imprecise. Predicate-focus sentences can also be uttered in the absence of a given proposition in which x represents the predicate. According to Lambrecht, the only proposition that can be assumed to be given with respect to a predicate-focus sentence such as *My car broke **down*** is a proposition to the effect that "the speaker's car is pragmatically available as a topic for discussion"; in other words, the given information is the proposition "the speaker's car is a topic for this utterance" (Lambrecht 1994: 226). This proposition is not directly related to the content of the sentence, as in constituent-focus sentences; furthermore, the focus *broke down* does not

---

2. Propositions of the form "x ate the doughnuts" are open propositions, that is, propositions containing a variable (Prince 1985, 1986). Dryer (1996: 512) points out that, technically speaking, open propositions cannot be given, in the sense of believed or known, "since they are not the type of thing that can be true or false" (see §6.1.2 on various conceptions of givenness). It would be more correct to say that the given proposition is the "existential closure of an open proposition" (Dryer 1996: 512); i.e., "there exists an x such that x ate the doughnuts." In the present study, given propositions are represented as open propositions, with the understanding that the open proposition is shorthand for the existential closure of that proposition.

identify a variable in this proposition. The given proposition is best characterized as a metalinguistic proposition regarding the topic of the sentence.[3]

The essential difference between predicate- and sentence-focus sentences, in Lambrecht's view, is that the latter do not have a topic. A topic is lacking in the sentence-focus sentence because it informs the addressee of an event rather than relating information about the subject (Lambrecht 1994: 124). In other words, *my car* is the topic of predicate-focus *My car broke **down*** but not of sentence-focus *My **car** broke down*. Sentence-focus sentences need not involve the given proposition "*x* happened" and can be uttered out of the blue (Lambrecht 1994: 124). Neither predicate-focus sentences nor sentence-focus sentences, then, need involve a given proposition with an unknown.

It can be concluded that the only type of focus that fits the strict definition of informational focus is constituent focus. Only constituent focus identifies an unknown in a given proposition and answers a *wh*-question. Both predicate-focus and sentence-focus sentences do not involve a piece of given information closely related to the content of the sentence. Furthermore, the difference between predicate and sentence focus has nothing to do with focus but concerns the presence or absence of a topic. Using the term *informational focus* to include predicate and sentence focus, therefore, obscures the very significant differences between constituent focus and the other two types.

Constituent focus is the only kind of focus marked by preposing in the casual English register (see §3.3.1.3), and, I contend, is the only type of focus marked by preposing in BH. Convincing evidence is lacking for the marking of sentence focus by preposing in BH, as discussed earlier in §3.3.7. Predicate focus is the pragmatically unmarked articulation (see §3.3.7) and, as such, would be expected to correspond to verb-first word order in BH.

In the following sections, I examine the concept of constituent focus (henceforth referred to simply as "focus") in more detail. The following sections explore the concept of givenness as it relates to focus.

6.1.2. Types of givenness: Pragmatic presupposition and activation

Two types of givenness can be distinguished with regard to informational focus: *pragmatic presupposition* and *activation*.[4] Pragmatically presupposed information is information that is part of the common ground of speaker and addressee, that is, information that the speaker assumes to be known or be-

---

3. In Lambrecht and Michaelis (1998), the two types of given information are clearly distinguished. Given information involving an open proposition is termed a "knowledge presupposition," and given information relating to sentence topic is termed a "topicality presupposition."

4. Although presupposition and activation are often discussed in relation to discourse entities represented by noun phrases, the concepts are equally applicable to the propositions represented by sentences (Dryer 1996: 483).

lieved by him and his addressee.[5] Activated information is information that is assumed by the speaker to be in the consciousness of the addressee at the time of the utterance.[6] Pragmatic presupposition and activation correspond roughly to the cognitive states of *long-term* and *short-term* (or *working*) *memory*.[7] Long-term memory stores all of a person's knowledge and beliefs and has a very large capacity. Short-term memory, on the other hand, has room for only a very small amount of information. Long-term memory is relatively stable, whereas short-term memory is in a state of flux, with items entering and leaving on a regular basis.

The relation between presupposition and activation is a subject that has not received adequate treatment in much of the linguistic literature. Activated entities are widely held to be a subset of presupposed entities.[8] Dryer (1996), however, shows that pragmatic presupposition and activation are logically distinct categories; that is, an entity can be activated but not pragmatically presupposed. Dryer (1996: 483) offers the proposition "the earth is flat" as an example of a proposition that may be in a person's consciousness (once it is mentioned by someone else), despite that person's lack of belief in the proposition.

When we talk about a construction marking a focus with respect to a given proposition, it must be clarified whether we mean that this proposition is presupposed or activated. In Prince's (1986: 209–10) view, focusing constructions

5. See, e.g., Karttunen (1974) and Stalnaker (1974). Pragmatic presupposition is not to be confused with semantic presupposition, which is an entailment of the sentence that is constant under negation. Clark and Haviland's (1977) "given" information is pragmatically presupposed information. Prince's (1981) term for pragmatic presupposition is *assumed familiarity*. Lambrecht (1994: 44) uses the term *pragmatic presupposition* somewhat differently to refer to mentally represented propositions that may or may not be believed (see n. 8).

6. For the term *activation*, see, for example, Gundel (1985); Chafe (1987); Gundel, Hedberg, and Zacharski (1993: 278); Lambrecht (1994); Kintsch (1998). The concept originates in Chafe's seminal article (1976: 30), in which given information is defined as "the knowledge which the speaker assumes to be in the consciousness of the addressee at the time of the utterance. In Prince (1981), the concept is termed "saliency."

7. On short-term and long-term memory, see, e.g., Kintsch (1998: 215–46). Kintsch's theory of memory and its role in comprehension is described in further detail in §6.1.3.

8. Prince (1985: 70), for example, writes that English topicalization marks a proposition "as representing 'shared knowledge', more particularly, Chafe-given [i.e., activated] knowledge" (text in brackets is mine). In another article (1986: 209), she states that focus-presupposition constructions mark a proposition as "salient shared knowledge"; that is, presupposed and activated. See Dryer (1996: 511–12) for further discussion of Prince's views. In the "givenness hierarchy" described by Gundel, Hedberg, and Zacharski (1993), activated entities are a subset of presupposed entities; however, this hierarchy does not specifically address propositions. A different taxonomy of givenness is Prince's (1981) "familiarity" scale. Despite its superficial resemblance to the givenness hierarchy referred to above, Prince's scale relates exclusively to states of pragmatic presupposition. Lambrecht (1994) also views activated propositions as a subset of presupposed ones, because presupposed propositions for him are those that are "mentally represented" (see n. 5 above); all activated propositions are thus presupposed by definition.

relate to a proposition that is both presupposed and activated.[9] Dryer (1996), however, demonstrates that different focusing constructions relate to different kinds of given information: accenting relates specifically to activated information (whether presupposed or not), while clefting relates specifies to presupposed information (whether activated or not). The pragmatic difference between accenting and clefting is illustrated by (133) and (134):

(133) A: Did anyone see Mary?
　　　 B: **John** saw her.

(134) A: Did anyone see Mary?
　　　 B: #It was John who saw her.

As Dryer notes, A's question activates the proposition "x saw Mary" but does not presuppose it, because the point of the question is precisely whether this proposition is true. In this context, *John* can be marked as a focus by accenting, as in (133), but cannot be marked as focus by a cleft construction, as shown by the inappropriateness of (134).[10]

6.1.3. Activation in a model of text comprehension

What kind of information do speakers/writers assume to be activated for their addressees, and how does this information become activated, that is, placed in short-term memory? I first consider written-speech contexts. It is proposed here that activated information for the reader of a text is information either contained in or inferrable from the previous sentence. Support for this claim can be gathered from current research on the process of text comprehension. A broad body of psycholinguistic research supports the theory that readers understand texts by constructing a coherent mental representation of the text (Singer 1990; Sanders and Spooren 2001). Short-term and long-term memory play key roles in building the mental representation. In the ensuing discussion, activation is examined in the light of a well-known comprehension model, Kintsch's "construction-integration" model (1998). The model is supported by a large number of laboratory experiments by Kintsch and others.

---

9. Prince (1986: 210) has stated that Yiddish-movement (see §3.3.1.2, p. 33 n. 47) differs from the aforementioned constructions in involving presupposed but not necessarily activated information (see also Prince 1988: 512–15). In later work (1992, 1999), however, she states that the given information in Yiddish-movement may be merely plausibly inferable and not necessarily presupposed.

10. Similarly, B may answer *Nobody saw her*, but not *It was **nobody** who saw her*. The first sentence, in which the focus is marked by accent alone, is acceptable because it marks the proposition "Somebody saw him" as activated. The cleft sentence is unacceptable because it presupposes the proposition "Somebody saw him," while its content contradicts this presupposition. For additional proofs that focusing by accent does not involve presupposition, see Dryer (1996).

The relevant aspect of Kintsch's theory for present purposes is the concept of *working memory*, which includes short-term memory as well as a section of long-term memory. Long-term memory, storing knowledge, beliefs, and experience, is a network of propositions, a large and intricately interconnected structure. Short-term working memory, in contrast, is an extremely small buffer containing up to four or perhaps seven "chunks" of information—about the amount of information contained in a single sentence (Kintsch 1998: 217, 411). Strictly speaking, the only information that is activated is the proposition currently in short-term working memory. This is not the only memory available to the reader, however. The reader also has near-instant access to all of the propositions in long-term memory that are directly linked to the proposition in the short-term memory. These easily retrievable propositions constitute the *long-term working memory*. Propositions in long-term working memory can be easily activated and placed in short-term memory and are known as *accessible* propositions.[11]

The essence of the comprehension process is described by Kintsch (1998: 93) as follows: "We comprehend a text, understand something, by building a mental model. To do so we must form connections between things that were previously disparate: the ideas expressed in the text and relevant prior knowledge." A reader builds a mental representation of the text in the form of a network of propositions derived from the text and stores it in long-term memory. As the reader proceeds through a text, a proposition is constructed corresponding to each sentence and stored in short-term working memory. After the sentence processing is completed, the proposition representing the sentence is copied to long-term memory and linked to the textual representation already stored there. Furthermore, additional propositions, drawn from the reader's knowledge and experience, are added to the representation and linked to the sentence representation. These propositions include, for example, bridging inferences regarding referring expressions in the text, inferences about causal connections between sentences in the text, and elaborative inferences that fill in details unspecified in the text (Kintsch 1998: 188–99).[12]

---

11. This term is from Dryer (1996: 481), although Dryer does not connect accessibility to long-term working memory. According to Dryer, accessible information is inferable from activated information and is therefore more easily activated than unrelated information. Accessible information is similar but not identical to Chafe's (1987; 1994: 29) "semi-active" information. Accessibility also has a different meaning in Ariel's Accessibility Theory (for a recent summary and discussion, see Ariel 2001). For Ariel, accessibility is a scalar property applicable to activated and nonactivated entities and refers to the ease of retrieval of an item from memory.

12. Higher-level propositions are also inserted into the text representation to represent the macrostructure of the text, that is, its main ideas and themes. On the various types of inferences made during text comprehension, see Singer (1990: 167–89); Kintsch (1998: 193–98); Graesser et al. (2001). A controversy exists over which types of inferences are

As the reader moves on to the next sentence, the central information contained in the previous sentence is retained in short-term memory in order to aid in comprehending the next sentence. All of the propositions in the text representation directly linked to the information in short-term memory, including inferred information, are in long-term working memory and can be quickly and easily converted to activated information. In short, when reading a sentence, the gist of the previous sentence is *activated* and information inferred from or directly linked to the previous sentence is *accessible*.

In Kintsch's model, activated and accessible propositions have much in common, both being part of working memory. Moreover, it is hard to draw a line between activated and accessible information, because information in long-term working memory can quickly and easily be activated and transferred to short-term memory. It is plausible, therefore, that both activated and accessible propositions can serve as given information in connection with a focusing construction. In fact, it can be argued that a focusing construction relating to an accessible proposition reflects an assumption that this proposition will have been activated by the reader. From this point, on I will use *activated* to refer to information in short-term memory as well as accessible information that is treated by the writer as activated.

The comprehension model as outlined above relates to text comprehension and does not include many aspects of spoken-language comprehension. In spoken discourse, information assumed to be in the consciousness of the addressee is not restricted to propositions derived from the preceding discourse but also includes propositions pertaining to the identities of speaker and addressee, their emotions and motivations, as well as elements of the real-world environment in which the dialogue takes place. All of this information cannot possibly fit into the small short-term memory buffer. Kintsch (1998: 411) suggests that this additional information should be thought of as located in permanently activated nodes in long-term memory. Focusing constructions in spoken discourse, then, may relate to activated parts of the addressee's mental representation of the preceding utterances, as well as additional information of the permanently activated type.

6.1.4. Focusing in Biblical Hebrew

Preposing in BH can serve as a focusing construction, as will be demonstrated by the statistical analysis in the next chapter. Left-dislocation may also have a focusing function, as noted by Khan (1988: 93–94).[13] Because the pragmatic analysis in the present work is restricted to the preposing construction,

---

typically generated during text comprehension and which only later during retrieval. Readers appear to vary greatly in the degree of inference that they perform during the comprehension process.

13. See, e.g., Gen 15:4, 44:17; Deut 1:36, 38, 39; 1 Kgs 22:14; 2 Kgs 17:36.

the term *focusing* is used as shorthand for focusing by preposing; similarly, a "focused clause" is one in which the focus has been marked by preposing.

Does BH focusing relate to activated or presupposed information? An examination of focusing in Genesis shows that activation is the relevant type of givenness for this construction. In narrative, focused clauses relate in every case to a proposition contained in or derived from the previous clause; in other words, the given proposition is assumed to be in short-term or long-term working memory. In direct speech, focused clauses relate to information derived from the previous dialogue or to information pertaining to the addressee's personal details, motivations, and perceptions of the environment. The activated proposition associated with a focused clause need not be presupposed, i.e., believed or known by the hearer. A full examination of focusing in BH is presented in chap. 8.

6.2. Topicalization

As described in §3.3.1.2, the term *topicalization* at first denoted a syntactic concept, later shifting to a syntactic-prosodic one; yet another use of the term is to denote a syntactic-pragmatic concept. The latter conception of topicalization is the most useful for investigating BH, a language for which we have no prosodic data.[14] It is important to keep in mind, of course, that corresponding structures in different languages may not have exactly the same pragmatic properties. Thus, the function of BH topicalization may be subtly different from topicalization in other languages. In order to determine whether topicalization exists in BH, however, we need to understand exactly what the function of topicalization is.

As discussed in §3.3.1.2, the linguistic literature cited in studies of BH is somewhat unclear on this crucial point, with topicalization variously characterized as marking discontinuity, continuity, or both. There are, however, other studies of topicalization that have not been fully taken advantage of by scholars of BH. These are addressed in §6.2.1. In §6.2.2, I present a new characterization of BH topicalization based on prior research on topicalization and on discourse connectives.

6.2.1. Prince's and Birner and Ward's characterization of topicalization

Prince and, subsequently, Birner and Ward have presented a theory regarding the function of topicalization that does not involve the concept of topic and is equally applicable to verb-first and subject-first languages.[15] Although their description of topicalization is open to challenge in some respects, it

---

14. On the cross-linguistic investigation of topicalization, see, e.g., Myhill (1985, 1992b) and Givón (2001).

15. See Prince (e.g., 1985, 1986, 1988, 1998); Ward and Prince (1991); Birner and Ward (1998).

provides significant insights relevant to BH. Its most important achievement is to provide a framework that unites the continuous and discontinuous uses of topicalization.

Prince and Birner and Ward see topicalization as having a double function. In §§6.2.1.1 and 6.2.1.2, I present a discussion and critical analysis of the two proposed functions.

6.2.1.1. Marking a partially ordered set relation pertaining to the preposed element

One function of topicalization according to Prince is to mark a relation between the preposed item and an item in the prior context. The preposed item may be an entity already evoked in the discourse, or else in a "salient [i.e., activated] set relation to something already evoked" (Prince 1985: 73; words in brackets are mine).[16] The former type is what has been called continuous topicalization, in which the preposed element is identical to an element mentioned earlier. The latter type, in which the preposed element is related to an earlier element, frequently standing in contrast with it, is what has been called discontinuous topicalization.

In later work by Ward and Prince (1991: 173), Prince's description of topicalization is reformulated to incorporate the idea of the "partially ordered set relation."[17] The partially ordered set relation, or "poset," includes a broad variety of logical relations, e.g., "A is identical to / a member of / subset of / type of / part of B," or "A and B are members of / subsets of / types of / parts of C." Two items belonging to a set stand in a poset relation to each other: {husband, wife}, {father, son}, {bread, wine}. "Functional dependency" relations, such as "A has a B" (e.g., a book has a cover), are *not* poset relations and, it is claimed, are not characteristic of topicalization.[18] According to Ward and Prince (1991), topicalization marks the preposed item as standing in a salient partially ordered set relation to an entity or entities already evoked in the discourse.[19]

---

16. Levinsohn (1990: 22) cites this definition, attributing it erroneously to Andrews (1985: 78). Levinsohn's understanding of topicalization is much broader than Prince's, including the use of preposing to mark all kinds of discontinuities, whether relating to the preposed constituent or to the thematic progression of the story.

17. The logical definition of this concept is highly technical and difficult to understand intuitively; according to Ward and Prince (1991:173), partially ordered sets "are defined by a partial ordering R on some set of referents, b, such that, for all b1, b2, and b3 that are elements of b, R is either reflexive, transitive, and antisymmetric… or, alternatively, irreflexive, transitive, and asymmetric." The linguistic application of the partially ordered set originates in Hirschberg (1991).

18. See Ward and Prince (1991: 175–76); Prince (1998: 8).

19. See also Prince (1998).

In Birner and Ward's (1998) modification of Prince's theory,[20] the description of topicalization is similar, except that it specifies that the entity to which the preposed item is related need not have been explicitly evoked in the prior context; it may be merely inferable from the prior context. The partially ordered set relation must be "contextually licensed" (Birner and Ward 1998: 20); that is, it must be directly derivable or inferrable from the context.

The partially ordered set relation involved in topicalization may be highly idiosyncratic and restricted to the particular discourse context; in Birner and Ward's (1998: 234) words, it may be "entirely ad-hoc." This point is illustrated by (135):

> (135) Philadelphia Inquirer, 8/31/1983 (Birner and Ward 1998: 234).
> It is nearly 8 and Ellerbee, back from dinner, tidies up some details in her narrow, windowless third floor office before moving down the hall to the studio. Her son and his friend pore over computer workbooks in a small area outside her office. Joshua and his 14-year-old sister, Vanessa, take turns spending Friday nights at the studio. "**Sleep** they can catch up on," Ellerbee says, "**Mom** they can't."

Example (135) contains paired topicalized clauses, with *sleep* and *Mom* as the respective preposed constituents. *Mom* is obviously meant to be related to the preceding *sleep*, despite the lack of any natural relation between the two concepts outside the given context. Birner and Ward (1998: 234) explain that these two items belong to an ad-hoc partially ordered set, {things children need}. This example and others like it raise the question whether the elaborate logical apparatus of the poset is really necessary for the description of topicalization. The possibility of ad-hoc posets means, in essence, that any items that constitute a pair in a given context qualify as a poset.[21] It can be argued that this loose conception of the relation between the linked items obviates the need for partially ordered set concept. The point is that the linked items in topicalization are contextually related in a way that is recognizable by the addressee.

6.2.1.2. Marking a focus in relation to a given proposition

Prince, as well as Birner and Ward, argue that in addition to marking a relation pertaining to the preposed constituent, topicalization simultaneously marks a different constituent as focus. The focus in a topicalized clause remains in its original position and is marked by accent alone. Thus in Prince's view, a sentence of the form *Cake I like to eat with a **spoon*** would only be appropriate in a context in which "I like to eat cake with an *x*" is an activated

---

20. Birner and Ward (1998) have extended and modified Prince's theory of topicalization to explain a wide variety of marked word-order constructions in English and other languages; my comments on their work are restricted to its ramifications for preposing.

21. I am indebted to Yael Ziv for this insight (personal communication).

proposition, and "spoon" is the new value for x.[22] Birner and Ward (1998) agree with Prince that most types of topicalization, except for those involving preposed locatives, mark a focus.

Gregory and Michaelis (2001: 1673 n. 8), raise doubts regarding the focus-marking function of topicalization. They note that the final accent in *Cake, I like to eat with a **spoon*** need not represent constituent focus but can just as well be interpreted as the unmarked articulation, in which the accent falls on the last lexical expression in the clause.[23] Thus, "I like to eat cake with an x" is not necessarily given information with respect to the clause.[24]

An examination of some of the examples of topicalization cited by Birner and Ward (1998) confirms that topicalization need not involve constituent focus. In examples (136) and (137), it is unlikely that the (presumably) accented constituent is interpretable as the focus.

(136) S. Pintzuk to G. Ward in conversation about Ph.D. exam
           (Birner and Ward 1998: 22)
       G: So, how'd it go?
       S: The historical question I had some problems with, but I think
           it's ok. The descriptive I just wrote a whole lot.

(137) M. Schultz to G. Ward in conversation (Birner and Ward 1998: 222)
       G: How could you take an exam with all those students pestering
           you?
       M: It wasn't easy, but they were all done by three-thirty, and I had
           until five. The hard part I left for the end.

In the underlined topicalized clause in (136), the accented constituent is presumably *problems*. Yet replacing this constituent with a variable yields a proposition that is neither activated nor inferrable: "The historical question I had some x (or had x) with." Similarly, in (137) *end* is presumably accented, but "The hard part I left for x" cannot be reasonably be considered an activated proposition in this context.

---

22. In Prince (1985), the given proposition is arrived at by replacing the accented constituent with a variable and by replacing the preposed constituent with the set containing it, that is, "I like to eat {types of foods} with an x." In Prince (1998: 293) the procedure is described somewhat differently: the preposed constituent is not replaced by the set containing it but is accompanied by an explicit representation of the set relation; that is, "I like to eat cake, a member of the set {types of food}, with an x." It is unclear to me how the latter formulation differs in its propositional content from the simpler version, "I like to eat cake with an x."

23. This is what Lambrecht calls the "predicate-focus" articulation, in which the focus is projected from the accented constituent over the entire verb phrase (see §3.3.7).

24. It can be further noted that, under the predicate-focus interpretation, "I do x" cannot be assumed to be given information either; see §6.1.1.

6.2.2. Topicalization in Biblical Hebrew: A discourse-connective device

In this section, I present a new characterization of the function of topicalization as it is manifested in BH. The description here is based in part on the insights of Prince and Birner and Ward but also draws on a different area of pragmatic research—the function of conjunct adverbials, also known as *discourse markers* or *discourse connectives* (see §5.2.1, p. 69 n. 13).

A problematic aspect of both Prince's and Birner and Ward's descriptions of topicalization is that they do not specify where the linked item or the item from which it is inferred is located in the previous discourse. It can be argued that without a specification of this sort their descriptions are too broad to be useful for cross-linguistic comparison: since most clause elements are related at least indirectly to something mentioned at some earlier point (especially in long narrative texts), nearly any preposed clause can by viewed as topicalized under these descriptions. In most of the cited examples in Birner and Ward, however, the source of the linked item is the *immediately preceding* context. It is unlikely that this is a coincidence.

As a working hypothesis, then, it is posited that topicalization indicates a contextual relation between the preposed constituent and another element in the immediately preceding context. An examination of the Genesis corpus, as described in the following chapters, reveals a large number of preposed clauses that satisfy this description, thus justifying the topicalization category for this language. There is also, however, a group of BH clauses in which the clause containing the preposed entity and the clause containing the item to which it is related are not immediately adjacent to each other. This type is addressed further in this section in the discussion of discourse connectives.

In another group of BH clauses, the preposed element is related to an element in the immediately *following* context, rather than the preceding context. In fact, a topicalized clause may occur at the beginning of a discourse, where the only possible relation must concern the following clause (see §9.3). It is probable that forward-pointing topicalization occurs in English as well, although this cannot be conclusively demonstrated from the examples cited by Birner and Ward.

As will be shown in chap. 9, ad-hoc links between entities bearing no natural relation are not uncommon in BH topicalization; the only requirement is that the linked entities bear a contextual relation which is perceptible by the addressee. As in English, BH topicalization does not necessarily involve a constituent focus.

Marking a relation between entities, however, is only one functional aspect of BH topicalization and, mostly likely, of English topicalization as well. Consider again example (135), repeated in (138):

(138) "**Sleep** they can catch up on, **Mom** they can't."

The ad-hoc contextual relation between *sleep* and *Mom* is hardly significant in and of itself. Rather, this relation serves to indicate a larger-scale relation between the clauses—in this case, contrast. In most cases of BH topicalization, a specific relation, usually contrast or similarity, exists between the topicalized clause and the clause containing the other linked entity. When the two linked items are identical, the relation between clauses is often one of explanation or restatement. Occasionally, the relation is one of temporal sequence.

In marking relations between clauses, BH topicalization bears a functional resemblance to discourse connectives, which are words or phrases that mark the relation between two adjacent sentences or text segments (Schiffrin 1987: 31; Fraser 1990, 1996; Schourup 1999).[25] Discourse connectives and the relations they signal have been studied by researchers in pragmatics as well as by psycholinguists. Relations between text segments, including causal, contrastive, and concessive relations, are frequently referred to as *coherence relations* (Sanders 1997; Sanders and Noordman 2000; Knott 2001; Sanders and Spooren 2001). Coherence relations are often left to the reader to infer and not explicitly signaled on the formal level. Alternatively, coherence relations may be signaled by discourse connectives such as *so*, *but*, *however*, and *similarly*. In the context of psycholinguistic theories of comprehension, discourse connectives are said to facilitate the building of a coherent text representation by guiding the reader in correctly linking the representations of the two segments (Sanders and Noordman 2000; Sanders and Spooren 2001).

Coherence relations are generally divided into two types: those that concern the content of the two segments, and those that concern the speaker's reasoning or the speech acts accomplished by the segments. These types are sometimes known as *semantic* and *pragmatic* relations, respectively (Van Dijk 1979: 449);[26] alternative terms are *external* and *internal* relations (Halliday and Hasan 1976: 240), and *ideational* and *rhetorical* relations (Redeker 1990). Sweetser (1990: 21) divides the pragmatic relation category into *epistemic* (relating to the speaker's beliefs or reasoning) and *speech act* relations. Following Sweetser, I will refer to three types of coherence relations: *content*, *epistemic*, and *speech-act* relations.[27]

The difference between the various types of relations is illustrated in (139). As the examples show, a single discourse connective can often signal more than one type of relation.

25. Many discourse connectives are conjunct adverbs or adverbials (see §5.2.1).

26. Van Dijk's use of the term *pragmatic* is narrower than the one adopted in the present work. I am using this term to include all aspects of the relations between clauses and their contexts, including the so-called semantic relations.

27. The question of whether epistemic and speech-act relations should be subsumed under a single category does not concern us here; for an attempt to settle this issue, see Knott (2001). On the relations signaled by discourse connectives in Modern Hebrew, see Abadi (1988).

(139) Semantic, epistemic, and speech-act relations (Knott 2001)
   a. Bill was starving, **so** he had a sandwich.
   b. Bill had five sandwiches, **so** he must have been starving.
   c. Bill is starving. **So** why isn't he eating?

In all three examples, the discourse connective *so* marks a cause-and-effect relation between the clauses, but in each case the relation is of a different type. In (139a), the discourse connective marks a relation between the contents of the two clauses. In (139b), *so* marks a relation concerning the speaker's reasoning: the clause *he must have been starving* represents a conclusion derived from the premise "Bill had five sandwiches." The sequence can be paraphrased as *Bill had five sandwiches. It may be concluded that he must have been starving.* In (139c), *so* marks a relation between the fact that Bill is starving and the speech act of questioning. The sequence can be paraphrased as *Bill is starving. Therefore I ask, "Why isn't he eating?"*

It is proposed here that topicalization is a kind of generalized discourse connective. By marking a link between the preposed item and a second item, topicalization cues the reader to the coherence relation between the segments containing these items,[28] a relation which specifically concerns the pair of linked items. The exact nature of the coherence relation is not specified, but is left to the reader's inference. In marking either forward-pointing or backward-pointing relations, topicalization resembles some BH conjuncts that may point either forward or backward. An example is הלא, which marks the justification for a preceding or a following clause (see §7.3.2.1, p. 117 n. 21).

Viewing topicalization as a discourse-connective device explains why in some cases in BH the linked items are not in adjacent clauses. As mentioned above, discourse connectives can link adjacent sentences or adjacent text segments of longer length. In cases in which the linked items in BH topicalization are not in adjacent clauses, the items nonetheless stand at the head of adjacent text segments.

A full examination of topicalization in BH is presented in chap. 9.

---

28. Blakemore (1987: 86) notes that discourse connectives do not always link segments in a single discourse, but may relate to a different speaker's utterance, as in (1), or even to the extratextual situation, as in (2):
   (1)   A: You take the first turning on the left.
         B: So I don't go past the hospital. (Blakemore 1987: 85)
   (2)   [Having seen someone arrive home laden with parcels]
         A: So you've spent all your money. (Blakemore 1987: 86)
Some of the examples of topicalization cited by Birner and Ward (1998) are similar to (1), linking the preposed item to an item in a different speaker's utterance, as in (3).
   (3)   A: You know **this album**?
         B: **This song** I know. (Birner and Ward 1998: 44)
This type of topicalization does not appear to occur in the Genesis corpus, but occurs in Jer 1:14, where the preposed מצפון 'from the north' in God's utterance is linked to צפונה 'the north' in Jeremiah's immediately preceding utterance.

Chapter 7
The Pragmatics of Preposing: A Statistical Analysis

In this chapter, the pragmatic function of preposing in the 401 marked preposed clauses in Genesis (see §3.6) is analyzed, with the aim of establishing the dominance of the information-structure concepts of focusing and topicalization.

7.1. Focusing and topicalization in preposed clauses

Table 6 shows the frequency of information-structure functions in preposed clauses in Genesis. Topicalization is shown to be a widespread function of preposing, occurring in 42.5% of all preposed clauses. Focusing is considerably less common, accounting for 12.4%. Including the seven clauses that are ambiguous—either focused or topicalized—the two information-structure functions account for 56.6% of preposing in Genesis.

A closer examination of the data reveals that the frequency of information-structure functions varies according to the syntactic function of the preposed constituent (subject vs. complement/adjunct)[1] and according to the register of the clause (narrative vs. direct speech). The figures are displayed in tables 7 and 8, respectively.[2] Table 7 shows that information-structure functions constitute the majority of complement/adjunct-preposed clauses, 68.6% of the total, but a minority of subject-preposed clauses, only 43.6%. The *chi*-square test shows that the difference between the two frequencies is statistically significant.

Table 8 shows that information-structure functions account for 66.7% of narrative clauses and a smaller portion, 50%, of direct-speech clauses. Again, the *chi*-square test shows that the difference between the two groups is statistically significant. In §§7.2 and 7.3, I examine complement/adjunct preposing and subject preposing separately. In each section, the functions of the preposed clauses in narrative is compared to their functions in direct speech.

---

1. As explained in §4.5, I do not systematically differentiate between complements and adjuncts, due to practical and theoretical difficulties in doing so.
2. As noted in §5.6 n. 77 (p. 88), in two of the 402 clauses, the syntactic function of the preposed constituent cannot be definitively determined. These clauses are omitted from table 7.

Table 6. Pragmatic functions of preposed clauses in Genesis.

	Number	*Percentage*
Focusing	50	12.4
Topicalization	171	42.5
Focusing/topicalization[3]	7	1.7
Residue	174	43.3
Total	402	

Table 7. Relation between syntactic function of the preposed constituent and pragmatic function of preposing.

Syntactic function		*Information structure*	*Other*	*Total*
Subject	No.	86	110	196
	%	43.9	56.1	
Complement/adjunct	No.	140	64	204
	%	68.6	31.4	
Total	No.	226	174	400
	%	56.5	43.5	

chi-square = 24.914
$p \leq .001$

7.2. Focusing and topicalization in complement/adjunct-preposed clauses

Table 7 shows that information-structure functions constitute 68% percent of all clauses with a preposed complement/adjunct. As mentioned in §3.3.5, it has been suggested that preposed time adjuncts may be preposed for no reason other than to provide a setting for the clause. I checked various representative time-adjunct types, examining all of the preposed occurrences in finite nonsubordinate clauses in the classical BH prose corpus. The expressions checked were מחר 'tomorrow', היום 'today', ביום 'on the . . . day', בחדש 'on the . . . month', בשנה/בשנת 'in the . . . year'; and temporal infinitive phrases

---

3. This category includes clauses that allow either a focused or a topicalized interpretation; i.e., Gen 8:17, 9:2, 18:7, 34:26, 34:29, 43:15 (בידכם), and 46:7.

**Table 8. Relation between register and
pragmatic function of preposing.**

Register		Information structure	Other	Total
Narrative	No.	108	54	162
	%	66.7	33.3	
Direct speech	No.	120	120	240
	%	50.0	50.0	
Total	No.	228	174	402
	%	56.7	43.3	

chi-square = 10.944
$p \leq .001$

**Table 9. Pragmatic functions of complement/adjunct
preposed clauses.**

Pragmatic function	Number	Percentage
Focusing	42	20.5
Topicalization	93	45.6
Focusing/topicalization	5	2.5
Residue	64	31.4
Total	204	

involving the prepositions כ, ב, or אחרי. Of the 123 clauses containing pre-posed expressions of these types, a total of 72% have an information-structure function. When this figure is compared to the 68% of complement/adjunct-preposed clauses that have an information-structure function, it can be seen that information-structure functions are at least as dominant in time-adjunct-preposed clauses as in complement/adjunct-preposed clauses in general. These results indicate that there is no reason to consider time-adjunct preposing to be functionally distinct from complement/adjunct preposing in general.

Table 9 shows the distribution of pragmatic functions in complement/adjunct preposed clauses. The table shows that topicalization is over twice as common as focusing in complement/adjunct preposed clauses, 45.6%, as compared to 20.5%.

**Table 10. Pragmatic functions of complement/adjunct-preposed clauses:
Narrative vs. direct speech.**

Register		Focus.	Topic.	Focus./ Topic.	Residue	Total
Narrative	No.	7	47	4	7	65
	%	10.8	72.3	6.2	10.8	
Direct speech	No.	35	46	1	57	139
	%	25.2	33.1	0.7	41.0	
Total	No.	42	93	5	64	204
	%	20.6	45.6	2.5	31.4	

In table 10, the functions of complement/adjunct preposing are tallied separately for narrative and direct speech.[4] Several interesting facts may be observed. First, the frequencies of focusing and topicalization constructions differ sharply in narrative and direct speech. In narrative, focusing (10.8%) is much less common than topicalization (72.3%). In direct speech, the frequencies of the two functions are more similar: 25.2% focusing and 33.1% topicalization. Comparing the size of the residue group in the two registers, we see that almost all the residue clauses are direct speech clauses. Of the 64 clauses in the residue column, 57 (89%) are in direct speech and only 7 (11%) are in narrative. Looked at another way, only 7 out of 65 narrative clauses (11%) are residue, whereas 57 out of 139 direct-speech clauses (41%) are residue.

It may be concluded from these figures that focusing and topicalization are the predominant and perhaps the only significant functions of complement/adjunct preposing in narrative. In direct speech, though focusing and topicalization still together account for the majority (58%) of complement/adjunct preposing, other factors, presently unclear, are obviously at work as well. In the ensuing discussion, I offer some tentative remarks regarding the residue, without attempting to give a systematic account.

7.2.1. The residue: Possible instances of focusing

A number of the clauses in the direct-speech residue may actually be intended to be focused. In the present study, clauses are classified as focused only if examination of the context makes it clear that a proposition relating

4. The *chi*-square test was not performed on this table. The *chi*-square test is not considered accurate for this table due to the presence of two cells with frequencies of less than 5.

to this focus is activated or accessible for the addressee. This procedure may
not identify all of the cases in which the speaker/writer is treating a particular
proposition as activated. The preposed clauses in (140) and (141), for example,
may have been intended to be focused, although they are not classified as such
due to lack of evidence of an activated proposition.

(140) Gen 29:25

ויהי בבקר והנה הוא לאה ויאמר אל לבן מה זאת עשית לי הלא **ברחל** עבדתי
עמך ולמה רמיתני:

And it came to pass in the morning, and behold, it was Leah; and Jacob
said to Laban, "What have you done to me? Surely **for Rachel** I served
you! And why have you deceived me?"[5]

(141) Gen 24:50

ויען לבן ובתואל ויאמרו **מי׳** יצא הדבר

And Laban and Bethuel answered, and said, "**From the LORD** the thing
has come."

In (140), it is hard to determine whether "I worked for you for *x*" is accessible
by inference from the preceding clause, מה זאת עשית לי 'What have you done to
me?' Nevertheless, it is certainly plausible that Jacob assumes that this proposition is accessible. Such an explanation is plausible for (141) as well.

A different phenomenon, known as *accommodation*, involves a speaker
treating a proposition as presupposed or activated, even though he knows this
is unlikely. An example given by Dryer is a speaker who says "Watch out, the
dog will bite you," even though he knows the addressee is unaware of any dog
nearby. By acting as if the existence of the dog is presupposed, the speaker in-
duces the addressee to adopt this presupposition.[6] The sentence serves as shorthand for "There is a dog nearby, and he is likely to bite you." Accommodation
may be at work in clauses such as (142).[7]

(142) Gen 12:7

וירא י׳ אל אברם ויאמר **לזרעך** אתן את הארץ הזאת

And the LORD appeared to Abram, and said, "**To your offspring** I will
give this land."

---

5. The translation follows NJPSV in giving הלא an asseverative rather than an interrogative
interpretation (see §5.2.1, p. 70 n. 19 for the distinction between the two). In this clause, הלא
marks the justification for the preceding rhetorical question, as explained further in §7.3.2.1.

6. Chafe (1976: 34) calls this a "quasi-given" state, where the speaker engages in a pre-
tense that conscious information is involved. On accommodation, see Lewis (1979); Dryer
(1996).

7. Similar instances are Gen 15:18–21, 24:7, and 31:15. See also Gen 21:6, where the
speaker is addressing a nonspecific audience or herself.

In this verse God speaks as if "I shall give this land to *x*" is an activated proposition, although there is no reason to assume that Abram was thinking about this proposition.

7.2.2. The residue: Fixed expressions with preposed word order

In some of the clauses in the direct-speech residue, preposing seems to be due to the presence of a fixed expression with characteristically preposed word order. This type of preposing does not have any pragmatic function at all. An example is the expression בי נשבעתי:

(143) Gen 22:16

ויאמר **בי נשבעתי** נאם י' כי יען אשר עשית את הדבר הזה

By myself I swear, says the LORD, that because you have done this

This expression occurs three times elsewhere, each time with preposed בי.[8] Although these other occurrences are not in the classical prose corpus, the striking resemblance to the word order in (143) seems to indicate a fixed expression.

Another recurring expression that is usually preposed is כדבר הזה or כדברים האלה with the meaning 'such and such', as used in direct speech:[9]

(144) Gen 32:20

ויצו גם את השני גם את השלישי גם את כל ההלכים אחרי העדרים לאמר **כדבר הזה** תדברון אל עשו במצאכם אתו:

He also instructed the second and the third and all who followed the droves, saying, "**Such and such** you shall say to Esau when you meet him."

(145) Gen 39:19

ויהי כשמע אדניו את דברי אשתו אשר דברה אליו לאמר **כדברים האלה** עשה לי עבדך

When his master heard the words which his wife spoke to him, saying "**Such and such** your servant did to me"

Another characteristically preposed formula is כל אשר אמר/צוה . . . אעשה/נעשה 'whatever *x* says/commands, I/we shall do':[10]

---

8. These are Isa 45:23; Jer 22:5, 49:13. The similar expression בי' נשבעתי 'by the LORD I swear' occurs in 2 Sam 19:8.

9. Additional examples include 1 Sam 18:24 and 2 Sam 17:6. In 2 Sam 14:3, the equivalent expression is not preposed.

10. Additional examples include Exod 24:3, 7; Josh 1:16. A similar formula has a left-dislocated structure instead of a preposed clause (Num 22:20, 23:26). Folmer (1995: 569–72) shows that in Aramaic texts of the Achaemenid period, phrases containing general relative clauses of the form כל . . . זי 'every *x* that' are usually preposed; this is also true of similar types such as מה זי 'whatever' and מן זי 'whoever'. (I am indebted to Richard Steiner for the

(146) Gen 31:16

וְעַתָּה **כֹּל אֲשֶׁר אָמַר אֱלֹהִים אֵלֶיךָ** עֲשֵׂה׃

And now, **whatever God has said to you**, do.

(147) Exod 19:8

וַיַּעֲנוּ כָל הָעָם יַחְדָּו וַיֹּאמְרוּ **כֹּל אֲשֶׁר דִּבֶּר יְיָ** נַעֲשֶׂה

And all the people answered together and said, "**Whatever the LORD has spoken** we will do."

(148) 2 Kgs 10:5

עֲבָדֶיךָ אֲנַחְנוּ **וְכֹל אֲשֶׁר תֹּאמַר אֵלֵינוּ** נַעֲשֶׂה

We are your servants, and **whatever you say to us** we will do.

A similar formula occurs in (149)–(151), with the head of the relative clause omitted.

(149) Gen 41:55

לְכוּ אֶל יוֹסֵף **אֲשֶׁר יֹאמַר לָכֶם תַּעֲשׂוּ**׃

Go to Joseph; **whatever he says to you**, you shall do.

(150) Gen 34:11

אֶמְצָא חֵן בְּעֵינֵיכֶם **וַאֲשֶׁר תֹּאמְרוּ אֵלַי** אֶתֵּן׃

Let me find favor in your eyes, and **whatever you say to me** I will give.

(151) 2 Sam 18:4

וַיֹּאמֶר אֲלֵיהֶם הַמֶּלֶךְ **אֲשֶׁר יִיטַב בְּעֵינֵיכֶם** אֶעֱשֶׂה

The king said to them, "**Whatever you think best** I will do."

7.3. Topicalization and focusing in subject-preposing constructions

Table 7 (p. 105) showed that focusing and topicalization account for only 43.9% of subject-preposed clauses. As discussed in chap. 3 (pp. 18–47), subject preposing appears to have a number of functions that relate to the clause as a whole, rather than to the preposed subject in particular; these include marking anteriority or a pair of simultaneous events (§3.1.2), marking a new narrative unit/scene (§3.1.3), or marking background information (§3.2). It is sometimes difficult to distinguish between the use of preposing for topicalization and the other functions. When a preposed subject is the same as an item in the preceding clause, for example, the clause fits the criterion for topicalization.[11] In

---

Folmer reference.) In BH, however, כל אשר phrases are not typically preposed. It is only in the formula exemplified by examples (146)–(148) that כל אשר is typically found in initial position.

11. In a case of this sort, the relation between linked items is one of identity. See §9.2 for further discussion.

Table 11. Pragmatic functions of subject-preposed clauses.

Pragmatic function	Number	Percentage
Focusing	9	4.6
Topicalization	75	38.3
Focusing/Topicalization	2	1.0
Residue	110	56.1
Total	196	

these cases, it is necessary to decide whether the preposing is for the purpose of linking the identical entities and the clauses containing them or whether the purpose is to mark a different function such as anteriority or simultaneity.

Table 11 shows the distribution of information-structure functions in subject-preposed clauses. Cases clearly intended to have a function relating to the clause as a whole are counted as residue even if the sentence could technically be taken as topicalization. If the data in table 11 are compared to the comparable data for complement/adjunct-preposed clauses in table 9 (p. 106), it can be seen that focusing is much less common in subject-preposed clauses. Only 4.6% of subject-preposed clauses are focused, as compared to 20.5% of complement/adjunct-preposed clauses. The frequency of topicalization in both groups is more similar: 38.3% of subject-preposed clauses and 45.6% of complement/adjunct-preposed clauses are topicalized. Turning to the residue, it can be seen that the residue of subject-preposed clauses is much larger than the residue of complement/adjunct clauses, at 56.1% as compared to 31.4%.

In table 12 (p. 112), the frequencies of information-structure functions in subject-preposed clauses are tabulated separately for narrative and direct speech. Although some differences may be noted between the two registers, the differences are probably not statistically significant.[12] Topicalization is much more common than focusing in both registers, although the frequency is somewhat higher in narrative, constituting 47.4% of the total, as compared to only 30.7% in direct speech. In both registers, focusing is a rare phenomenon, occurring in 3.2% of narrative clauses and 5.0% of direct-speech clauses. Interestingly, the residue of subject preposing constitutes nearly 50% or more of the clauses in both registers. This contrasts with the residue of complement/adjunct preposing in narrative, which is quite small (see table 10, p. 107). Although the sizes of the residues in narrative and direct speech are comparable,

---

12. The *chi*-square test cannot be performed on this table because one of the cells has a frequency of 0.

**Table 12. Pragmatic functions of subject-preposed clauses:
Narrative versus direct speech.**

Register		Focus.	Topic.	Focus./ Topic.	Residue	Total
Narrative	No.	3	45	0	47	95
	%	3.2	47.4	0	49.5	
Direct Speech	No.	5	31	2	63	101
	%	5.0	30.7	2.0	62.4	
Total	No.	8	76	2	110	196
	%	4.1	38.8	1.0	56.1	

the functional distribution of the residue clauses differs considerably in the two registers, as I discuss next.

7.3.1. The residue of subject-preposed narrative clauses

About three-quarters of the subject-preposed clauses in the narrative residue (34 clauses) appear to have a function relating to the clause as a whole. The function of preposing in the remaining third of the residue is not clear. In §§7.3.1.1–7.3.1.4, I list of the functions that were identified, which are marking anteriority, simultaneity, background information, or the beginning of a new narrative unit or a scene within the narrative. Because these have already been discussed in detail in chap. 3, I merely cite examples of each type from the Genesis corpus and elsewhere.

The examples cited include, wherever possible, an instance with a preposed lexical expression and an instance with a preposed pronoun. The pronominal examples serve as evidence that functions relating to the entire clause are marked by preposing the subject, as opposed to a complement or adjunct: in most of the pronominal examples, a complement or adjunct is present that could have been preposed, but instead the normally dropped subject pronoun is retained in order to produce the desired subject-verb order.

7.3.1.1. Anteriority

Preposing to mark anteriority is shown in (152) and (153). The anterior preposed clause can often be rendered with the English past perfect, as in these examples.[13]

---

13. Additional examples from the Genesis corpus include Gen 20:4 and 31:19. Additional representative examples from the classical BH prose corpus include Josh 2:6; 1 Sam 9:15, 30:1.

(152) Gen 31:33–34

ויבא לבן באהל יעקב ובאהל לאה ובאהל שתי האמהת ולא מצא ויצא מאהל
לאה ויבא באהל רחל: ורחל לקחה את התרפים ותשמם בכר הגמל ותשב עליהם

And Laban went into Jacob's tent, and into Leah's tent, and into the
tent of the two maidservants, and he did not find them. And he came
out of Leah's tent, and he entered Rachel's tent. And Rachel had taken
the household gods, and she put them in the camel cushion, and she sat
upon them.

(153) Josh 2:4–6

ותאמר כן באו אלי האנשים ולא ידעתי מאין המה: ויהי השער לסגור בחשך
והאנשים יצאו לא ידעתי אנה הלכו האנשים רדפו מהר אחריהם כי תשיגום:
והיא העלתם הגגה ותטמנם בפשתי העץ הערכות לה על הגג:

And she said, "True, the men came to me, and I did not know where they
were from. And the gate was [about] to be closed, at dark, and the men
went out; I do not know where the men went; pursue them quickly, for
you will overtake them." And she had brought them up to the roof, and
she hid them under the stalks of flax which she had laid out on the roof.

7.3.1.2. Simultaneity

Preposing can be used to mark a simultaneous event. In several instances,
the preposed clause is simultaneous with an immediately preceding nonverbal
or participial clause:[14]

(154) Gen 38:25

הוא מוצאת והיא שלחה אל חמיה לאמר לאיש אשר אלה לו אנכי הרה

She was being brought out, and she sent word to her father-in-law, saying "By the man to whom these belong, I am with child."

In (155), a triplet of preposed finite clauses denotes three simultaneous or
nearly simultaneous events:[15]

---

14. Appears in chap. 3 as (7) (p. 23). Additional examples from the Genesis corpus include 29:9, 38:25, and 44:3. Additional representative examples from the classical BH prose
corpus include Judg 18:3; 1 Sam 9:11; 1 Kgs 20:39.

15. As discussed in §3.1.2, it seems likely that simultaneity and near-simultaneity constitute a single pragmatic category. Pairs of finite preposed simultaneous clauses occur, for
example, in Josh 2:8, Judg 18:22, 1 Sam 9:5, and 2 Sam 2:24.

(155) Gen 19:23–24

השמש יצא על הארץ ולוט בא צערה: וי׳ המטיר על סדם ועל עמרה גפרית ואש
מאת י׳ מן השמים:

The sun rose on the earth, and Lot came to Zoar. And the Lord rained
upon Sodom and on Gemorrah sulfur and fire from the Lord from heaven.

In two cases, a preposed clause follows a ויהי clause with which it is simultaneous: [16]

(156) Gen 15:12

ויהי השמש לבוא ותרדמה נפלה על אברם

And the sun was setting, and a deep sleep fell upon Abraham.

7.3.1.3. Background information

A preposed clause may provide background information that is pertinent to
the narrative as it is unfolding. This function partially overlaps with the anteriority category, as anterior events often constitute background information.
Background information, however, may be a current state or event: [17]

(157) Gen 48:9–10

ויאמר יוסף אל אביו בני הם אשר נתן לי אלהים בזה ויאמר קחם נא אלי
ואברכם: ועיני ישראל כבדו מזקן לא יוכל לראות ויגש אתם אליו וישק להם
ויחבק להם:

And Joseph said to his father, "They are my sons, whom God has given
me here." And he said, "Bring them to me, please, and I will bless them."
And Israel's eyes were dim with age; he could not see. And Joseph
brought them near him; and he kissed them and embraced them.

(158) Gen 42:22–23

ויען ראובן אתם לאמר הלוא אמרתי אליכם לאמר אל תחטאו בילד ולא שמעתם
וגם דמו הנה נדרש: והם לא ידעו כי שמע יוסף כי המליץ בינתם:

And Reuben answered them, "Did I not tell you, 'Do not sin against the
boy?' And you did not listen. And behold, there comes a reckoning for
his blood." And they did not know that Joseph understood, for there was
an interpreter between them.

---

16. The other example is Gen 22:1. In a different pattern, the ויהי clause is a bare verbal
form without a temporal adverbial, followed by two preposed simultaneous clauses (Gen
15:17 and 27:30, ויהי אך). See §4.4.2 for the syntactic analysis of ויהי clauses adopted in the
present work.

17. An additional example is Gen 37:3.

7.3.1.4. New narrative unit or new scene within the narrative

In several instances, preposing marks the beginning of a new narrative unit:

(159) Gen 16:1

ושרי אשת אברם לא ילדה לו ולה שפחה מצרית ושמה הגר:

And Sarai, Abram's wife, had not borne him children. And she had an Egyptian maidservant, and her name was Hagar.

(160) Gen 39:1

ויוסף הורד מצרימה ויקנהו פוטיפר סריס פרעה שר הטבחים איש מצרי מיד
הישמעאלים אשר הורדהו שמה:

And Joseph was taken down to Egypt. And Potiphar, an officer of Pharaoh, the captain of the guard, an Egyptian, bought him from the Ishmaelites who had brought him down there.

Both (159) and (160) occur at the beginning of a פרשה סתומה 'closed portion' (see §3.1.3).[18]

Somewhat more frequently, subject-preposing marks the clause as beginning a new scene within a narrative unit. The new scene is characterized by new participants and/or a new setting:[19]

(161) Gen 24:61–62

ותקם רבקה ונערתיה ותרכבנה על הגמלים ותלכנה אחרי האיש ויקח העבד את
רבקה וילך: ויצחק בא מבוא באר לחי ראי

And Rebekah and her maids arose, and they mounted the camels and followed the man; and the servant took Rebekah, and he went his way. And Isaac had come from Beer-lahai-roi

(162) Gen 26:25–26

ויבן שם מזבח ויקרא בשם י' ויט שם אהלו ויכרו שם עבדי יצחק באר:
ואבימלך הלך אליו מגרר ואחזת מרעהו ופיכל שר צבאו:

And he built an altar there, and he called upon the name of the Lord, and he pitched his tent there. And Isaac's servants dug a well there. And Abimelech went to him from Gerar, and Ahuzzath his adviser and Phicol the commander of his army.

7.3.2. The residue of subject-preposed direct speech clauses

The residue of subject-preposing in direct speech is more difficult to categorize than the narrative residue. The functions described above were not

---

18. Additional examples include Gen 3:1, 4:1, and 21:1. The latter two clauses are at the beginning of a פרשה סתומה.

19. Additional examples include Gen 13:14, 18:17, 34:5 (ויעקב), and 37:36.

found in this group. Only 11 clauses (17.5%) in the residue of subject-preposed direct speech clauses fall into plausible pragmatic categories, as discussed in §§7.3.2.1–7.3.2.3.

7.3.2.1. Justification

A specialized use of preposing is found in several clauses traditionally considered to be circumstantial clauses. As discussed in §3.1.2 (pp. 20–21), although narrative texts exhibit ample instances of nonverbal and participial circumstantial clauses, finite circumstantial clauses are scarce in these texts. The examples cited in the literature are mostly found in direct speech and typically follow a directive or a rhetorical question. The distinctive environment of these preposed clauses points to a different interpretation of this marked construction. I propose that preposing in these verses has the pragmatic function of marking the justification for the preceding utterance:

(163) Gen 24:56

אל תאחרו אתי וי' הצליח דרכי

Do not delay me. And (= for) the Lord has made my journey successful.

In (163), the preposed clause וי' הצליח דרכי marks the justification for the preceding directive אל תאחרו אתי.[20] The coordinated phrases may be idiomatically rendered 'Do not delay me, for the Lord has prospered my way'.

In examples (164)–(166), the justification provided by the preposed clause relates to the implication of a rhetorical question. Rhetorical yes-no questions imply an assertion with the opposite polarity of the question (Pope 1972: 46). For example, "Didn't I just tell you that yesterday?" implies the assertion "I told you that yesterday." Question-word rhetorical questions frequently imply that the answer is a null set; for example, "Who could pass that test" implies "Nobody could pass that test" (Pope 1972: 59). Examples of preposing to justify rhetorical questions include:

(164) Gen 24:31

למה תעמד בחוץ ואנכי פניתי הבית ומקום לגמלים:

Why do you stand outside? And (= for) I have prepared the house and a place for the camels.

(165) Gen 18:13

למה זה צחקה שרה לאמר האף אמנם אלד ואני זקנתי:

Why did Sarah laugh, and say, "Shall I indeed bear a child? And (= for) I am old."

---

20. See also Gen 26:27 and 32:12. Examples found in the classical BH prose corpus include Judg 21:7; 1 Sam 15:6, 16:1, 28:16.

(166) Gen 18:17–18

המכסה אני מאברהם אשר אני עשה: ואברהם היו יהיה לגוי גדול ועצום

Shall I hide from Abraham what I am about to do? <u>And (= for) Abraham</u>
<u>shall become a great and mighty nation</u>

In (164), the rhetorical question למה תעמד בחוץ 'Why do you stand outside?'
implies the assertion "There is no reason for you to stand outside." The subsequent preposed clause, ואנכי פניתי הבית 'I have prepared the house', supplies a
justification for this implication. In (165), the question האף אמנם אלד 'Shall I
indeed bear a child?' implies "I will not bear a child." The preposed clause, ואני
זקנתי 'I am old', supports this prediction. The relation between the rhetorical
question and preposed clause in (166) is comparable.

Preposing for justification is an alternative to marking with the clausal adverb הלא (see §5.2.1). As in the case of preposing, utterances justified by הלא
are usually directives or rhetorical questions (Moshavi 2007b):[21]

(167) Gen 19:20

הנה נא העיר הזאת קרבה לנוס שמה והוא מצער אמלטה נא שמה **הלא** מצער
הוא

Behold, that city is near enough to flee to, and it is a little place. Let me
escape there. **Surely** it is a little place

(168) Gen 44:4–5

למה שלמתם רעה תחת טובה: **הלוא** זה אשר ישתה אדני בו

Why have you repaid good with evil? **Surely** this is the one from which
my master drinks

The similarity between justificational clauses marked by preposing and justificational clauses marked by הלא is illustrated by the close-to-minimal pair
in (169) and (170):

---

21. See also, e.g., Gen 19:20, 44:5; Judg 6:14, 11:7 (appears as example 170); 1 Sam
17:29; 2 Sam 11:20; 2 Kgs 6:32. The interpretation of justificational הלא as a clausal adverb
is supported by its interchangeability with הנה. Representative examples of הנה justifying a
directive include Gen 16:2; 27:2–3, 6–8; 42:2; for הנה justifying a rhetorical question, see,
e.g., Gen 25:32; 1 Sam 20:2, 28:9. Unlike הנה, which almost always precedes the justified
utterance, הלא may precede or follow. When a justificational הלא clause contains a preposed
element, הלא occurs in front of the preposed element, in the characteristic position of the
clausal adverb (e.g., Gen 20:5, 29:25, 31:15; Josh 22:20; Judg 4:14, 11:7; 1 Kgs 1:13). For
further discussion on distinguishing the clausal adverb from interrogative הלא, see Moshavi
(forthcoming).

(169) Gen 26:27

מדוע באתם אלי ואתם שנאתם אתי ותשלחוני מאתכם:

Why have you come to me? And (= for) you hate me and sent me away
from you.

(170) Judg 11:7

הלא אתם שנאתם אותי ותגרשוני מבית אבי ומדוע באתם אלי עתה כאשר צר
לכם:

Surely you hate me, and you drove me out of my father's house. Why
have you come to me now when you are in trouble?

The justification in (169) is the segment ואתם שנאתם אתי ותשלחוני מאתכם;
in (170), it is the very similar הלא אתם שנאתם אותי ותגרשוני מבית אבי. The
supported rhetorical question in both cases is מדוע באתם אלי. In (170), the
justificational segment is marked by הלא (and by preposing), whereas in (169)
it is marked by preposing alone. One difference between marking justification
by הלא as opposed to preposing is that הלא may precede or follow the justified
utterance,[22] but the preposed clause always follows.

Example (169) illustrates that preposing may mark a justification that is a
segment longer than a clause. The justification in this example includes the
clause following the preposed one, ותגרשוני מבית אבי. In such cases, only the
first clause in the segment is preposed.

7.3.2.2. Affirmation

In several cases, a preposed first-person pronoun occurs in a promise to
carry out a certain action.[23] The exact pragmatic function of preposing in this
group is difficult to characterize; to say that the pronoun is "emphatic" is hardly
sufficient. Nevertheless, the pattern exemplified by these clauses is undoubtedly significant. It could be that this category and the category of boasting, described in §7.3.2.3 (p. 119), are subtypes of a broader category the parameters
of which are currently unclear.

(171) Gen 21:24

ויאמר אברהם אנכי אשבע:

And Abraham said, "I swear."

(172) Gen 47:30

ויאמר אנכי אעשה כדברך:

And he said, "I will do as you have said."

22. For הלא preceding, see, e.g., Gen 37:13; Judg 15:2, 11; 1 Sam 9:21, 26:15.
23. See Waltke and O'Connor 1990: §16.3.2b. Additional examples are Gen 38:17 and
50:21. Additional clear examples from the classical BH prose corpus are Exod 8:24; Judg
6:18, 17:10; 1 Kgs 2:18, 21:7; 2 Kgs 6:3.

7.3.2.3. Boasting

Joüon-Muraoka (§146a) note that preposed first-person pronouns occur in boasts, as in the well-known instances in the Mesha inscription. Genesis contains one clause of this type:

(173) Gen 14:23

ולא תאמר <u>אני העשרתי את אברם</u>:

And you shall not say, "<u>I made Abram rich.</u>"

An additional example from the classical BH prose corpus is shown in (174).[24]

(174) 2 Sam 1:16

ויאמר אליו דוד דמך על ראשך כי פיך ענה בך לאמר <u>אנכי מתתי את משיח י'</u>:

"And David said to him, "Your blood be on your own head! Your own mouth testified against you, saying, '<u>I put the LORD's anointed to death.</u>'"

7.4. Conclusion

Statistical analysis of the pragmatic functions of preposing in the Genesis corpus reveals a complex picture in which information-structure functions play the leading roles, accompanied by various other functions, not all of which can be currently identified. Focusing and topicalization account for 56.6% of all preposed clauses, with topicalization being over three times as common as focusing. The actual numbers of focused clauses may be somewhat higher, because some plausible cases were excluded due to lack of textual evidence of activation. In comparison to information-structure functions, which constitute the majority of preposed clauses, functions relating to the clause as a whole (i.e., marking anteriority, simultaneity, background information, the start of a new scene or episode, justification, affirmation, and boasting) together constitute only 11.2% of preposed clauses over all. Preposing in fixed expressions accounts for an additional 1.5%. The function of preposing in the remaining 30.6% of clauses is currently unclear; nearly all of these (83.7%) are in direct speech.

Complement/adjunct preposing and subject-preposing exhibit distinct functional patterns; these patterns also vary according to discourse register. Complement/adjunct preposing in narrative is almost exclusively for the purpose of focusing or topicalization. In direct speech, however, information-structure functions constitute only three-fifths of the preposed-complement/adjunct total. Much of the residue of complement/adjunct preposed clauses in direct speech is hard to characterize, but in some of the cases preposing appears to reflect a fixed expression and does not have a pragmatic function. Almost half

---

24. An additional example is 1 Kgs 1:5.

of subject-preposed clauses have information-structure functions; the number is a bit higher in narrative and lower in direct speech. Although the relative sizes of the subject-preposed residues are comparable for the two discourse registers, most of the clauses in the narrative residue have a function relating to the clause as a whole, while most of the residue of direct speech lacks a specific explanation. A new function of subject-preposing in direct speech was identified: the marking of the justification for a preceding request or rhetorical question.

The impression that word order in direct speech is "freer" than in narrative can be explained as the result of a combination of two factors. First, as noted in §5.6 (table 3, p. 87), preposing is more frequent in direct speech than in narrative. Second, the proportion of preposed clauses with no clearly identifiable pragmatic function or other explanation is higher in direct speech. While in narrative only 12.3% of the preposed clauses have no clear function, in direct speech the percentage is 42.9%. Put another way, 83.6% of the unexplained preposed clauses are in direct speech.

In the following chapters, I discuss focused clauses and topicalized clauses in more detail, examining them from a syntactic and pragmatic perspective.

Chapter 8

The Focused Clause

This chapter examines BH preposed clauses with a focusing function (henceforth referred to as focused clauses). The analysis is based on the 50 focused clauses in Genesis and selected clauses from elsewhere in the classical prose BH corpus. In §8.1, I describe the preposed constituent in the focused clause. In §8.2, I examine the activated proposition to which the focused clause relates. In §8.3, I set out a taxonomy of focused clauses based on how the clause is to be interpreted with respect to the relevant activated information. In §8.4, I discuss a special type of focusing known as *focus of negation*. In §8.5, I discuss the relevance of focusing to a particular stylistic device. Conclusions are presented in §8.6. In the citations in this chapter, focused clauses are marked by underlining and focuses by bold type.

8.1. Syntactic description of the preposed constituent

The preposed constituent in the focused clause may be a subject, complement, or adjunct:

(175) Subject

בלעדי **אלהים** יענה את שלום פרעה:

Not I. **God** will give Pharaoh a favorable answer. (Gen 41:16)

(176) Complement

בני יעקב באו על החללים ויבזו העיר אשר טמאו אחותם: **את צאנם ואת בקרם**
ואת חמריהם ואת אשר בעיר ואת אשר בשדה לקחו:

And the sons of Jacob came upon the slain, and plundered the city, because they had defiled their sister. **Their flocks and their herds and their asses, and whatever was in the city and whatever was in the field** they took. (Gen 34:27–28)

(177) Adjunct

כל רמש אשר הוא חי לכם יהיה לאכלה **כירק עשב** נתתי לכם את כל:

Every moving thing that lives, for you shall be for food. **Like the green grasses**, I give you everything. (Gen 9:3)

121

Table 13. Syntactic function of the preposed constituent in focused clauses in Genesis.

Function	Number	Percentage
Subject	8	16
Complement/adjunct	42	84
Total	50	

Table 14. Syntactic category of the preposed constituent in focused clauses in Genesis.

Category	Number	Percentage
Noun phrase	29	58
Prepositional phrase	21	42
Total	50	

Focusing is primarily associated with complement/adjunct preposing. Table 13 shows that 84% of focused clauses have a preposed complement or adjunct. Table 14 shows that 58% of focused clauses have a preposed noun phrase, and 42% have a preposed prepositional phrase. Other syntactic categories, such as adverbs or adjectives, do not occur as preposed constituents in focused clauses in the Genesis corpus.

Although the preposed constituent in a focused clause is commonly referred to as the focus of the clause, this is not entirely accurate. Because preposing is normally performed on entire clause-level constituents, material that belongs to the activated proposition is often preposed along with the focus. This phenomenon is particularly common when the preposed item is a prepositional phrase. In these cases, it is usually the noun phrase governed by the preposition that is the focus:

(178) Gen 19:2

וַיֹּאמֶר הִנֶּה נָּא אֲדֹנַי סוּרוּ נָא אֶל בֵּית עַבְדְּכֶם וְלִינוּ וְרַחֲצוּ רַגְלֵיכֶם וְהִשְׁכַּמְתֶּם וַה
לַכְתֶּם לְדַרְכְּכֶם וַיֹּאמְרוּ לֹּא כִּי **בָרְחוֹב** נָלִין:

And he said, "My lords, please turn aside to your servant's house and spend the night, and wash your feet. And [= then] you may rise early and go on your way." And they said, "No. **In the square** we will spend the night."

The preposed constituent is בָרְחוֹב 'in the street', but the focus is הָרְחוֹב 'the street'. The focused clause relates to the proposition "We will spend the night in x," activated by Laban's invitation, סוּרוּ נָא אֶל בֵּית עַבְדְּכֶם וְלִינוּ. The clause asserts "x = the street." The preposition ב is necessarily preposed along with its noun phrase, despite being extraneous to the focus.

In the focused clauses cited in this chapter, the preposed element is bolded in its entirety, whether or not it is identical with the focus.

8.2. The activated proposition

As noted in §6.1.4, focusing in BH relates the focus to an activated proposition. In §8.2.1, I describe the formal relation between the focused clause and the relevant activated proposition. In §8.2.2, I discuss the means by which the activated proposition acquires this cognitive status. In §8.2.3, I discuss the issue of activation versus pragmatic presupposition in the focused clause.

8.2.1. The relation between focused clause and activated proposition

In focused clauses that express statements, the relevant activated proposition consists of the proposition expressed by the clause, with a variable "x" substituted for the focus. In (179), for example, the activated proposition is "You did x to me," with a variable substituted for the complement מעשים אשר לא יעשו.

(179) Gen 20:9

מה עשית לנו ומה חטאתי לך כי הבאת עלי ועל ממלכתי חטאה גדלה **מעשים**
אשר לא יעשו עשית עמדי:

What have you done to us, and how have I sinned against you, that you have brought such great guilt on me and my kingdom? **Things that ought not to be done** you have done to me.

When the focused clause is a question, request, or command, its relation to the activated proposition is more indirect, because these illocutionary types do not themselves express propositions. The activated proposition in these types of clause is the one expressed by the statement most resembling the clause:

(180) Gen 23:3–6

ויקם אברהם מעל פני מתו וידבר אל בני חת לאמר: גר ותושב אנכי עמכם תנו
לי אחזת קבר עמכם ואקברה מתי מלפני: ויענו בני חת את אברהם לאמר לו:
שמענו אדני נשיא אלהים אתה בתוכנו **במבחר קברינו** קבר את מתך

And Abraham rose up from before his dead, and spoke to the Hittites, saying, "I am a resident alien among you; give me a burying place among you, and [= so that] I may bury my dead from before me." And the Hittites answered Abraham, saying to him, "Hear us, my lord; you are a prince of God among us. **In the choicest of our burial places** bury your dead."

The activated proposition associated with the underlined focused clause is "You will bury your dead in x."

8.2.2. The source of the activated proposition

The given information in BH focusing relates to an activated proposition, that is, a proposition assumed to be in short-term or long-term working memory (see §§6.1.2–6.1.3). Activated information for the reader of a written text includes propositions derived directly from the previous clause; elements in the mental representation of the text that are directly linked to the previous clause may be activated as well. The mental representation incorporates inferences based on the reader's knowledge and experience; thus information not explicitly referred to in the text may nonetheless constitute activated information.

In (181), the activated proposition "I will require the life of man from x" is derived directly from the previous clause, with the addition of an unspecified argument:

(181) Gen 9:5

ואך את דמכם לנפשתיכם אדרש **מיד כל חיה** אדרשנו

But for your own life-blood I will require a reckoning. **Of every beast** I will require it

The first clause, ואך את דמכם לנפשתיכם אדרש, activates the proposition "I will require your life-blood of x"; the source argument is not present in the surface structure of the clause. The focused clause supplies the value "every beast" for x.

In (182), the activated proposition "He will father x" is derived by entailment from the preceding clauses.[1]

(182) Gen 17:20

הנה ברכתי אתו והפריתי אתו והרביתי אתו במאד מאד **שנים עשר נשיאם** יוליד

Behold, I bless him and I will make him fruitful and exceedingly numerous. **Twelve princes** he will father

In (183), the activated proposition is inferred from the preceding clause:

(183) Gen 24:37–38

וישבעני אדני לאמר לא תקח אשה לבני מבנות הכנעני אשר אנכי ישב בארצו: אם לא **אל בית אבי** תלך ואל משפחתי ולקחת אשה לבני:

And my master made me swear, saying, "You shall not take a wife for my son from the daughters of the Canaanites, in whose land I dwell. But **to my father's house and to my family** you shall go, and take a wife for my son."

---

1. See also, e.g., Gen 35:11.

Abraham's command to the servant not to take a wife for Isaac from the Canaanites implies that he must go elsewhere to find a wife for Isaac; that is, "You
will go to *x* to take a wife for Isaac." The focused clause identifies "my father's
house" as the value for *x*.

In spoken discourse, activated information includes textually derived information in the mental representation of the preceding dialogue, as well as
extra-textual information pertaining to the speaker's and addressee's personal
details, their motivations, and their perceptions of the environment. Direct
speech in the Bible may be treated like spoken discourse for the purposes of
analyzing focusing. Although direct speech in the Bible is not an exact rendition of spoken discourse, as discussed in §§1.2 and 4.4.3, it nevertheless
represents the quoted citation from the perspectives of the quoted speaker and
addressee. Focusing in direct speech relates to information activated for the
quoted addressee, rather than for the reader of the citation. Either textual or
extratextual sources of information, therefore, may be relevant in analyzing
direct-speech focusing.

An example of extra-textual activation is shown in (184):

(184) Gen 30:16

ייבא יעקב מן השדה בערב ותצא לאה לקראתו ותאמר **אלי** תבוא כי שכר שכ
רתיך בדודאי בני

And Jacob came from the field in the evening, and Leah went out to meet
him, and she said, "**To me** you will come, for I have hired you with my
son's mandrakes."

Because Leah knows that Jacob is heading for Rachel's tent, she takes the
proposition "Jacob will go to *x*" as information activated by the extratextual
situation. Her statement, אלי תבוא, replaces "Rachel," the value for *x* activated
for Jacob, with a new value, "Leah."[2]

When a person comes to see someone else, the proposition "I have come" is
treated as activated extratextual information. An adjunct describing the purpose
of the visit can be marked as a focus in relation to this activated proposition:[3]

(185) Gen 47:2–4

ומקצה אחיו לקח חמשה אנשים ויצגם לפני פרעה: ויאמר פרעה אל אחיו מה
מעשיכם ויאמרו אל פרעה רעה צאן עבדיך גם אנחנו גם אבותינו: ויאמרו אל
פרעה **לגור בארץ** באנו

And from among his brothers he took five men and presented them to
Pharaoh. And Pharaoh said to his brothers, "What is your occupation?"

---

2. This clause is of the substitutional type, where the focus replaces a previously activated value for *x* (see §8.3.3).

3. An additional example of this type is 1 Sam 16:5.

And they said to Pharaoh, "Your servants are shepherds, as our fathers also were." And they said to Pharaoh, "**To sojourn in the land** we have come."

(186) Judg 15:11–12

וירדו שלשת אלפים איש מיהודה אל סעיף סלע עיטם ויאמרו לשמשון הלא
ידעת כי משלים בנו פלשתים ומה זאת עשית לנו ויאמר להם כאשר עשו לי כן
עשיתי להם: ויאמרו לו **לאסרך** ירדנו לתתך ביד פלשתים

And three thousand men of Judah went down to the cleft of the rock of Etam, and said to Samson, "Surely you know that the Philistines are rulers over us. What have you done to us?" And he said to them, "As they did to me, so have I done to them." And they said to him, "**To bind you** we have come down, so that we may give you into the hands of the Philistines."

8.2.3. Activation versus pragmatic presupposition in the focused clause

Propositions that are activated are generally presupposed as well, as (187) illustrates:

(187) Judg 1:1–2

וישאלו בני ישראל בי' לאמר מי יעלה לנו אל הכנעני בתחלה להלחם בו: ויאמר
י' **יהודה** יעלה

And the Israelites inquired of the LORD, saying "Who shall go up first for us against the Canaanites to fight against them?" And the LORD said, "**Judah** shall go up."

The question מי יעלה לנו both presupposes and activates the proposition "x will go up with us first against the Canaanites." That is, the question reflects the Israelites' assumption that both they and God believe the truth of this proposition. By uttering the question, the people activate this proposition for the addressee, God. God answers with a focused clause supplying a value for the x: יהודה יעלה 'Judah shall go up [first against the Canaanites]'.

Despite the general association between presupposition and activation, presupposition is not a necessary condition for focusing, as shown by the following examples:

(188) Gen 23:3–6[4]

ויקם אברהם מעל פני מתו וידבר אל בני חת לאמר: גר ותושב אנכי עמכם תנו
לי אחזת קבר עמכם ואקברה מתי מלפני: ויענו בני חת את אברהם לאמר לו:
שמענו אדני נשיא אלהים אתה בתוכנו **במבחר קברינו** קבר את מתך

And Abraham rose up from before his dead, and spoke to the Hittites, saying, "I am a resident alien among you; give me a burying place site among you, and [= so that] I may bury my dead from before me." And

4. Appears above as (180) (p. 123).

the Hittites answered Abraham, saying to him, "Hear us, my lord; you
are a prince of God among us. **In the choicest of our burial places** bury
your dead."

(189) Gen 43:11–13

ויאמר אלהם ישראל אביהם אם כן אפוא זאת עשו קחו מזמרת הארץ בכליכם
והורידו לאיש מנחה מעט צרי ומעט דבש נכאת ולט בטנים ושקדים: וכסף
משנה קחו בידכם ואת הכסף המושב בפי אמתחתיכם תשיבו בידכם אולי משגה
הוא: **ואת אחיכם** קחו וקומו שובו אל האיש:

And their father Israel said to them, "If it is so, then do this: take some
of the choice fruits of the land in your bags, and carry down to the man
a present, a little balm and a little honey, gum, resin, pistachio nuts, and
almonds. And double the money take with you; and the money that was
returned in the mouth of your sack bring back with you; perhaps it was
an oversight. And **your brother** take, and go again to the man.

In (188), the focused clause במבחר קברינו קבר את מתך relates to Abraham's
earlier request to the children of Het to give him a burial place. Abraham's
request activates the proposition "Abram will bury his dead in x," but does not
presuppose it: in fact, Abram implies that he will have no burial place for Sarah
if the children of Het do not accede to his request. In (189), the focused clause
relates to the proposition activated by Jacob's previous command, i.e., "You
will take x." The value for x supplied in the focused clause is added to the items
Jacob has already specified (on additive focus, see §8.3.4.) Again, the proposition "You will take x" is not presupposed. In general, focusing in commands
and requests involves activation but not presupposition.[5]

8.3. A taxonomy of focused clauses

The focus in a focused clause supplies a value for a variable x in the activated proposition; in other words, a focused clause containing a focus f asserts
the identifying proposition "$x = f$" with respect to an activated proposition p. In
some cases, a value for x (let us call it v) is already activated for the addressee
at the time that he processes the clause. In this case, an identifying proposition
of the form "$x = v$" is activated for the addressee. In §§8.3.1–8.3.4, I propose
a taxonomy of focused clauses based on the relation between the new proposition "$x = f$" and the proposition "$x = v$," if a proposition of the latter type is
activated. Four types of focusing are distinguished: *identificational, descriptive, substitutive,* and *additive.*[6]

---

5. For other examples of focusing in commands or requests, see, e.g., Gen 20:15, 44:2,
43:12, and 47:6.

6. A different taxonomy is found in Dik (1989: 282), where six types are distinguished: completive, parallel, replacing, expanding, restricting, and selecting; see also Dik
et al. (1981). This taxonomy is followed in Rosenbaum (1997) and Heimerdinger (1999).

8.3.1. Identificational focusing

In identificational focusing, the value of *x* is unknown to the addressee at the time of clause processing, that is, there is no currently activated proposition "*x* = *v*." Identification is the most common type of focusing, constituting about three-fifths of the focused clauses in Genesis.[7] The classic case of identificational focus, as cited in the linguistic literature, is the answer to a previously posed question. An example from BH is (187) above (p. 126).[8] This type of focusing is quite rare in BH. The only remotely similar example in Genesis is (190):

(190) Gen 20:9 [9]

מה עשית לנו ומה חטאתי לך כי הבאת עלי ועל ממלכתי חטאה גדלה **מעשים** **אשר לא יעשו** עשית עמדי:

What have you done to us? And how have I sinned against you, that you have brought such great guilt on me and my kingdom? **Things that ought not to be done** you have done to me.

The focused clause echoes the rhetorical question posed just before by the same speaker, מה עשית לנו 'What have you done to us?' Although on the surface this looks like identificational focus, an interpretation such as this misses the implication of the rhetorical question.[10] In contrast to the genuine question, an RQ is not a request for information but an implicit assertion (Ilie 1994: 38, 45; Schmidt-Radefeldt (1977: 376–77). The assertion implied by Abimelek's question is "You have done a terrible thing."[11] Because the focus, "things that

---

Completive focus corresponds to my identificational focus, replacing focus is the same as substitutional focus, and expanding focus is the equivalent of my additive focus. Restricting focus, in which a compound value for *x* is reduced to a simple one, and selecting focus, in which one of a number of alternative values for *x* is selected, are not recognized as separate categories in my scheme. The former is included in the substitutive category and the latter in the identificational category. Parallel focus refers to contrasted items in a pair of clauses, as in *John and Bill came to see me. **John** was nice, but **Bill** was rather boring. John* and *Bill* are not informational focuses, according to the definition of focusing set out in §§3.3.1.3 and 6.1; thus, there is no need here for the parallel category. As mentioned in §3.3.5, Dik defines focus in terms of importance rather than in terms of new and given information.

7. Representative examples of identificational focused clauses from the classical BH prose corpus include Num 9:3; Deut 24:19, 20, 21; Judg 1:2, 2:29; 1 Sam 1:27.

8. See also Judg 6:29.

9. Appears as (179) above (p. 123).

10. I am indebted to Yochanan Breuer for pointing this out.

11. Question-word rhetorical questions frequently imply that the answer is the null set; e.g., "Who could pass that test" implies "Nobody could pass that test" (Pope 1972: 59). Although the question מה עשית "what have I done" usually has the interpretation "I have done nothing" in the Bible (see, e.g., Num 22:28; 1 Sam 20:1, 26:18, 29:8), the question "What have you done" usually implies "You have done a terrible thing" (see e.g., Gen 3:13, 4:10, 12:18, 26:10, 29:25, 31:26).

ought not to be done," is merely a reformulation of the value for *x* that has already been activated ("a terrible thing"), this is actually descriptive focus (see §8.3.2).

More commonly, identificational focusing answers a question that could appropriately be asked by the hearer/reader, not one that has actually been asked: [12]

(191) Gen 34:27–28 [13]

בני יעקב באו על החללים ויבזו העיר אשר טמאו אחותם: **את צאנם ואת בקרם ואת חמריהם ואת אשר בעיר ואת אשר בשדה** לקחו:

And the sons of Jacob came upon the slain, and plundered the city, because their sister had been defiled. **Their flocks and their herds, their asses, and whatever was in the city and in the field** they took.

(192) Gen 9:5 [14]

ואך את דמכם לנפשתיכם אדרש **מיד כל חיה** אדרשנו

But for your life-blood I will surely require a reckoning. **Of every beast** I will require it.

In (191), the previous clause ויבזו העיר 'they plundered the city' entails the proposition "they took *x*." This proposition can appropriately be the subject of a question: "What did they take?" The focused clause supplies the answer: את צאנם ואת בקרם . . . 'Their flocks, their cattle', and so on. Similarly, in (192), the reader may ask subsequent to reading the first clause, "Of whom will God require the blood?" The preposed clause indicates the answer: מכל חיה 'Of every beast'. [15]

When the focus in an identifying clause is an adjunct, the focus supplies a previously unspecified detail regarding the circumstances of the event described in an activated proposition. Consider (193) and (194): [16]

(193) Gen 23:11

השדה נתתי לך והמערה אשר בו לך נתתיה **לעיני בני עמי** נתתיה לך

I give you the field, and I give you the cave that is in it. **In the presence of my people** I give it to you.

12. See also, e.g., Gen 17:20 (שנים עשר נשיאים) and 35:11.

13. Appears as (176) above (p. 121).

14. Appears as (181) above (p. 124).

15. An additional value for *x* is supplied in the continuation of the verse; the latter clause is an example of additive focus (see §8.3.4.)

16. See also, e.g., Gen 7:20, 9:3 (כירק עשב), 20:5 (בתם לבבי), and 41:11. In the latter verse, the preposed element is an adjunct phrase containing the word איש: **איש כפתרון חלמו** חלמנו '**Each man according to the interpretation of his dream** we dreamed.' The word איש cannot be the subject of the clause, as is evident from the mismatch in person and number between איש and the verb (additional examples are Gen 41:12 and 49:28).

(194) Gen 17:10–12

זאת בריתי אשר תשמרו ביני וביניכם ובין זרעך אחריך המול לכם כל זכר:
ונמלתם את בשר ערלתכם והיה לאות ברית ביני וביניכם: **ובן שמנת ימים**
ימול לכם כל זכר לדרתיכם יליד בית ומקנת כסף מכל בן נכר אשר לא מזרעך
הוא:

This is my covenant, which you shall keep, between me and you and
your offspring after you: every male among you shall be circumcised.
You shall circumcise the flesh of your foreskins, and it shall be a sign of
the covenant between me and you. **At the age of eight days** every male
among you shall be circumcised throughout your generations, whether
the slave born in your house, or bought with your money from any for-
eigner who is not of your offspring.

In (193), the clause preceding the focused one activates the proposition "I give
the cave to you." Although this proposition does not appear to contain a variable *x* corresponding to the adjunct "in the presence of my people," a variable
is present in covert form. Every proposition admits an unspecified number of
adjuncts regarding the circumstances of the event (e.g., time, place, manner, and
cause). The proposition "I give the field to you" is thus more fully represented
as "I give the field to you at time *x*, in place *y*, in manner *z*, for reason *a*," and
so on. The phrase לעיני בני עמי 'In the eyes of my people' supplies the value for
an implicit adjunct variable in the activated proposition. In (194), similarly, the
focus בן שמנת ימים 'at eight days old' supplies the value for an implicit adjunct
in the proposition activated by v. 10, "Every male will be circumcised."

8.3.2. Descriptive focusing

Descriptive focusing presents an alternate or more explicit description for
an already identified variable. In descriptive focusing, a proposition of the form
"*x* = *v*" is activated for the hearer/reader at the time of processing the clause,
such that *v* and the new value, *f*, are referentially identical. In other words, the
focused clause asserts the proposition "*x* = *f*," where "*f* = *v*." Clauses of the
descriptive-focus type do not answer a potential question, because the hearer/
reader already has an activated value for *x*.

Descriptive focusing appears to be rare in BH. The Genesis corpus contains
only three examples, two of which are shown in (195) and (196). The third is
(190), p. 128 above. The expressions representing *v* and *f* are bold.

(195) Gen 6:17

ואני הנני מביא את המבול מים על הארץ לשחת **כל בשר אשר בו רוח חיים**
מתחת השמים כל אשר בארץ יגוע:

And I, behold, I will bring a flood—waters upon the earth—**to destroy**
all flesh in which is breath of life from under the sky. Everything
that is on the earth shall perish.

(196) Gen 7:21–22

ויגוע כל בשר הרמש על הארץ בעוף ובבהמה ובחיה ובכל השרץ השרץ
על הארץ וכל האדם: כל אשר נשמת רוח חיים באפיו מכל אשר בחרבה
מתו:

And **all flesh that crawls upon the earth, of the birds, and of the
cattle, and of the beasts, and of all the swarming creatures that
swarm upon the earth, and every human being**, perished. <u>**Everything
in whose nostrils was the breath of life, from all that are on the dry
land,**</u> died.

In (195), the proposition "*x* will die" is an activated proposition, inferred from
the first clause. A value for *x* is already supplied by this first clause: "all flesh
in which is breath of life." The focus of the preposed clause, כל אשר בארץ
'everything that is on the earth', denotes the same set of referents as the former
value but is a new way of describing this set. The focus in (196), כל אשר נשמת
רוח חיים באפיו 'everything in whose nostrils was the breath of life', bears a
similar relation to the expression in the previous verse, 'all flesh that crawls
upon the earth'.

8.3.3. Substitutional focusing

Substitutional focus replaces an old value for *x* with a new one. In this type
of focus, a value *v* has previously been activated for *x*, and the new value, *f*, is
not referentially identical to *v*. Substitutional focus carries with it the implication that the previous value for *x* is to be rejected; that is, the assertion "*x* = *f*"
implies the negation of the activated proposition "*x* = *v*."

In many cases of substitutional focus, the proposition "*x* = *v*" has been negated by the speaker immediately prior to the utterance of the focused clause.[17]
The substitutional focused clause in this environment answers a potential question that could be asked: if *x* is not *v*, then what is *x*? Focused clauses that
replace previously negated values for *x* are frequently introduced by one of the
conjuncts כי אם, כי, or אם לא, each in the sense 'rather'. The adverb signifies
that the new value is to be substituted for the previously rejected one. Examples are shown in (197) and (198), with *v* and *f* marked in bold.[18]

---

17. The negation of the proposition "*x* = *v*" does not remove this proposition from the
hearer's consciousness, because the negated proposition remains in short-term memory; it
does, of course, strip it of presupposed status if it previously had this status.

18. Representative examples with כי from the classical BH prose corpus include 1 Sam
8:7 and 10:19. Representative examples with כי אם are Num 10:30 and 2 Kgs 17:40. This
phrase אם לא in this sense occurs in Gen 24:38. On the elliptical כי clause, see §8.4.

(197) Gen 19:2 [19]

ויאמר הנה נא אדני סורו נא אל **בית עבדכם** ולינו ורחצו רגליכם והשכמתם
והלכתם לדרככם ויאמרו לא כי **ברחוב** נלין:

And he said, "My lords, please turn aside to **your servant's house** and
spend the night, and wash your feet. And you may rise early and go on
your way." They said, "No. **In the square** we will spend the night."

(198) Gen 35:10

ויאמר לו אלהים שמך יעקב לא יקרא שמך עוד **יעקב** כי אם **ישראל** יהיה שמך

And God said to him, "Your name Jacob, your name will no longer be
called **Jacob**. Rather, **Israel** will be your name."

Lot's request in (197) activates the proposition "You will spend the night at
x" and, along with it, the proposition "*x* = my house." The three men reject
this value for *x* with their response, לא 'No', and then specify "the street" as
the substitute. In (198), God rejects the value "Jacob" for *x* in the proposition
"Your name will be *x*." "Israel" is then substituted for the rejected value.

In other cases, the focused clause follows immediately after the explicit or
implicit rejection of the old value, with no introductory conjunct: [20]

(199) Gen 41:16 [21]

ויען יוסף את פרעה לאמר בלעדי **אלהים** יענה את שלום פרעה:

Joseph answered Phraoh, saying, Not I. "**God** will give Pharaoh a favorable answer."

(200) Gen 42:7–9

ויאמר אלהם מאין באתם ויאמרו מארץ כנען **לשבר אכל**: ויכר יוסף את אחיו
והם לא הכרהו: ויזכר יוסף את החלמות אשר חלם להם ויאמר אלהם מרגלים
אתם **לראות את ערות הארץ** באתם:

And he said to them, "Where do you come from?" And they said, "From
the land of Canaan, **to buy food**." And Joseph recognized his brothers,
and they did not recognize him. And Joseph remembered the dreams
which he had dreamed of them; and he said to them, "You are spies. **To
see the nakedness of the land** you have come."

In (199), the activated proposition is "*x* will give Pharaoh a favorable answer,"
with the associated proposition "*x* = Joseph." Both propositions can be inferred indirectly from Pharaoh's statement in the previous verse, ואני שמעתי
עליך לאמר תשמע חלום לפתר אתו 'I have heard about you that you can interpret

---

19. Appears as (178) above (p. 122).
20. See also, e.g., Judg 8:23.
21. Appears as (175) above (p. 121).

dreams'. This statement serves as an indirect directive to Joseph to interpret the dream and, presumably, to supply a favorable interpretation. Joseph first negates the proposition "x = Joseph" with בלעדי 'Not I', that is, "it is not I who will give you a favorable interpretation." A focused clause follows, substituting "God" as the correct value for x. In (200), Joseph's statement מרגלים אתם 'you are spies' implicitly rejects the brothers' earlier assertion that they came with the purpose of buying food. In other words, the proposition "x = buy food" is rejected with respect to the proposition "We have come in order to x." The focused clause substitutes a different value for x, "see the nakedness of the land."

In some cases of substitutional focus, the old value v has not been previously rejected, and the question *What is x?* is not appropriate. In example (184), repeated here as (201), the focused clause is substitutional, despite the fact that it is conversation-initial. As discussed above, the speaker substitutes "Leah" for the previously activated value, "Rachel."

(201) Gen 30:16

ייבא יעקב מן השדה בערב ותצא לאה לקראתו ותאמר **אלי** תבוא כי שכר שכ
רתיך בדודאי בני

And Jacob came from the field in the evening, and Leah went out to meet him, and she said, "**To me** you will come, for I have hired you with my son's mandrakes."

8.3.4. Additive focusing

Additive focusing resembles substitutional focus in that there is a previously activated value for x that is not referentially identical to the focus f. Additive focus, however, does not imply the negation of the proposition "x = v" but implies that f is to be added to v. The result is a new identifying proposition in which the two values form a compound expression: "x = v + f." Additive focus does not answer a potential question, because the addressee has no way of knowing that another value is to be added to v. An example of additive focus is (202):

(202) Gen 35:12

ואת הארץ אשר נתתי לאברהם וליצחק **לך** אתננה **ולזרעך אחריך** אתן את
הארץ:

The land that I gave to Abraham and Isaac I give **to you**. And **to your offspring after you** I give the land.

The first clause activates the proposition "I give the land to x" and the associated proposition "x = you." The focused clause adds a new value "your offspring after you," yielding the proposition "x = you and your offspring after you." Additive focusing differs from other types of focus in that it generally begins with the conjunction ו; [22] the other types are almost always asyndetic.

Additional examples of additive focusing appear in (203)–(205). [23]

(203) Gen 9:5 [24]

ואך את דמכם לנפשתיכם אדרש **מיד כל חיה** אדרשנו **ומיד האדם מיד איש אחיו** אדרש את נפש האדם:

But for your life-blood I will require a reckoning. Of **every beast** I will require it. And **of man, of every man for that of his fellow man** I will require the life of man.

(204) Gen 8:18–19

ויצא נח ובניו ואשתו ונשי בניו אתו: **כל החיה כל הרמש וכל העוף כל רומש על הארץ למשפחתיהם** יצאו מן התבה:

And **Noah and his sons and his wife and his sons' wives with him** came out. **Every beast, every creeping thing, and every bird, everything that creeps upon the earth**, by families came out of the ark.

(205) Gen 43:11–13 [25]

ויאמר אלהם ישראל אביהם אם כן אפוא זאת עשו קחו מזמרת הארץ בכליכם והורידו לאיש מנחה **מעט צרי ומעט דבש נכאת ולט בטנים ושקדים: וכסף משנה** קחו בידכם . . . **ואת אחיכם** קחו

And their father Israel said to them, "If it is so, do this: take some of the choice products of the land in your baggage, and carry them down as a gift for the man—**some balm and some honey, gum, resin, pista-**

---

22. Gen 8:19 is an exception to this generalization.

23. Additional examples are Gen 17:27, 34:25–26, and 44:2. Gen 34:25–26 is an excep5 tional case of additive focusing, in that *f* is included in *v* rather than added to it: ויהרגו כל זכר ואת חמור ואת שכם בנו הרגו לפי חרב 'And they killed all the males. And they killed **Hamor and his son Shechem** by the sword'. Some examples of additive focus from the classical BH prose corpus are Exod 36:10; Lev 26:29; Num 6:3; Deut 17:17; 1 Kgs 6:22.

24. My interpretation of this verse follows the cantillation marks, in accordance with NJPSV. Some translations, such as RSV, consider ומיד האדם 'and of man' to be appended to the end of the previous (also focused) clause, yielding 'Of every beast I will require it, and of man'. The second focused clause would then be **מיד איש אחיו** אדרש את נפש האדם 'Of every man for his fellow man I will require the life of a man'. According to this clause division, the first focused clause relates to the proposition "I will require it [i.e., the life of man] of *x*," and asserts "*x* = every beast and man." The second focused clause asserts "*x* = every man for his fellow man." This value is a subset of the set denoted by the previous focus and is a different way of describing that set. The focus in this interpretation bears characteristics of additive and descriptive focusing.

25. Appears on p. 127 above as (189).

chio nuts, and almonds. And **double the money** take with you. . . . And
your brother take.

The last clause, ואת אחיכם קחו, adds their brother to the other items the brothers are to take. The previous clause, וכסף משנה קחו בידכם, is an additive-focus
clause as well, assuming that the expression קחו בידכם is not meant to be taken
literally and the money was to be placed in the brothers' bags along with the
gifts.

Additive focusing is functionally similar to the focusing adverb גם. For
example, the preposing construction in (202) may be replaced by or supple-
mented with גם:[26]

(206) Paraphrase of Gen 35:12 with גם

ואת הארץ אשר נתתי לאברהם וליצחק לך אתננה ונתתי את הארץ גם לזרעך
אחריך:

The land that I gave to Abraham and Isaac, to **you** I give it. And I give
the land **also to your offspring after you**.

Additive focusing by preposing and focusing by גם are not pragmatically
identical: the two devices involve different kinds of given propositions. Focusing by preposing, as we have seen, relates to an activated but not necessarily presupposed proposition. The focusing adverb, in contrast, may relate to
a proposition that is presupposed but not activated. In (207), for example, the
relevant proposition was introduced much earlier in the discourse and is no
longer activated in the consciousness of the reader.

(207) Gen 27:30–31

ויהי כאשר כלה יצחק לברך את יעקב ויהי אך יצא יצא יעקב מאת פני יצחק
אביו ועשו אחיו בא מצידו: ויעש **גם הוא** מטעמים

And it came to pass when Isaac finished blessing Jacob; and it came to
pass—Jacob had scarcely gone out from the presence of Isaac his father,
and Esau his brother came in from his hunting. And **he also** had prepared
delicacies.

The clause ויעש גם הוא מטעמים asserts "*x* = Esau" with respect to the presupposed proposition "*x* prepared delicacies," with the implication that the value
"Esau" is added to an earlier value, "Rebekah." The information that Rebekah
prepared delicacies is presented much earlier in the story, in v. 14. The relatively large distance between the גם clause and the source of the given proposition is apparently no barrier to the use of the focusing adverb. The use of
preposing to mark additive focus in this context, in contrast, would be inappropriate and unclear, because the presupposed proposition is no longer activated.

---

26. As discussed in §5.4.1, focus adverbs can also be combined with preposing.

8.4. Focus of negation

There are two ways in which negation and focusing can operate together in a clause, as illustrated in (208) and (209):

(208) A: Is there anyone who didn't finish the assignment?
       B: **Mary** didn't finish it.

(209) A: Did anyone finish the assignment? [27]
       B: I don't know. I know **Mary** didn't finish it.

Mary is marked as the focus by accenting in (208) and (209), both of which involve clause-level negation. Nevertheless, the two clauses have different pragmatic interpretations. The focused clause in (208) relates to the activated negative proposition, "x did not finish the assignment," and asserts "x = Mary." In (209), the activated proposition is the affirmative "x finished the assignment," and the focused clause asserts "x is not Mary." [28] The negation here is external to the activated proposition. This type of focus is termed "focus of negation." [29]

As seen above, ordinary focusing with negation and focus of negation are not distinguishable by pitch accent in English; in both types, the focus is accented. The cleft construction, however, does distinguish the two types:

(210) A: Who did not finish the assignment?
       B: It was **Mary** who didn't finish it.

(211) A: Who finished the assignment?
       B: I don't know. I know it wasn't **Mary** who finished it.

Example (210) is the cleft equivalent of the ordinary focusing structure with negation in (208), and (211) is the cleft equivalent of the focus-of-negation structure in (209). In the cleft versions, the given propositions must be pragmatically presupposed and are not necessarily activated (although in these examples they are). The cleft in (211) would be inappropriate as an answer to the question in (209), because there the proposition "x finished the assignment" is not presupposed (i.e., the speaker does not know if anyone finished).

In BH, ordinary focusing with negation and focus of negation are represented by two distinct forms of preposing, in a manner reminiscent of English clefting. An example of ordinary focusing with negation is the additive clause in (212). [30]

27. The example is adapted from Dryer (1996: 490).
28. Note that in both cases the proposition is activated but not presupposed, because the speaker does not know whether there is any such x. See further the next paragraph.
29. Huddleston and Pullum (2002: 796). See also Jackendoff (1972: 255), where the phenomenon is termed "association of negation with focus," and Horn (1989: 515–16).
30. No examples of this type were found in the Genesis corpus.

(212) Num 6:3

מיין ושכר יזיר חמץ יין וחמץ שכר לא ישתה וכל משרת ענבים לא ישתה

From **wine and intoxicants** he shall separate himself. **Vinegar made from wine or intoxicants** he shall not drink. And **all juice of grapes** he shall not drink

The activated presupposition in this case is "He will not drink *x*." The focused clause adds "any juice of grapes" to the items already identified as values for *x*.

Focus of negation is rare in BH but unmistakable, due to its unique syntactic structure. As opposed to all other instances of clause-level negation, where the negative particle and the verb form an inseparable unit, the focus-of-negation structure places the negative particle before the preposed focus. An example is (213).

(213) Gen 45:5–8

ועתה אל תעצבו ואל יחר בעיניכם כי מכרתם אתי הנה כי למחיה שלחני אלהים
לפניכם: כי זה שנתים הרעב בקרב הארץ ועוד חמש שנים אשר אין חריש
וקציר: וישלחני אלהים לפניכם לשום לכם שארית בארץ ולהחיות לכם לפליטה
גדלה: ועתה לא **אתם** שלחתם אתי הנה כי **האלהים**

And now do not be distressed, or angry with yourselves that you sold me here, for it was to preserve life that God sent me before you. For it is two years that the famine has been in the land; and there are yet five years in which there will be neither plowing nor harvest. And God sent me before you to preserve for you a remnant on earth, and to keep you alive in a great deliverance. And now, it was not **you** who sent me here; rather **God** [sent me here].

The proposition involved in the underlined focused clause is "*x* sent me here," activated by the previous clause, וישלחני אלהים לפניכם 'and God sent me before you'. By assigning responsibility for his exile to Egypt to God, Joseph implicitly rejects the brothers' culpability. The following focused clause explicitly specifies that the brothers are not ultimately responsible for what happened. To this end, Joseph utilizes a focus-of-negation clause that asserts "*x* is not you" with respect to the affirmative proposition "*x* sent me here." [31]

31. In this analysis the focus-of-negation structure is understood as involving clause-level negation, like the English accented-focus construction "I know **Mary** didn't finish it" (example 209, p. 136 above). An alternate analysis is presented in Snyman and Naudé (2003); Snyman (2004). Utilizing the framework of the Minimalist Program, they argue that the BH focus-of-negation construction involves "constituent negation" rather clause-level negation. The concept of constituent negation is different from the word-level negation exhibited in, e.g., הם קנאוני בלא אל 'They incensed me with non-gods' (Deut 32:21). Thus, it is not argued that Gen 45:8 should be rendered as 'Non-you sent me here' but rather as 'Not-you sent me here'. See also Waltke and O'Connor (1990: §39.3.2) on clausal versus "item" (i.e., constituent) negation. A variation of Snyman and Naudé's analysis is proposed by the editors (see n. 33 below).

The focus-of-negation construction in BH is often assumed to be the equivalent of the English focus-of-negation cleft, above, *It is not x that y*. This is true, however, only when the relevant activated proposition happens to be presupposed as well. In (213), the given proposition is both activated and presupposed, and a cleft translation is perfectly appropriate. In other instances of BH focus of negation, however, the activated proposition is not presupposed. Here the assertion "*x is not f*" does not imply that there is a correct value for *x*; the implication of the focused clause may in fact be that there is no value at all for which the activated proposition is true. An English cleft rendering is odd and/or misleading for focused clauses of this type, as shown by (214).

(214) Num 16:28–29

ויאמר משה בזאת תדעון כי י׳ שלחני לעשות את כל המעשים האלה כי לא
מלבי: אם כמות כל האדם ימתון אלה ופקדת כל האדם יפקד עליהם <u>לא י׳</u>
שלחני:

And Moses said, "By this you shall know that the LORD has sent me to do all these things, [and] that it has not been of my own devising. If these men die as all people do, and if their fate be the fate of all people, **the LORD** did not send me."

The focused clause in (214), ‏לא י׳ שלחני, asserts "*x* is not the LORD" with respect to the activated proposition "*x* sent me." The activated proposition is derived from Moses' previous statement, ‏בזאת תדעון כי י׳ שלחני 'by this you shall know that the Lord has sent me'. At first glance, the focused clause has an appropriate cleft rendering: 'It is not the LORD who sent me'. This cleft, however, implies that someone other than God sent Moses. If God did not send Moses, however, Moses must have fabricated his mission, as Moses implies in the previous verse: ‏כי לא מלבי 'it has not been of my own devising'. The intent of the conditional in v. 29 is "If these men die a normal death then **the LORD** did not send me, that is to say, **no one** sent me." It is clear, then, that "*x* sent me" is activated but not presupposed information. The cleft rendering inappropriately converts the activated presupposition into a presupposed one and blocks the intended implication that no one sent Moses.

An additional example of this type is (215).

(215) Num 16:15

ויחר למשה מאד ויאמר אל י׳ אל תפן אל מנחתם לא **חמור אחד** מהם נשאתי

And Moses was very angry, and he said to the LORD, "Do not pay heed to their offering. I have not taken one ass from them"

The focused clause ‏לא חמור אחד מהם נשאתי asserts "*x* is not one ass" with respect to the activated proposition "I took *x* from them."[32] The inappropriate-

32. The previous context does not make it clear how the proposition "I took *x*" has been activated. Although this sort of clause would not be counted as focused according to the strict

ness of the cleft rendering here is obvious: "It is not a single ass that I took"
implies that the speaker is guilty of a different theft, whereas Moses' actual
intent is "I did not take (even) a single ass—in fact, I didn't take anything!" [33]

Focus-of-negation clauses involving presupposition are often followed
by an elliptical clause beginning with the clausal adverb כי 'rather' or כי אם
'rather'. [34] The second clause functions as a substitutional-focus clause, supplying the correct value for x in the activated proposition:

(216) Deut 5:3

לא את אבתינו כרת י' את הברית הזאת כי **אתנו אנחנו אלה פה היום כלנו
חיים**

It is not **with our fathers** that the LORD made this covenant; rather, with
us, we who are here today, all of us alive, [He made this covenant].

The focus-of-negation clause in (216) relates to the proposition "The LORD
made this covenant with x," activated by Moses' utterance in the previous
verse: י' אלהינו כרת עמנו ברית בחרב 'The LORD our God made a covenant with
us at Horeb'. The activated proposition is also presupposed, because the addressees presumably accept Moses' assertion that a covenant took place. The
focus-of-negation clause asserts "x is not our fathers" and is followed by an
elliptical clause כי אתנו 'Rather, with us, we who are here today, all of us alive,
[He made this covenant]'. [35] The כי clause provides the correct value for x, "us."

---

criteria I followed in classifying the Genesis corpus, it is included in the discussion here
for purposes of illustration. Because the לא + preposed constituent structure has virtually
no other uses besides focus-of-negation, it is reasonable to assume that focus of negation is
involved in (215) as well. Furthermore, it is intuitively obvious that Moses intends the clause
to be focused. This is plausibly viewed as a case of accommodation (§7.2.1, pp. 108–109),
where in his agitation Moses treats the proposition as activated even though this is not necessarily the case for his addressee.

33. The editors suggest that one can explain the difference between focus-of-negation
clauses that can be rendered by clefts and those that cannot by means of the clause-negation/
constituent-negation distinction. Examples such as (213) and (216) below, where the cleft
is an appropriate rendering, involve constituent negation, whereas examples that cannot be
rendered by clefts, such as (214) and (215), involve clause-level negation. In contrast, I am
claiming that the same level of negation is involved in both cases and that the difference
between the two groups of clauses is solely due to the type of givenness involved.

34. See also (213), above. For an example with כי אם, see (217) below. The particles כי
and כי אם seem largely interchangeable in this usage. Follingstad, however, distinguishes
between the two, claiming that כי אם has scope over a constituent and marks it for replace-
ment (i.e., substitutional) focus (2001: 563–66), whereas כי has scope over the entire clause,
marking it for "assertive" focus (2001: 569–83).

35. Although the כי (אם) clause following a focus-of-negation clause usually undergoes
ellipsis, the full version is occasionally attested, e.g., Lev 21:14 (Richard Steiner, personal
communication). The editors argue that כי following a focus-of-negation clause does not
start a new clause. Rather, כי is the continuation of the focused constituent. In Gen 45:8
(example (213), p. 137 above), it is claimed, there is a discontinuous two-part subject, לא
אתם כי האלהים 'not you but God'. This interpretation is dependent on a constituent-negation

Example (217) is a somewhat complex case of a focus-of-negation clause
followed by a כי אם clause:

(217) Gen 32:28–29

ויאמר אליו מה שמך ויאמר יעקב: ויאמר לא **יעקב** יאמר עוד שמך כי אם
ישראל

And he said to him, "What is your name?" And he said, "Jacob." And he
said to him, "Your name shall no longer be called **Jacob**; rather, [your
name will be called] **Israel**."

In this example it seems that the adverb עוד is external to the activated proposition, along with the negative; in other words, the activated proposition is "Your
name will be *x*," inferred from Jacob's prior assertion that his name is Jacob,
and the clause asserts "*x* will no longer be Jacob." The focused clause is followed by an elliptical כי אם clause identifying the correct value for *x*, "Israel."

8.5. The stylistic use of focusing

Focusing may be used to achieve a stylistic effect. An example is the "re-
peating verb" structure discussed by Blau (1972) and Paran (1989), among
others, in which a verb is repeated over the course of two or more adjacent
clauses.[36] The second half of the structure typically exhibits preposing and a
perfect verb form. Examples are shown in (218)–(220).

(218) Lev 23:11

והניף את העמר לפני י ' לרצנכם ממחרת השבת יניפנו הכהן

He shall elevate the sheaf before the LORD for acceptance in your behalf;
on the day after the sabbath the priest shall elevate it.

(219) Lev 4:12

ושרף אתו על עצים באש על שפך הדשן ישרף:

And he shall burn it on a fire of wood; on the ash heap it shall be burned.

---

analysis (see n. 31 above). If clause-level negation is involved, לא is not part of the subject;
and the two-part subject would have to be אתם כי האלהים, which is impossible from both the
syntactic and the semantic perspective. Against the two-part subject analysis, as the editors
themselves note, is the fact that the verb in Gen 45:8 agrees with the negated אתם, rather than
with האלהים. A further argument is the occurrence of כי אם after clauses that clearly involve
clause-level negation and hence exclude the possibility of a two-part subject, e.g., ויאמר לא
עכרתי את ישראל כי אם אתה ובית אביך 'I did not bring trouble on Israel; rather you and you
father's house [brought trouble on Israel]' (1 Kgs 18:18; see also Num 26:33, 1 Sam 2:15,
1 Kgs 22:18). Because כי אם introduces an elliptical clause in these verses, it seems most probable that כי אם following a focus-of-negation clause introduces an elliptical clause there too.

36. See §3.1.1 for additional references. As mentioned in §3.1.1, Paran terms this structure the "circular inclusio." According to Paran (1989: 49), the circular inclusio is characteristic of the Priestly style and appears more than 100 times in the Priestly source in legal and
cultic contexts alone. For further references, see Paran (1989: 49–50).

(220) Gen 41:12 [37]

ויפתר לנו את חלמתינו איש כחלמו פתר

And he interpreted our dreams to us; each man according to his dream
he interpreted

As Blau points out, in each cases the double clause structure can be condensed
into a single clause. Example (218) could have been expressed as והניף את
העמר לפני י׳ לרצנכם ממחרת השבת 'he shall elevate the sheaf before the Lord
for acceptance in your behalf on the day after the Sabbath', and (219) could
have been expressed as ויפתר לנו את חלומתינו איש כחלומו 'and he interpreted
our dreams to us, each man according to his dream'.

In the light of the above discussion of focusing, it can be seen that the preposed clause in the repeating-verb structure is a focused clause. The second
sentence is preposed not simply to create an inclusio but in order to mark the
preposed element as the focus in relation to the proposition expressed by the
first clause. All three clauses involve identificational focus. The examples are
repeated in (221)–(223), with the focused clauses underlined and focuses bold.

(221) Lev 23:11

והניף את העמר לפני י׳ לרצנכם **ממחרת השבת** יניפנו הכהן

(222) Gen 41:12

ויפתר לנו את חלמתינו **איש כחלמו** פתר

(223) Lev 4:12

ושרף אתו על עצים באש **על שפך הדשן** ישרף׃

On the level of the clause, stylistic focusing is indistinguishable from ordinary
focusing. What makes these structures "stylistic" is that the writer has intentionally set up the first clause as a lead-in to the focused clause, when the same
idea could have been expressed more economically by a single clause.

A particularly elaborate example of focusing for stylistic effect is (224),
cited in Blau (1972: 235):[38]

(224) Gen 1:27

ויברא אלהים את האדם בצלמו **בצלם אלהים** ברא אתו **זכר ונקבה** ברא אתם׃

And God created man in His image; **in the image of God** He created
him; **male and female** he created them.

37. Paran (1989: 78–79) views this example as exceptional in that it is not from the
Priestly source. He also views its style as different from the one usually employed in the
Priestly source.
38. Although this verse is often taken to be poetry, the appearance of a stylistic device
such as the repeated-verb structure does not necessarily justify the classification of the verse
as poetry, as discussed further on in this section.

In this three-part structure the initial clause, ויברא אלהים את האדם בצלמו, provides the activated proposition for the following focused clause, בצם אלהים
ברא אתו. This is technically speaking descriptive focus, although the old value
v and the new value *f* are semantically identical. The two values differ only
with regard to the form of the expressions involved: where *v* contains an enclitic pronoun, *f* substitutes the lexical expression אלהים. Next comes an identificational focus clause, זכר ונקבה ברא אתם. The verb ברא 'created' recurs in
each of the three clauses in the structure, all of which can be condensed into a
single clause, ויברא אלהים את האדם בצלמו זכר ונקבה 'And God created man in
His image, male and female'.

Although on the level of the clause there is nothing exceptional about stylistic focusing, it is worth investigating why in these cases the speaker has chosen
to use a repeated-verb structure with focusing, rather than a simpler mode of
expression. It is plausible that in many cases the repeated-verb structure has
a specific pragmatic function.[39] Pragmatics operates on the discourse level as
well as the clause level, motivating the speaker both to express an idea as a
particular combination of clauses and to structure those clauses in particular
ways. A plausible hypothesis for some of the examples of stylistic focusing is
that they draw the listener's attention to a constituent that might be otherwise
overlooked or insufficiently appreciated. Bendavid (1971: 857) states that the
repeated verb structure has the purpose of giving "weight to each piece of new
information individually"; a similar view is expressed in Paran (1989).[40] In
(223), for example, the identificational focus על שפך הדשן is brought to attention to stress that it is here and nowhere else that the offering is to be burnt.
The concept of attentional focus (see §3.3.1.3) may prove to be useful in understanding this type of function. In other cases, as in (224), focusing may be
motivated more by esthetics than by pragmatics.

A separate issue is whether "stylistic" focusing serves as an indication that
a segment of text is poetry rather than prose. Example (224), for example, is
considered poetry in many Bible translations, including NRSV, NAB, and NJB.
Although investigation of this issue is beyond the scope of this work, it is
worthwhile to note that "poetic" devices are widespread even in ordinary language use. As Jakobsen (1967: 302) writes, "Any attempt to reduce the sphere
of poetic function to poetry or to confine poetry to poetic function would be a

---

39. Stylistic devices often have pragmatic functions, although in some cases the function is purely esthetic. Watson (1984: 32–34) states that poetic devices may have functions
related to structure or esthetics, among other functions. Structural functions are pragmatic,
whereas esthetic functions are not. According to Wimsatt (1967: 369 n. 31) the meaning of
stylistic devices may be "emotive," function that may or may not be included in pragmatics.

40. Paran suggests that the device is also intended to facilitate memorization of the text
(1989: ix). According to Blau (1972: 237), the device reflects an oral style that was originally
used to express an afterthought. He also suggests that the preposed element serves as the
"psychological predicate" of the previous sentence.

delusive oversimplification."[41] Devices such as parallelism and repetition are not exclusive to poetic or even elevated discourse, but can be found in everyday language as well.[42] It should not be surprising, therefore, to find devices such as stylistic focusing in prose texts.

8.6. Conclusion

The activated proposition relating to a focused clause may be derived from the textual or extratextual context. Activation frequently goes hand-in-hand with presupposition, but there are many examples of focused clauses in which presupposition is not involved. Focusing in commands and requests generally does not involve presupposition.

Focused clauses may be identificational, descriptive, substitutional, or additive, depending on the relation the focus bears to previously activated values for x. Substitutional clauses that replace previously negated values for x may be introduced by the conjuncts כי, כי אם, or אם לא. Additive focusing and the focusing adverb גם are in some ways similar, but the two devices involve different types of given information. The focusing adverb relates to presupposed but not necessarily activated information, whereas additive focusing by preparing relates to activated but not necessarily presupposed information.

Focus of negation is a special type of focusing with a distinct syntactic form. Like ordinary focus, focus of negation also relates to an activated but not necessarily presupposed proposition. The English cleft is an appropriate rendering only for focus-of-negation constructions involving presupposition. Focus-of-negation clauses involving presupposition may be followed by an elliptical כי or כי אם clause supplying the correct value for x.

There are stylistic uses of focusing in which a repetitive structure is intentionally set up containing a focused clause. The purpose of a structure of this sort may be to set up the focused constituent as a focus of attention.

41. I am indebted to Michael O'Connor for bringing this reference to my attention. See also Berlin (1985: 3–5).

42. According to Muilenberg (1953), repetition is a characteristic stylistic feature of biblical narrative as well as poetry. See also Holes (1995), who shows that repetition and parallelism can be found in the everyday speech of certain communities of nonliterate Arabic speakers, and Johnstone (1991), who discusses the use of repetition and parallelism in different types of nonpoetic Arabic discourse. See also the discussion in §1.2.

Chapter 9

The Topicalized Clause

In this chapter, I describe BH topicalization, based on the 171 occurrences in Genesis and selected additional examples from the classical BH prose corpus. Topicalization highlights a link between the preposed item and a second item in an adjacent text segment, cueing the addressee to a coherence relation between the linked segments. Because segments linked by topicalization are most frequently single clauses, I refer to them as clauses, except when larger segments are concerned. The item linked to the preposed item is termed the "counterpart" of the preposed item.

In §9.1, I examine the preposed constituent and its counterpart from a syntactic perspective. In §9.2, I examine the nature of the link between the preposed item and counterpart. In §9.3, I examine the structure of the segments linked by topicalization. In §9.4, I describe the coherence relations obtaining between the linked segments. In the citations in this chapter, preposed clauses are marked by underlining, and the preposed items and their counterparts are bold.

9.1. Syntactic description of the preposed constituent and its counterpart

The preposed constituent in the topicalized clause may be a subject, complement, or adjunct:

(225) Subject

ויקרא לו **לבן** יגר שהדותא ו**יעקב** קרא לו גלעד:

Laban called it Jegar-sahadutha; and **Jacob** called it Galeed. (Gen 31:47)

(226) Complement

את בנתם נקח לנו לנשים ו**את בנתינו** נתן להם:

We will take **their daughters** for ourselves as wives, and **our daughters** we will give to them. (Gen 34:21)

144

**Table 15. Syntactic function of the preposed constituent in
topicalized clauses in Genesis.**

Function	Number	Percentage
Subject	76	44.4
Complement/adjunct	93	54.4
Unclear	2	1.2
Total	171	

**Table 16. Syntactic category of the preposed constituent in
topicalized clauses in Genesis**

Category	Number	Percentage
Noun phrase	101	59.1
Prepositional phrase	68	39.8
Infinitive clause	1	0.6
Adverb	1	0.6
Total	171	

(227) Adjunct

ויחפש **בגדול** החל **ובקטן** כלה

And he searched: **with the eldest** he began, and **with the youngest** he
ended. (Gen 44:12)

Table 15 shows the frequency of the various syntactic functions of the preposed constituents in topicalized clauses from Genesis. Complement/adjunct-
preposed topicalization is somewhat more common than the subject-preposed
type. As shown in table 16, the preposed constituent is most frequently a noun
phrase but may also be a prepositional phrase or, more rarely, an infinitive
clause or adverb. About 60% of preposed constituents are noun phrases.

In contrast to the preposed item, the counterpart of the preposed item need
not be present in the surface structure of the text. A subject counterpart in (228)
and a complement counterpart in (229) have been deleted from the surface
structure.[1] The deleted items are indicated in brackets.

(228) Gen 35:18

ותקרא [**רחל**] שמו בן אוני **ואביו** קרא לו בנימין:

And [**Rachel**] called his name Ben-oni, and **his father** called his name
Benjamin.

---

1. See also, e.g., Gen 22:5 and 24:53.

(229) Gen 20:15–16

ויאמר אבימלך [**לאברהם**] הנה ארצי לפניך בטוב בעיניך שב: **ולשרה** אמר הנה
נתתי אלף כסף לאחיך

And Abimelech said [**to Abraham**], "Behold, my land is before you; dwell where it pleases you." And **to Sarah** he said, "Behold, I give your brother a thousand pieces of silver"

In exceptional cases, the counterpart of the preposed item is not a phrase, but an entire clause, or even a group of coordinated clauses. In (230), for example, the word זאת, used as a pro-clause, has as its counterpart the several clauses following, marked in bold.[2]

(230) Gen 42:33–34

בזאת אדע כי כנים אתם **אחיכם האחד הניחו אתי ואת רעבון בתיכם קחו
ולכו: והביאו את אחיכם הקטן אלי**

By this I shall know that you are honest men: **one of your brothers leave with me, and for the famine of your households take [something], and go. And bring your youngest brother to me**.

9.2. The link between the preposed item and its counterpart

The link between the preposed item and its counterpart generally pertains to the referents of the linked items, rather than to the expressions themselves.[3] Because preposing is normally performed on entire clause-level constituents, the preposed constituent may contain material that is irrelevant to the link with the counterpart. Prepositions are extraneous to the link:

(231) Gen 10:10–11

ותהי ראשית ממלכתו בבל וארך ואכד וכלנה **בארץ שנער: מן הארץ ההוא**
יצא אשור

And the beginning of his kingdom were Babel, Erech, and Accad and Calneh[4] **in the land of Shinar**. **From that land** Ashur went forth[5]

---

2. The topicalized clause in (230) is forward-linking (see §9.3), with the preposed item and its counterpart linked by a relation of identity. The counterpart itself contains two items linked by topicalization: אחיכם האחד 'one of your brothers' is linked to את רעבון בתיכם '[something for] the famine of your households'. The former is to be left behind and the latter taken back to Canaan. Additional examples of clauses or groups of clauses serving as counterparts are Gen 42:15–16, 18–20; 43:11–13; 45:17–18.

3. In Gen 48:11, however, the link concerns the meaning of the preposed infinitive clause ראה פניך 'seeing your face' and the meaning of the following verse.

4. The NRSV translates 'all of them' instead of 'Calneh', emending the vocalization to כֻּלָּנָה.

5. The NRSV translates 'From that land he went into Assyria', taking Ashur as the object rather than the subject of the clause.

In (231), מן 'from' is extraneous to the link of identity obtaining between the referent of הארץ ההוא and the referent of the preceding ארץ שנער.[6]

A noun that is part of an idiomatic expression may also be extraneous to the link:

(232) Gen 43:9

אנכי אערבנו מידי תבקשנו

I will be surety for him; **from my hand** you shall require him.

Preposed מידי in the second clause has אנכי in the preceding clause as its counterpart. The word ידי is part of the idiomatic expression בקש מיד 'hold responsible' and has no independent meaning and hence no reference. The link obtains between the referents of אנכי and the coreferential enclitic pronoun in the phrase מידי. A more idiomatic rendering of the verse would be 'I will be surety for him; you may hold **me** responsible', with the linked items marked in bold.

An examination of topicalization in Genesis and elsewhere reveals a wide variety in the links obtaining between the linked items. The common denominator in all cases is a contextual relation between the referents of the preposed item and counterpart; that is, the referents function as a pair in the discourse context. I refer to the referents of the linked items as A and B, where A is the item found in the first segment and B is in the second segment.

In most instances of topicalization, A and B have been mentioned just before the linked segments in a way that establishes them as a pair. Examples are shown in (233) and (234).[7]

(233) Gen 1:4–5

וירא אלהים את האור כי טוב ויבדל אלהים בין האור ובין החשך: ויקרא
אלהים **לאור** יום **ולחשך** קרא לילה

And God saw that the light was good; and God separated between the light and the darkness. And God called **the light** Day, and **the darkness** He called Night.

(234) Gen 29:16–17

וללבן שתי בנות שם הגדלה לאה ושם הקטנה רחל: ועיני **לאה** רכות **ורחל**
היתה יפת תאר ויפת מראה:

And Laban had two daughters; the name of the older was Leah, and the name of the younger was Rachel. And **Leah**'s eyes were weak, and **Rachel** was beautiful in form and beautiful in appearance.

6. See also, e.g., Gen 9:19, 10:32, 12:16, and 41:44.
7. Additional representative examples include Gen 3:16; 4:2, 5; 12:16; 13:12; 31:47; 36:4; and 40:21–22.

In (233), light and darkness are mentioned together in the preceding verse; similarly, in (234) Rachel and Leah are named just before as Laban's two daughters. In these examples, as in many others, A and B bear a logical relation that automatically establishes a contextual link: light and darkness are opposites, and Rachel and Leah are members of the set of Laban's children.

In some cases, neither A nor B has been previously mentioned, but they nevertheless bear a logical relation to each other. An example is (235), in which the linked items, the pure animals and the impure animals, are mentioned for this first time. Since these constitute subsets of the set of all animals, a link between them is automatically established.[8]

(235) Gen 7:2

מכל **הבהמה הטהורה** תקח לך שבעה שבעה איש ואשתו **ומן הבהמה אשר לא טהרה הוא** [תקח לך] שנים איש ואשתו:

Of **every clean animal** you shall take for yourself seven pairs, a male and its mate; and **of every animal that is not clean** [you shall take] two, a male and its mate.

Logical relations are not necessary for linkage by topicalization. In many cases, the link is ad hoc, restricted to the particular context:[9]

(236) Gen 18:33

וילך י׳ כאשר כלה לדבר אל אברהם **ואברהם** שב למקמו:

And **the Lord** departed when He had finished speaking to Abraham; and **Abraham** returned to his place

Abraham and God are not a natural pair, but they are linked by the prior context by virtue of being mutually engaged in conversation. Another ad-hoc pair is shown in (237).

(237) Gen 47:19

למה נמות לעיניך גם **אנחנו** גם **אדמתנו** קנה אתנו ואת **אדמתנו** בלחם ונהיה **אנחנו ואדמתנו** עבדים לפרעה ותן זרע ו[**אנחנו**] נחיה ולא נמות **והאדמה לא** תשם:

Why should we die before your eyes, both **we** and **our land**? Buy **us** and **our land** in exchange for food, and **we** and **our land** will be slaves to Pharaoh; and give us seed and (= that) [**we**] may live, and not die, and **the land** may not become desolate."

---

8. See also Gen 19:3, where the preposed מצות 'unleavened bread' bears a part-whole relation to משתה 'a feast' in the previous clause.

9. The idea of the ad hoc link is discussed in Birner and Ward (1998: 234). Note that these scholars use the term *link* somewhat differently to refer to the referent of the preposed constituent rather than to a relation between that referent and another item (1998: 20).

The topicalized clause והאדמה לא תשם is linked to the previous two clauses, ונחיה ולא נמות. The preposed element האדמה is linked to the implicit subject pronoun in the preceding segment, אנחנו (i.e., the people). A contextual link between the land and the people was established previously in the verse, where the people propose to sell themselves and their land to Pharaoh. The pair אנחנו/גויתנו and אדמתנו occur in coordinated or appositive phrases no less than three times in the preceding text (shown above in bold), making the link impossible to miss.

In some cases a previously nonexistent ad hoc relation is established by the linked clauses themselves:

(238) Gen 27:15–16

ותקח רבקה את בגדי עשו בנה הגדל החמדת אשר אתה בבית ותלבש [**אותם**]
את יעקב בנה הקטן: **ואת ערת גדיי העזים** הלבישה על ידיו ועל חלקת צואריו:

Then Rebekah took the best clothes of Esau her older son, which were with her in the house, and she put [**them**] on Jacob her younger son; and **the skins of the kids** she put upon his hands and upon the smooth part of his neck.

In this example, A is the referent of the omitted object אותם in the first under-lined clause, that is, Esau's clothes mentioned in the previous verse. B is the goat skins. It is hard to think of a natural relation obtaining between Esau's clothes and the goat skins, outside of this particular context. Nevertheless, be-cause the clauses referring to these items describe similar actions performed with the two items—both are used to clothe Jacob—a link is established be-tween the two. Other unnatural pairs of this sort include, among others: the wood of a wagon and the cows pulling the wagon (1 Sam 6:14), the head of the dead Philistine and his weapons (1 Sam 17:54), and a household idol and a goat's hair quilt (1 Sam 19:13).[10] The link between each of these pairs is perfectly comprehensible in its context: the wood and the cows are both used in preparing a sacrifice, the Philistine's head and his weapons are retrieved from the battlefield as war trophies, and the idol and quilt are used to simu-late the form of David's body lying under the covers. Idiosyncratic examples like these make it clear that logical relations like partially ordered set relations (see §6.2.1.1), even if involved in some instances of topicalization, are beside the point.

A notable type of link is between two items with identical reference. The first item is often a lexical expression and the second a coreferential expres-sion containing a personal pronoun (independent or enclitic), as in (239), or a demonstrative pronoun, as in (240).[11]

10. The last example bears a striking relation to (238).
11. For additional examples, see, e.g., Gen 2:10; 10:11; 25:10; 36:13; and 42:15.

(239) Gen 4:20

וַתֵּלֶד עָדָה אֶת **יָבָל הוּא** הָיָה אֲבִי יֹשֵׁב אֹהֶל וּמִקְנֶה:

And Adah bore **Jabal**; **he** was the father of those who dwell in tents and amidst cattle.

(240) Gen 22:20–23

וַיֻּגַּד לְאַבְרָהָם לֵאמֹר הִנֵּה יָלְדָה מִלְכָּה גַם הִוא בָּנִים לְנָחוֹר אָחִיךָ: **אֶת עוּץ בְּכֹרוֹ וְאֶת בּוּז אָחִיו וְאֶת קְמוּאֵל אֲבִי אֲרָם: וְאֶת כֶּשֶׂד וְאֶת חֲזוֹ וְאֶת פִּלְדָּשׁ וְאֶת יִדְלָף וְאֵת בְּתוּאֵל**: וּבְתוּאֵל יָלַד אֶת רִבְקָה **שְׁמֹנָה אֵלֶּה** יָלְדָה מִלְכָּה לְנָחוֹר אֲחִי אַבְרָהָם:

And it was told to Abraham, saying, "Behold, Milcah also has born children to your brother Nahor: **Uz the first-born, and Buz his brother, and Kemuel the father of Aram, and Chesed, and Hazo, and Pildash, and Jidlaph, and Bethuel.**" And Bethuel fathered Rebekah. **These eight** Milcah bore to Nahor, Abraham's brother.

The lexical expression may also be repeated in place of a pronoun, as in (241).[12] In many cases both items are pronouns, as in (242).[13]

(241) Gen 36:1–3

וְאֵלֶּה תֹּלְדוֹת **עֵשָׂו** הוּא אֱדוֹם: **עֵשָׂו** לָקַח אֶת נָשָׁיו מִבְּנוֹת כְּנָעַן אֶת עָדָה בַּת אֵילוֹן הַחִתִּי וְאֶת אָהֳלִיבָמָה בַּת עֲנָה בַּת צִבְעוֹן הַחִוִּי: וְאֶת בָּשְׂמַת בַּת יִשְׁמָעֵאל אֲחוֹת נְבָיוֹת:

These are the descendents of **Esau**, that is, Edom. **Esau** took his wives from the Canaanites: Adah the daughter of Elon the Hittite, Oholibamah the daughter of Anah the daughter of Zibeon the Hivite, and Basemath, the daughter of Ishmael, the sister of Nebaioth.

(242) Gen 9:19

שְׁלֹשָׁה אֵלֶּה בְּנֵי נֹחַ **וּמֵאֵלֶּה** נָפְצָה כָל הָאָרֶץ:

These three were the sons of Noah; and **from these** the whole world branched out.

9.3. The linked segments

In the simplest and most common situation, topicalization links two adjacent clauses. The second clause is generally topicalized, pointing back to the previous one. This is termed *backward-linking* topicalization. The preceding clause most often has normal word order:[14]

---

12. Additional examples include Gen 1:27; 7:19; 8:5; 9:23; 11:27; 40:13, 19; and 41:50.
13. Additional examples include Gen 9:19, 10:32, 31:39, 36:14, 41:40, 43:9, and 46:4.
14. These are the "chiastic" structures discussed by Andersen and Khan (see §3.1.1). Additional representative examples include Gen 1:5, 1:10, 4:2, 12:12, 18:33, 24:53, 25:5–6, 25:33–34, 31:47, 33:16–17, 35:18, 37:11, 40:21–22, and 41:51–52.

(243) Gen 4:4–5

וישע י׳ **אל הבל ואל מנחתו**: **ואל קין ואל מנחתו** לא שעה

And the Lord paid heed **to Abel and his offering**, and **to Cain and his offering** He paid no heed.

(244) Gen 37:11

ויקנאו בו **אחיו ואביו** שמר את הדבר:

And **his brothers** were jealous of him, and **his father** kept the matter in mind.

Backward-linking topicalizations are almost always coordinated with the previous clause with the conjunction ו, as in (243) and (244). When the linked items have identical reference, the topicalized clause is often asyndetic, as in (245):

(245) Gen 40:12–13

שלשת השרגים **שלשת ימים** הם: **בעוד שלשת ימים** ישא פרעה את ראשך והשיבך על כנך

The three branches are **three days**. In another three days Pharaoh will lift up your head and return you to your post.

Forward-linking topicalization points ahead to a subsequent clause, which usually undergoes topicalization as well.[15] A particularly clear-cut example of forward-linking topicalization is the underlined clause in (246), which occurs in the absence of any preceding discourse:

(246) Gen 2:16–17

ויצו י׳ אלהים על האדם לאמר: **מכל עץ הגן** אכל תאכל: **ומעץ הדעת טוב ורע** לא תאכל ממנו כי ביום אכלך ממנו מות תמות:

And the Lord God commanded the man, saying, "**From every tree of the garden** you may eat; and **from the tree of the knowledge of good and evil**, you shall not eat from it, for on the day that you eat from it you shall die."

The initial underlined clause marks a relation between the preposed מכל עץ הגן and the expression in the following clause, מעץ הדעת טוב ורע.

Forward-linking topicalization is almost always asyndetic.[16] The syndesis/asyndesis opposition between backward- and forward-linking topicalization

---

15. These are Andersen's (1974) and Khan's (1988) "parallel" structures (see §3.1.1). An exception to this rule is Gen 45:17, where a forward-linking topicalization is followed by a clause with normal word order.

16. One exception is Gen 50:20, where the *waw* is attached to the first topicalized clause, rather than the second, as would be expected: **ואתם** חשבתם עלי רעה **אלהים** חשבה לטבה למען עשה כיום הזה להחית עם רב: 'And **you** intended me harm, **God** intended it for good, to bring it about that many people should be kept alive, as they are today'.

guides the addressee in correctly identifying the linked segment. If the topicalized clause is syndetic, the linked segment precedes. If it is asyndetic, the
linked segment lies ahead. Additional examples of forward-linking topicalization are shown in (247) and (248).[17]

(247) Gen 41:13

ויהי כאשר פתר לנו כן היה **אתי** השיב על כני **ואתו** תלה:

And as he interpreted to us, so it came to pass: **me** he restored to my office, and **him** he hanged.

(248) Gen 13:11–12

ויפרדו איש מעל אחיו: **אברם** ישב בארץ כנען **ולוט** ישב בערי הככר:

And they separated from each other. **Abram** dwelt in the land of Canaan,
and **Lot** dwelt among the cities of the plain.

When the linked clause following a forward-linking topicalization contains
material identical to the former clause, the repetitious material may be gapped:

(249) Gen 7:2 [18]

מכל הבהמה הטהורה תקח לך שבעה שבעה איש ואשתו **ומן הבהמה אשר
לא טהרה הוא** [תקח לך] שנים איש ואשתו:

Of every clean animal you shall take for yourself seven pairs, a male
and its mate; and **of every animal that is not clean** [you shall take] two,
a male and its mate.

The counterpart of the preposed item is at the head of the gapped clause, and
the verb, along with other material identical to that in the topicalized clause,
has been omitted. The gapped material is shown in brackets.[19]

In several instances, a forward-linking topicalization is followed by left-
dislocation:[20]

---

17. See also, e.g., Gen 3:2; 14:4; 31:38, 40; 34:9, 21; 42:19, 33; and 44:12, as well as
examples (249)–(250).

18. Appears as (235) above (p. 148).

19. A similar example is Gen 31:40. This verse shows that verb gapping does occur in
BH prose, contrary to O'Connor's (1980: 401) denial of this possibility, discussed above in
§1.2. Additional examples of verb-gapping in prose can be found in (254) below. See Kugel
(1981: 321–22) for some additional examples.

20. An additional example is Gen 3:2. In Exod 1:22, a left-dislocation is followed by a
topicalized clause.

(250) Gen 2:16 ²¹

ויצו י׳ אלהים על האדם לאמר: **מכל עץ הגן** אכל תאכל. **ומעץ הדעת טוב ורע**
לא תאכל ממנו כי ביום אכלך ממנו מות תמות:

And the Lord God commanded the man, saying, "**From every tree of
the garden** you may eat; and **from the tree of the knowledge of good
and evil**, you shall not eat from **it**, for on the day that you eat from it you
shall die."

The linked items in this example are מכל עץ הגן and מעץ הדעת טוב ורע. The
first item is preposed, and the second is dislocated, with a resumptive enclitic
pronoun.

When the segments linked by topicalization are larger than a single clause,
the preposed item and its counterpart occur in the first clause of their respective
segments. Large discourse segments are often involved when the linked items
are time adverbials. The segments include all of the clauses referring to events
occurring at the designated time:

(251) Gen 8:13–14

ויהי **באחת ושש מאות שנה בראשון באחד לחדש** חרבו המים מעל הארץ
ויסר נח את מכסה התבה וירא והנה חרבו פני האדמה: **ובחדש השני בשבעה**
ועשרים יום לחדש יבשה הארץ:

And it came to pass **in the six hundred and first year, in the first
[month], on the first day of the month**, the waters dried up from the
earth. And Noah removed the covering of the ark, and he looked, and
behold, the surface of the ground was dry. And **in the second month, on
the twenty-seventh day of the month**, the earth was dry.

The first segment encompasses all of the clauses in v. 13, and the second segment consists of the topicalized clause in v. 14.

Although topicalization most frequently links two segments, chains of
linked segments also occur: ²²

(252) Gen 3:14–19

ויאמר י׳ אלהים **אל הנחש** כי עשית זאת ארור אתה מכל הבהמה. . . . **אל**
האשה אמר הרבה ארבה עצבונך והרנך. . . . **ולאדם** אמר כי שמעת לקול
אשתך:

And the Lord God said to the serpent, "Because you did this, you are
more cursed than all beasts. . . ." **To the woman** he said, "I will greatly
increase your pangs in childbearing. . . ." And **to Adam** he said, "Because you listened to the voice of your wife"

21. Appears above as (246).
22. See also Gen 42:36, where the first two segments are nonverbal clauses and the third
a topicalized clause.

(253) Gen 14:4–6

שתים עשרה שנה עבדו את כדרלעמר **ושלש עשרה שנה** מרדו: **ובארבע**
עשרה שנה בא כדרלעמר והמלכים אשר אתו ויכו את רפאים בעשתרת קרנים
ואת הזוזים בהם ואת האימים בשוה קריתים: ואת החרי בהררם שעיר עד איל
פארן אשר על המדבר:

Twelve years they served Chedorlaomer, and **in the thirteenth year**
they rebelled. And **in the fourteenth year** Chedorlaomer came, and the
kings who were with him, and they defeated the Rephaim at Ashteroth-
karnaim, and the Zuzim at Ham, and the Emim at Shaveh-kiriathaim,
and the Horites in their hill country of Seir as far as El-paran, which is
by the wilderness.

Each of these examples contains three linked segments. In (252), a normal
clause is followed by two topicalized clauses, each of which includes a direct-
speech citation.[23] Example (253) contains three segments, the first two consisting of one clause each and the last probably extending to the end of v. 6.

A particularly long chain from the classical BH prose corpus is shown in
(254); only part of the chain appears in the citation.

(254) Num 7:12–83 (excerpt)

ויהי המקריב **ביום הראשון** את קרבנו נחשון בן עמינדב למטה יהודה: וקרבנו
קערת כסף אחת שלשים ומאה משקלה מזרק אחד כסף שבעים שקל בשקל
הקדש שניהם מלאים סלת בלולה בשמן למנחה: כף אחת עשרה זהב מלאה
קטרת: פר אחד בן בקר איל אחד כבש אחד בן שנתו לעלה: שעיר עזים אחד
לחטאת: ולזבח השלמים בקר שנים אילם חמשה עתודים חמשה כבשים בני
שנה חמשה זה קרבן נחשון בן עמינדב: **ביום השני** הקריב נתנאל בן צוער נשיא
יששכר. . . . . **ביום השלישי** [הקריב] נשיא לבני זבולן אליאב בן חלן

The one who offered his offering **on the first day** was Nahshon the son
of Amminadab, of the tribe of Judah; and his offering was one silver
plate whose weight was a hundred and thirty shekels, one silver basin of
seventy shekels, according to the shekel of the sanctuary, both of them
full of fine flour mixed with oil for a meal offering; one golden ladle of
ten shekels, filled with incense; one bull of the herd, one ram, one lamb
in its first year, for a burnt offering; one goat for a sin offering; and
for the sacrifice of well being, two oxen, five rams, five he-goats, and
five yearling lambs. This was the offering of Nahshon the son of Amminadab. **On the second day** Nethanel the son of Zuar, the leader of Is-
sachar, made an offering. . . . **On the third day** the leader of the children
of Zebulun, Eliab son of Helon [made an offering]

23. As discussed in §4.4.3, the syntactic status of direct-speech citations is uncertain,
making it hard to determine how many nonsubordinate clauses there are in each segment.

The complete chain contains 12 segments. The first clause in each segment contains a time adverbial: ביום הראשון, ביום השני and so on. The first segment opens with a clause with normal word order, and the second segment begins with a backward-linking topicalized clause. The initial clause in the rest of the segments has a preposed time adverbial and a gapped verb; for example, ביום השלישי [הקריב] נשיא לבני זבולן אליאב בן חלן 'On the third day the leader of the children of Zebulun, Eliab son of Helon [made an offering]' (v. 24). [24]

9.4. Coherence relations between segments linked by topicalization

Topicalization marks a coherence relation obtaining between the linked clauses or segments, a relation concerning the pair of linked items. The specific relation involved in each case is left to the reader's inference. Coherence relations are categorized as content, epistemic, or speech-act relations, as described in §6.2.2.

In most cases of topicalization the clauses or segments stand in a relation of *opposition* or *similarity*. The categorization of these coherence relations is a matter of debate. Halliday and Hasan (1976: 242) view opposition and similarity as pragmatic (i.e, epistemic) relations, whereas Sanders et al. (1992) categorize them as semantic (i.e., content). In my view, opposition and similarity are epistemic relations, relating to speaker reasoning: the opposition or similarity between the segments exists in the mind of the speaker rather than in the real world. The distinction between opposition and similarity is to some degree subjective and is not fully determined by the content of the sentences (see §9.4.2).

In some cases, the coherence relation involved in topicalization is of the speech-act type. A relation of similarity concerning speech acts is termed *addition*. Other speech-act relations associated with topicalization are *elaboration*, *summary*, and *paraphrase*. A type rare in the Genesis corpus but amply attested elsewhere is the content relation of *temporal succession*. [25] It is likely that other coherence relations are possible as well but do not occur in the corpus.

The coherence relations associated with topicalization are explored in more detail in §§9.4.1–9.4.5.

9.4.1. Opposition

Segments linked by topicalization most frequently stand in a relation of opposition: the linked items in the segments are marked in order to highlight the difference between what is said about them. The opposition between the two segments might be expressed in English by the conjunct adverbial *in contrast*; the closest equivalent in BH is אולם, although use of this conjunct is much less

24. Another long chain involving fronted time adverbials is found in the passage describing the offerings for the Sabbath and festivals (Num 28:9–29:38).
25. In a few cases, it is difficult to identify a specific coherence relation; these are Gen 2:10; 7:18–19; 10:11; 19:6, 10–11; 25:10; and 46:32.

common than topicalization. Opposition is a binary relation; thus, this relation is to be found in pairs of linked segments but not in topicalization chains.

Oppositional segments may consist of a normal word-order clause followed by a backward-linking topicalization or a forward-linking topicalization followed by a backward-linking one. The linked clauses often exhibit parallel syntactic and lexical structure, as in (255) and (256). The linked clauses in these examples have an identical syntactic structure and involve the same verb. The opposition is between the postverbal constituents in both clauses.[26]

(255) Gen 41:51–52

ויקרא יוסף **את שם הבכור** מנשה כי נשני אלהים את כל עמלי ואת כל בית אבי:
ואת שם השני קרא אפרים כי הפרני אלהים בארץ עניי:

And Joseph called **the name of the first-born** Manasseh, "For God has made me forget all my hardship and my father's entire house." And **the name of the second** he called Ephraim, "For God has made me fruitful in the land of my affliction."

(256) Gen 4:2

ויהי **הבל** רעה צאן **וקין** היה עבד אדמה:

And **Abel** was a keeper of sheep, and **Cain** was a tiller of the soil.

When oppositional segments exhibit parallel structure, it is often possible to interpret the last constituent in the second clause as a focus. In (254), for example, we are told that Joseph had two sons and named the first Menasseh. This activates by inference the proposition that he also named the second son, that is, "He named the second *x*." The topicalized clause supplies the value for *x*, "Ephraim." Similarly, in (256) "a tiller of the soil" is identified as the value for *x* with respect to the indirectly activated proposition "Cain was *x*." Although "Ephraim" and "a tiller of the soil" satisfy the pragmatic conditions for focus, they are not marked as such on the syntactic level, because they stand in their usual position in the clause.

Topicalized clauses such as (255) and (256) are indistinguishable structurally and semantically from others that do not have a focus. An example of the latter is (257).

(257) Gen 35:18[27]

ותקרא [**רחל**] שמו בן אוני **ואביו** קרא לו בנימין:

And [**Rachel**] called his name Ben-oni; and **his father** called his name Benjamin.

---

26. Additional representative examples include Gen 1:10, 2:16–17, 4:5, 7:2, 12:12, 13:12, 14:21, 15:10, 25:5–6, and 50:20.

27. Appears above as (228) (p. 145).

The two clauses in this example are syntactically and semantically parallel, just as in the examples above. Here, however, there is no part of the topicalized clause that can be interpreted as a focus, because the fact that Jacob gave Benjamin a different name is unexpected information that is not inferrable from the preceding clause.

When the linked segments do not exhibit parallel structure, as is often the case, there is no possibility of an unmarked focus. The opposition is inferred from the content of the two clauses:[28]

(258) Gen 42:3–4

וירדו **אחי יוסף עשרה** לשבר בר ממצרים: **ואת בנימין אחי יוסף** לא שלח
יעקב את אחיו כי אמר פן יקראנו אסון

And **ten of Joseph's brothers** went down to buy grain in Egypt. And **Benjamin, Joseph's brother**, Jacob did not send with his brothers, for he said, "Lest disaster befall him."

(259) Gen 12:15–16

ותקח **האשה** בית פרעה: **ולאברם** היטיב בעבורה

And **the woman** was taken into Pharaoh's house. And **with Abram** it went well because of her.

In (258), an opposition is drawn between the 10 brothers' going down to Egypt and Benjamin's remaining in Canaan. The topicalized clause does not state straightforwardly that Benjamin did not go down but relates this fact indirectly by stating that Jacob did not send him. In (259), an opposition is drawn between the tragic event of Sarai's abduction to the palace and the benefits accruing to Abram as a result.

An interesting variety of opposition is found in cases in which the linked referents refer to a set and a member of that set, respectively. The first clause makes a statement regarding set A, and the second clause makes a directly contradictory statement regarding member B. In order to reconcile the two statements, the addressee is forced to conclude that the expression apparently designating set A actually refers to all members of A except for B. Examples include (260) and (261).

(260) Gen 2:16 [29]

ויצו י' אלהים על האדם לאמר: **מכל עץ הגן** אכל תאכל **ומעץ הדעת טוב ורע**
לא תאכל ממנו כי ביום אכלך ממנו מות תמות:

And the Lord God commanded the man, saying, "**From every tree of the garden** you may eat; and **from the tree of the knowledge of good**

---

28. Additional representative examples include Gen 6:6–8, 17:20–21, 29:17, 33:14, 48:11, and 50:24.

29. Appears as (246) and (250) above (p. 151 and p. 153, respectively).

and evil, you shall not eat from it, for on the day that you eat from it you shall die."

(261) Gen 41:54

ותחלינה שבע שני הרעב לבוא כאשר אמר יוסף ויהי רעב <u>**בכל הארצות ובכל**</u>
<u>**ארץ מצרים**</u> היה לחם:

And the seven years of famine began to come, as Joseph had said. And there was famine in **all of the lands**, and **in all the land of Egypt** there was bread.

In (260), man is given permission to eat from every tree in the garden. The subsequent clause makes it clear that this means every tree except for the Tree of Knowledge. Similarly, in (261), כל הארצות actually means all of the lands except for the land of Egypt.[30] Recognizing the link between the items in the two segments and the coherence relation between the segments is critical for the proper understanding of the first segment. By explicitly marking the links, topicalization plays an important role in guiding the addressee to the intended semantic interpretation.

Another interesting type of oppositional topicalization involves an *a fortiori* argument (קל וחמר 'the argument from the minor to the major'). In this type of argument, a speaker argues for a proposition *p* by asserting or implying a weaker version of *p*, from which the stronger version naturally follows: "if the 'minor' has this or that property then the 'major' must undoubtedly have it" (Jacobs 1972: 221). An example is (262).

(262) Gen 44:8

הן **כסף אשר מצאנו בפי אמתחתינו** השיבנו אליך מארץ כנען ואיך נגנב מבית
אדניך **כסף או זהב**

Behold, **the money which we found in the mouth of our sacks**, we brought back to you from the land of Canaan, and how could we have stolen from your master's house **silver or gold**?

The linked items are כסף אשר מצאנו בפי אמתחתנו and כסף או זהב. The first segment is a forward-linking topicalized clause with the clausal adverb הן,[31] and

---

30. A slightly different type is לכלם נתן לאיש חלפות שמלת **ולבנימן** נתן שלש מאות כסף **וחמש חלפת שמלת** 'To each of them he gave a change of clothing, and **to Benjamin** he gave 300 pieces of silver and five changes of clothing' (Gen 45:22). The topicalized clause does not contradict the literal meaning of the previous one, because Benjamin, like his brothers, received a change of clothing (following most translations, which take חלפות as referring to a single set of clothing.) Instead, the contradiction is between the implication of the first clause that the brothers (including Benjamin) received *only* a change of clothing and the following assertion that Benjamin received a large sum of money in addition to five changes of clothing.

31. On the use of הן in *a fortiori* arguments, see Blau (1993: §103.2); Garr (2004: 332).

the second segment is a rhetorical question. The rhetorical question implies the assertion "We did not steal gold or silver from Joseph's house." Topicalization highlights the "minor/major" relation between the linked items: "the money which we found in the mouth of our sack" is money that the brothers could have been justified in keeping, whereas they had no right to "silver or gold" from Joseph's house. "If we returned the money that we could have kept for ourselves," the brothers say, "we certainly would not steal Joseph's money."

The use of topicalization in *a fortiori* arguments occurs elsewhere in the classical BH prose corpus as well, as shown in the following examples.

(263) Exod 6:12

הן **בני ישראל** לא שמעו אלי ואיך ישמעני **פרעה**

Behold, **the Israelites** have not listened to me, and how should **Pharaoh** listen to me?

(264) 2 Kgs 10:4

הנה **שני המלכים** לא עמדו לפניו ואיך נעמד **אנחנו**:

Behold, **the two kings** could not withstand him, and how can **we** withstand [him]?

(265) Judg 14:16 [32]

הנה **לאבי ולאמי** לא הגדתי **ולך** אגיד

Behold, I have not told **my father or my mother**, and **you** I should tell?

(266) 1 Kgs 8:27

הנה **השמים ושמי השמים** לא יכלכלוך אף כי **הבית הזה אשר בניתי**:

Behold, **heaven and the highest heaven** cannot contain you; how much less **this house which I have built**.

As in (262) above (p. 158), the arguments in these examples start with a topicalized clause beginning with הן or הנה, followed by a rhetorical question. In (265), the rhetorical question is topicalized as well. In (266), the topicalized clause is followed by an elliptical clause introduced with אף כי 'how much more so'.[33] Everything in the elliptical clause has been omitted except for the linked item. In each case, a forward-linking topicalization highlights a "minor/ major" relation between the linked items and an oppositional relation between the segments.

---

32. The rhetorical question here is unmarked, lacking an interrogative particle or adverb.

33. For additional examples (not necessarily involving topicalization of a finite clause) of the הן/הנה . . . אף כי sequence, see 1 Sam 23:3 and 2 Sam 16:11. The phrase אף כי occurs without preceding הן/הנה in 1 Sam 14:29–30; Prov 15:11; 19:7, 10. See Labuschagne (1973: 7) and Stec (1987: 479–80).

9.4.2. Similarity

Segments linked by topicalization frequently stand in a relation of similarity, a relation that might be expressed in English by the conjunct *similarly* or *likewise*. The distinction between opposition and similarity is not completely determined by the content of the clauses but depends on whether the speaker views what is said about the linked items as different or similar. As such, similarity and opposition are epistemic rather than content relations. The distinction between opposition and similarity is at times very subtle, and some similar segments are apt to be taken at first glance as oppositional. Unlike the relation of opposition, the similarity relation may obtain in a chain of linked segments.

A relation of similarity is obvious when closely related things are stated about each of the linked items. A chain of topicalized segments of this type from the classical BH prose corpus is shown in (267):

(267) Deut 7:5

כי אם כה תעשו להם **מזבחתיהם** תתצו **ומצבתם** תשברו **ואשירהם** תגדעון **ופסיליהם** תשרפון באש

But thus shall you do to them: **their altars** you shall break down, and **their pillars** you shall smash, and **their sacred posts** you shall cut down, and **their graven images** you shall burn with fire.

The verbs in the linked clauses denote various types of destruction. The series of topicalized clauses highlights the common action that is to be performed on all of the cultic objects mentioned in the clauses.[34]

Paradoxically, a relation of similarity may exist even when what is stated about the linked items involves antonyms or near-antonyms:

(268) Gen 46:4

אנכי ארד עמך מצרימה **ואנכי** אעלך גם עלה

I will go down with you to Egypt, and **I** will also bring you up.

Although the verbs ארד and אעלך are near-antonyms from a semantic perspective, the clauses in their entirety are more similar than oppositional: the point is that God will be with Jacob both at the start and the conclusion of the exile to Egypt. A similar example is (269):

(269) Gen 34:9 [35]

והתחתנו אתנו **בנתיכם** תתנו לנו **ואת בנתינו** תקחו לכם:

Intermarry with us. **Your daughters** give to us, and **our daughters** take for yourselves.

---

34. Other representative examples of chains with a relation of similarity from the classical BH prose corpus include 1 Sam 8:11–17; 2 Sam 12:3; 2 Kgs 3:19, 23:11–13. See also the pairs of linked segments in Josh 11:6, 9.

35. See also Gen 34:16, Deut 7:3.

Although תתנו and תקחו are antonymous, the topicalized clauses are similar in that they describe two ways in which intermarrying may take place. As such, they serve as an elaboration of the introductory clause, והתחתנו אתנו.

In several cases, segments that appear to be oppositional at first glance are revealed on further reflection to be of the similarity type:[36]

(270) Gen 18:33 [37]

וילך י' כאשר כלה לדבר אל אברהם **ואברהם** שב למקמו:

And **the LORD** departed when he had finished speaking to Abraham; and [similarly] **Abraham** returned to his place

In this verse, the similarity between God's and Abram's departure is highlighted, rather than an opposition between their different destinations or between God's going and Abram's returning. In rendering the verse, *similarly* yields a more suitable result than *in contrast*: 'And God left when he finished speaking to Abram. Similarly/in contrast Abram returned to his place'.

Topicalization chains in genealogy passages involve the similarity relation. This is a frequent type of topicalization in Genesis:[38]

(271) Gen 4:18

ויולד לחנוך את **עירד ועירד** ילד את **מחויאל ומחייאל** ילד את **מתושאל**
ומתושאל ילד את למך:

And **Irad** was born to Enoch; and **Irad** fathered **Mehujael**, and **Mehujael** fathered **Methushael**, and **Methushael** fathered Lamech.

The point here is the continuation of the chain of lineage, rather than an opposition between the names.[39]

9.4.3. Addition

The additive relation pertains to speech acts rather than speaker reasoning and can be paraphrased as "I say in addition." In English, conjuncts such as *furthermore* and *moreover* mark an additive relation, and in BH the conjunct גם may be used for this purpose, as an alternative to or in combination with

36. See also, e.g., Gen 1:20, 22; and 45:14. A number of cases are ambiguous, admitting either oppositional or similarity interpretations; these include Gen 24:53, 25:33–34, 31:40, 32:1–2, and 40:21–22.

37. Appears as (237) above (p. 148).

38. Additional representative examples of topicalized clauses in genealogy passages include Gen 10:8, 13–14, 15–18, 24 (2×), 25, 26–29; 11:12, 14, 27 (2×).

39. In this example and others like it, there is an ambiguity regarding the counterparts of the preposed items. In the second clause, for example, Irad may be linked with the previous mention of this individual in the preceding clause (bold). Alternatively, Irad may be linked with his father, Enoch.

topicalization. Examples of topicalization with the additive relation include:[40]

(272) Gen 42:36

ויאמר אלהם יעקב אביהם אתי שכלתם **יוסף** איננו ו**שמעון** איננו ואת <u>בנימן</u>
<u>תקחו</u>

And Jacob their father said to them, "You have bereaved me: **Joseph** is
no more, and **Simeon** is no more, and **Benjamin** you would take."

(273) Gen 44:9 [41]

אשר ימצא אתו מעבדיך ומת וגם <u>**אנחנו** נהיה לאדני לעבדים</u>:

Whichever of your servants it is found with, he shall die, and furthermore, **we** will be my lord's slaves.

In (272), Jacob justifies his assertion that he has been and will be bereaved by
the brothers with a three-part proof. Two nonverbal clauses are followed by a
topicalized clause. In (273), the brothers specify two penalties they will incur
if the thief is among them. The first clause takes the form of a left-dislocation,
whereas the second is a topicalized clause containing the conjunct גם.[42]

9.4.4. Elaboration, summary, and paraphrase

Elaboration, summary, and *paraphrase* are coherence relations that concern
speech acts. There are no linguistic markers that explicitly signal the elaboration relation in English or in BH; the summary and paraphrase relations can be
marked in English by *to sum up* and *that is to say,* respectively. Topicalization
involving elaboration, summary, or paraphrase generally involves segments
with identical linked items.

In one pattern of the elaborative type, a forward-linking topicalization with
a preposed demonstrative pronoun is followed by a segment consisting of several clauses:[43]

(274) Gen 45:17–18

ויאמר פרעה אל יוסף אמר אל אחיך **זאת** עשו טענו את בעירכם ולכו באו
ארצה כנען: וקחו את אביכם ואת בתיכם ובאו אלי

And Pharaoh said to Joseph, "Say to your brothers, '**Thus** you shall do:
**load up your beasts and come to the land of Canaan. And take your
father and your households, and come to me.**'"

---

40. Clauses linked by an additive relation usually resemble each other in content, making it hard at times to determine whether similarity or addition is intended. Ambiguous examples include Gen 31:38, 39:8, and 41:40.

41. The word גם should be interpreted here as a conjunct rather than a focusing adverb
(see §5.2). See also Gen 21:26.

42. An additional example with גם is Gen 44:9.

43. Additional examples include Gen 42:15–16, 18–20, 33–34; 43:11–13; and 45:19.

In a second pattern of elaboration, an initial segment is followed by a backward-linking topicalization with a preposed lexical expression:[44]

(275) Gen 40:12–13[45]

שלשת השרגים **שלשת ימים** הם: **בעוד שלשת ימים** ישא פרעה את ראשך
והשיבך על כנך

Then Joseph said to him, "The three branches are **three days.** In another three days Pharaoh will lift up your head and return you to your post."

A summary relation can be observed in (276), which has a backward-linking topicalized clause with a preposed demonstrative pronoun.[46]

(276) Gen 22:20–23 [47]

ויגד לאברהם לאמר הנה ילדה מלכה גם הוא בנים לנחור אחיך: **את עוץ בכרו**
ואת בוז אחיו ואת קמואל אבי ארם: ואת כשד ואת חזו ואת פלדש ואת
ידלף ואת בתואל: ובתואל ילד את רבקה **שמנה אלה** ילדה מלכה לנחור אחי
אברהם:

And it was told to Abraham, "Behold, Milcah also has born children to your brother Nahor: **Uz the first-born, and Buz his brother, and Kemuel the father of Aram, and Chesed, and Hazo, and Pildash, and Jidlaph, and Bethuel.**" And Bethuel fathered Rebekah. **These eight** Milcah bore to Nahor, Abraham's brother.

In (277), the linked segments are related by a paraphrase relation.[48]

(277) Gen 43:9 [49]

אנכי אערבנו **מידי** תבקשנו

I will be surety for him; **from my hand** you shall require him.

9.4.5. Temporal succession

Temporal succession is a relation that pertains to the contents of the two segments and involves segments with linked temporal adjuncts. Although Genesis contains only examples of this coherence relation, the type occurs frequently in the larger classical BH prose corpus. The linked segments range from single clauses to large units; long topicalization chains also occur. Examples of single-clause segments follow:

---

44. Additional examples include Gen 8:5, 11:27, 36:1–3, and 40:18–19.
45. Appears as (245) above (p. 151).
46. An additional example is Gen 36:13.
47. Appears as (240) above (p. 150).
48. An additional example is the very similar Gen 31:39.
49. Appears above as (232) (p. 147).

(278) Exod 23:12 [50]

שֵׁשֶׁת יָמִים תַּעֲשֶׂה מַעֲשֶׂיךָ **וּבַיּוֹם הַשְּׁבִיעִי** תִּשְׁבֹּת

Six days you shall do your work, and **on the seventh day** you shall rest.

(279) 2 Sam 11:12

וַיֹּאמֶר דָּוִד אֶל אוּרִיָּה שֵׁב בָּזֶה גַּם **הַיּוֹם וּמָחָר** אֲשַׁלְּחֶךָ

Then David said to Uriah, "Remain here **today** also, and **tomorrow** I will send you off."

(280) 1 Kgs 6:37–38

בַּשָּׁנָה הָרְבִיעִית יֻסַּד בֵּית יְ' בְּיֶרַח זִו: **וּבַשָּׁנָה הָאַחַת עֶשְׂרֵה בְּיֶרַח בּוּל הוּא הַחֹדֶשׁ הַשְּׁמִינִי** כָּלָה הַבַּיִת לְכָל דְּבָרָיו וּלְכָל מִשְׁפָּטָיו

In the fourth year the foundation of the house of the LORD was laid, in the month of Ziv. And **in the eleventh year, in the month of Bul, that is the eighth month**, the house was finished in all its parts, and according to all its specifications.

An example involving larger segments is (281).[51] Each segment describes a sequence of events that begins at the time specified by the linked adjunct at its head. The first segment extends from v. 3 to v. 7, and the second segment probably extends from v. 8 to v. 21.

(281) 2 Kgs 25:3–8

בְּתִשְׁעָה לַחֹדֶשׁ וַיֶּחֱזַק הָרָעָב בָּעִיר [52] וְלֹא הָיָה לֶחֶם לְעַם הָאָרֶץ וַתִּבָּקַע הָעִיר וְכָל אַנְשֵׁי הַמִּלְחָמָה הַלַּיְלָה דֶּרֶךְ שַׁעַר בֵּין הַחֹמֹתַיִם אֲשֶׁר עַל גַּן הַמֶּלֶךְ וְכַשְׂדִּים עַל הָעִיר סָבִיב וַיֵּלֶךְ דֶּרֶךְ הָעֲרָבָה: . . . . **וּבַחֹדֶשׁ הַחֲמִישִׁי בְּשִׁבְעָה לַחֹדֶשׁ הִיא שְׁנַת תְּשַׁע עֶשְׂרֵה שָׁנָה לַמֶּלֶךְ נְבֻכַדְנֶאצַּר מֶלֶךְ בָּבֶל** בָּא נְבוּזַרְאֲדָן רַב טַבָּחִים עֶבֶד מֶלֶךְ בָּבֶל יְרוּשָׁלִָם: וַיִּשְׂרֹף אֶת בֵּית יְ' וְאֶת בֵּית הַמֶּלֶךְ וְאֵת כָּל בָּתֵּי יְרוּשָׁלִַם וְאֶת כָּל בֵּית גָּדוֹל שָׂרַף בָּאֵשׁ. . . .

On the ninth day [in the fourth month][53] and the famine was severe in the city and there was no food for the people of the land. And the city was breached; all the soldiers [fled] by night through the gate between

---

50. It is common for the first-time adjunct to express duration and the second-time adjunct to express a point in time immediately following the specified time span, as in this example. Additional representative examples from the classical BH prose corpus include Exod 22:29; 31:17; 35:2; Lev 12:2–3; 15:28–29; 19:23–24; Deut 15:12; Josh 6:3–4; 1 Kgs 8:65–66; 2 Kgs 11:3–4.

51. See also (253) and (254) (p. 154), above. Other examples include the synchronistic verses in Kings in which preposed time adverbials mark long segments describing a king's reign, for example, וּבִשְׁנַת עֶשְׂרִים לְיָרָבְעָם מֶלֶךְ יִשְׂרָאֵל מָלַךְ אָסָא מֶלֶךְ יְהוּדָה 'And in the twentieth year of Jeroboam the king of Israel, Asa the king of Judah became king' (1 Kgs 15:9).

52. The temporal adverbial is connected to its clause by a conjunction (see §5.5.2).

53. Following the standard translation, the phrase "in the fourth month" is filled in from the parallel passage in Jer 52:6.

the double walls, which is by the king's garden, and the Chaldeans were all around the city. And they went in the direction of the Arabah. . . . **And in the fifth month, on the seventh day of the month (that was the nineteenth year of King Nebuchadnezzar, king of Babylon)** Nebuzaradan, the captain of the bodyguard, a servant of the king of Babylon, came to Jerusalem. And he burned the house of the LORD, and the king's house and all the houses of Jerusalem; and every great house he burned down.

The events in the first segment do not necessarily all precede the events in the second; that is, it is not clear that Zedekiah reached Babylon before the seventh day of the fifth month. The segments are nevertheless temporally successive in that the first sequence begins prior to the inception of the second sequence.

9.5. Conclusion

Topicalization functions as a discourse-connective device, signaling that the marked clause bears a coherence relation to an adjacent discourse segment, either preceding or following. Topicalization marks the preposed item as linked to an item in the first clause of the adjacent segment; the linked items bear a contextual relation which may be of a logical or ad hoc nature.

The specific coherence relation between the linked segments is not specified by topicalization. By examining the segments in the light of the linked items, the addressee infers the intended relation between the clauses. The most common relations are opposition and similarity, both of which are epistemic relations. Opposition always obtains between a pair of linked segments, while similarity may involve a topicalization chain. Oppositional segments may or may not exhibit parallel semantic and syntactic structure. In some cases, the relation between the linked items is crucial to the semantic interpretation of the two segments, as in the case of literally contradictory segments. Oppositional segments also occur in *a fortiori* arguments, highlighting the "major/minor" relation crucial to the argument.

Topicalization may involve a speech act relation such as addition, elaboration, summary, or paraphrase. The last three types are characteristic of topicalization involving identical linked items. When linked time adjuncts are involved, the coherence relation is the content relation of temporal succession. This type may involve a chain of long discourse segments, each describing a series of sequential events.

The topicalized clause, at least in the Genesis corpus, always occurs in the context of a second segment to which it is related. In contrast, the focused clause can occur as an isolated clause, relating to information activated by the extratextual situation.

Topicalization does not mark a constituent as focus. Although in a subset of oppositional topicalized clauses, it is possible to view the final constituent as a focus from a pragmatic perspective, this constituent is not syntactically marked in any way.

Chapter 10
Conclusion

The purpose of this study was to investigate BH preposing from a syntactic and pragmatic perspective, using the Genesis corpus as the basis of a statistical analysis. To this end, syntactic categories were defined, making possible the delineation and classification of clause units. Preposing was distinguished from other similar syntactic constructions and the preposed constituent distinguished from other preverbal elements such as clausal adverbs, negative particles, and left-dislocated elements. The various preverbal elements were ranked in terms of their degree of detachment from the clause. Marked preposing was distinguished from syntactically obligatory preposing, which lacks a pragmatic function.

The thesis was advanced that the majority of instances of preposing can be classified as either focusing or topicalization. In order to substantiate this thesis it was necessary to develop a clear and precise understanding of these two concepts, which have been understood in a variety of ways in the linguistic literature and in the literature on BH word order. Focusing was defined based on the concept of informational focus and was put in the context of a current psycholinguistic theory of text comprehension. The distinction between activation and presupposition was shown to be crucial for the proper understanding of BH focusing. Theories on the English topicalization construction were explored in order to glean insights regarding BH topicalization. A new conception of BH topicalization as a discourse-connective device was presented. It was shown that the pragmatic functions of focusing and topicalization are of two different types. Both address the interpretation of the clause in its context, but the relevant context in the case of focusing is information in the hearer's consciousness, and the context in the case of topicalization is an adjacent text segment.

A statistical analysis of Genesis was presented, demonstrating that focusing and topicalization account for about 57% of the preposed clauses in the corpus; this figure is higher (67%) in narrative clauses and lower (50%) in direct-speech clauses. The actual figures may be slightly higher, because it is likely that some clauses in the residue were intended as focused clauses, despite the lack of contextual evidence for an appropriate activated proposition.

In contrast to the relatively high frequency of information-structure functions, functions relating to the clause as a whole, such as marking simultaneity,

167

anteriority, background information, the beginning of a narrative unit, justification, affirmation, or boasting, together characterize a little more than one-tenth of the clauses. The explanation for the preposing in 31% of clauses is currently unclear; the overwhelming majority of the unexplained clauses are in direct speech. Thus, functions discussed in this work provide a relatively complete account of preposing in narrative and account for preposing in direct speech to a lesser degree.

The statistical analysis revealed significant differences between preposing patterns in direct speech and in narrative. The impression that word order in direct speech is "freer" than in narrative is due to two factors: first, direct speech has a significantly higher incidence of preposing than narrative, and, second, direct speech has a higher proportion of preposed clauses the pragmatic function of which is unclear.

It was shown that preposing for focus in BH relates to an activated but not necessarily presupposed proposition. Despite the fact that BH focused clauses are often rendered with a cleft sentence in English, the English constructions most equivalent to BH focusing are focusing by accent marking and preposing (in the casual register), both of which relate to activated propositions. The presupposition/activation distinction clarifies several important points regarding BH preposing for focus, including the fact that yes-no questions and commands, which often do not involve presupposition, may be focused. The distinction also helps to explain how additive focusing by preposing differs from focusing by גם, an adverb that can relate to a presupposed but non-activated proposition. It also explains why some focus-of-negation clauses cannot be appropriately translated with an English negative cleft sentence: because clefts relate to presupposed information, a cleft is an appropriate translation for focus-of-negation only when the relevant activated proposition happens to be presupposed as well.

As a discourse-connective device, topicalization functions in a manner similar to the clausal adverb of the conjunct type (see §5.2.1). Like conjuncts, topicalization can link single clauses or larger adjacent segments. Like the conjunct הלוא, topicalization can create a link to a preceding or a following segment. Both topicalization and conjuncts are used to indicate a coherence relation between discourse segments, such as opposition, addition, elaboration, and summarizing. Nevertheless, there are important differences between the two devices. First, conjuncts are usually specific to a particular coherence relation; for example, אולם indicates contrast and גם an additive relation on the speech-act level (see §5.2.1, p. 72 n. 24, and §9.4.3). Topicalization, however, marks a range of coherence relations. A feature unique to topicalization is the link it highlights or creates between two items and the connection between this link and the coherence relation obtaining between the clauses. For example, while the conjunct גם can be used to connect clauses with an overall thematic similarity but no specific parallel elements, the similarity in additive topicalization directly concerns the pair of linked items.

By highlighting a relation such as opposition or similarity, topicalization gives the hearer/reader a nuanced appreciation of the contribution of the clause to its context. At times, understanding the coherence relation signaled by topicalization is essential for the correct interpretation of the linked clauses. In seemingly self-contradictory units in which the linked items are a set and a member of that set, topicalization assists the reader in inferring which proposition is actually expressed by the first clause. In the *a fortiori* argument, the hearer/reader's acceptance of the argument hinges on the recognition of a "minor/major" relation between the items linked by topicalization.

Although the present research has underlined the importance of information-structure functions for the understanding of preposing, the fact that a third of the clauses remain unexplained means that the picture is far from complete. Future research is needed to illuminate the function of preposing in clauses that are not focused or topicalized and do not have any of the clause-level functions discussed here. Other avenues of research unexplored here include the syntactic and pragmatic analysis of preposing in subordinate clauses and the investigation of the pragmatics of marked constructions such as double preposing, preposing with focus adverbs, and left-dislocation. Like preposing, left-dislocation can be used for focusing and topicalization. An issue worthy of investigation is whether Polak's (1999, 2001, 2003) distinction of various direct speech and narrative styles (see §1.2) sheds further light on the statistical distribution of the various functional types of preposing. An important topic explored by Lunn (2006) and worthy of continued investigation is the degree to which pragmatic functions such as focusing and topicalization play a role in the word order of biblical poetry.

The concepts of focusing and topicalization as developed in this work lead to a richer understanding of the importance of preposing for the pragmatic interpretation of the sentence. Focusing and topicalization are conceived here as syntactic-pragmatic categories that have equivalents in English and other languages. The findings of this study, therefore, are potentially relevant to marked constructions in other languages as well. As such, this study plays a part in the cross-linguistic investigation of marked forms with a pragmatic contribution to sentence meaning.

References

Abadi, Adina
1988   תחביר השיח של העברית החדשה [*Discourse syntax of contemporary Hebrew*]. Jerusalem: Magnes.

Aejmelaeus, Anneli
1986   Function and interpretation of כי in Biblical Hebrew. *JBL* 105: 193–209.

Alter, Robert
1996   *Genesis: Translation and commentary*. New York: Norton.

Andersen, Francis I.
1970   *The Hebrew verbless clause in the Pentateuch*. Journal of Biblical Literature Monograph Series 14. Nashville: Abingdon.

1974   *The sentence in Biblical Hebrew*. Janua Linguarum Series Practica 231. The Hague: Mouton.

Andersen, Francis I., and Forbes, A. Dean
1983   "Prose particle" counts of the Hebrew Bible. Pp. 165–83 in *The Word of the Lord shall go forth: Essays in honor of David Noel Freedman in celebration of his sixtieth birthday*, ed. Carol L. Meyers and M. O'Connor. American Schools of Oriental Research Special Volume Series 1. Winona Lake, IN: Eisebrauns.

Andrews, Avery
1985   The major functions of the noun phrase. Pp. 62–154 in *Clause structure*, vol. 1 of Shopen 1985.

Ariel, Mira
2001   Accessibility theory: An overview. Pp. 29–87 in Sanders, Schilperoord, and Spooren 2001.

Azar, Moshe
1972   סימני הצרכה, מלות הדרכה והיחידות המילוניות של הפועל: עיון תחבירי וסמנטי בפעלים בעלי משלימים [A syntactic and semantic approach to verbs governing prepositional phrases]. *Leš* 36: 220–27, 282–86.

1993   לקראת הבנת המשפט הממוקד בעברית בת-זמננו [Towards an understanding of the focused clause in contemporary Hebrew]. Pp. 87–99 in vol. 1 of העברית שפה חיה: קובץ מחקרים על הלשון בהקשריה החברתיים-תרבותיים בעקבות כנס אורנים תש"ן [*Hebrew: A living language. Studies on the language in social and cultural contexts*], ed. Uzi Arnon, Rina Ben-Shahar, and Gideon Toury. Haifa: University of Haifa Press.

Bailey, Nicholas A.
2004   A second look at double preverbal constituents. Review of Gross (2001). *HS* 45: 253–76.

Bailey, Nicholas A., and Levinsohn, Stephen H.
1992   The function of preverbal elements in independent clauses in the Hebrew narrative of Genesis. *JTT* 5: 179–207.

Bandstra, Barry L
1982   *The syntax of particle KY in Biblical Hebrew and Ugaritic.* Ph.D. diss. Yale University.
1992   Word order and emphasis in Biblical Hebrew narrative: Syntactic observations on Genesis 22 from a discourse perspective. Pp. 109–23 in Bodine 1992.

Battistella, Edwin L.
1996   *The logic of markedness.* New York: Oxford University Press.

Ben-Asher, Mordechai
1973   להבחנה בין מושא עקיף ותיאור-פועל [On the distinction between indirect object and adverbial]. Pp. 54–71 in עיונים בתחביר העברית החדשה [*Studies in modern Hebrew syntax*]. Tel Aviv: Hakibbutz Hameuhad.

Bendavid, Abba
1958   כיצד סדר נושא ונשוא [On the order of subject and predicate]. *LešLaʿam* 9: 67–75, 97–107, 149–65.
1971   לשון מקרא ולשון חכמים [*Biblical Hebrew and Mishnaic Hebrew*], vol 2: דקדוק ותרגילי סגנון [*Grammar and style*]. Tel Aviv: Dvir.

Ben-Ḥayyim, Zeʾev
2000   *A grammar of Samaritan Hebrew: Based on the recitation of the Law in comparison with the Tiberian and other Jewish traditions,* rev. and trans. Abraham Tal. Jerusalem: Magnes.

Ben-Horin, Gad
1976   Aspects of syntactic preposing in spoken Hebrew. Pp. 193–207 in *Studies in Modern Hebrew syntax and semantics: The transformational generative approach,* ed. Peter Cole. Amsterdam: North-Holland.

Bergen, Robert D., ed.
1994   *Biblical Hebrew and discourse linguistics.* Dallas: SIL.

Bergsträsser, Gotthelf
1962   *Hebräische Grammatik,* part 2: *Verbum,* ed. E. Kautzch. Hildesheim: Olms.

Berlin, Adele
1985   *The dynamics of Biblical parallelism.* Bloomington: Indiana University Press.

Berman, Ruth A.
1980   The case of an (S)VO language: Subjectless constructions in modern Hebrew. *Lang* 56: 759–76.
1997   Modern Hebrew. Pp. 312–33 in *The Semitic languages,* ed. Robert Hetzron. Routledge Language Family Descriptions. London: Routledge.

Birner, Betty J., and Gregory Ward
1998   *Information status and noncanonical word order in English.* Studies in Language Companion Series 40. Amsterdam: Benjamins.

Blakemore, Diane

1987   *Semantic constraints on relevance*. Oxford: Blackwell.

Blau, Joshua

1959   Adverbia als psychologische un grammatische Subjekte/Prädikate im Bibel-
        hebräisch. *VT* 9: 130–37.

1972   על חזרת הנשוא במקרא [On the repetition of the predicate in the Bible]. Pp.
        234–40 in ליוור י׳ של לזכרו מחקרים :ישראל ותולדות המקרא [*Bible and Jewish
        history: Studies in Bible and Jewish history dedicated to the memory of Ja-
        cob Leiver*], ed. Benjamin Uffenheimer. Tel Aviv: Tel Aviv University Press.
        Repr., pp. 124–30 in עברית בבלשנות עיונים [*Studies in Hebrew linguistics*] by
        Joshua Blau. Jerusalem: Magnes, 1996.

1973a   כיצד להבחין בהוראה בין מושא עקיף לתיאור [How to distinguish between indi-
        rect objects and adverbials in teaching]. *Leš* 37: 202–4.

1973b   על מבנה המשפט השמני בתורה [On the structure of the nominal sentence in the
        Bible]. Review essay on Andersen 1970. *Leš* 37: 69–74.

1977   *An adverbial construction in Hebrew and Arabic: Sentence adverbials in
        frontal position separated from the rest of the sentence*. Proceedings of the
        Israel Academy of Sciences and Humanities 6/1. Jerusalem: Israel Academy
        of Sciences and Humanities.

1993   *A grammar of biblical Hebrew*. 2nd ed. Porta Linguarum Orientalium n.s. 12.
        Wiesbaden: Harrassowitz.

Bloch, Alfred

1946   *Vers und Sprache im altarabischen: Metrische und syntaktische Untersuc-
        hungen*. Acta Tropica Supplementa 5. Basel: Recht & Gesellschaft.

Bloch, Ariel A.

1986   *Studies in Arabic syntax and semantics*. Wiesbaden: Harrassowitz.

Bodine, Walter R., ed.

1992   *Linguistics and Biblical Hebrew*. Winona Lake, IN: Eisenbrauns.

1995   *Discourse analysis of biblical literature: What it is and what it offers*.
        SBLSemeiaSt. Atlanta: Scholars Press.

Bolkestein, A. Machtelt

1998   What to do with topic and focus? Evaluating pragmatic information. Pp. 193–
        214 in *Functional grammar and verbal interaction*, ed. Mike Hannay and
        A. Machtelt Bolkestein. Studies in Language Companion Series 44. Amster-
        dam: Benjamins.

Bosch, Peter, and van der Sandt, Rob, eds.

1999   *Focus: Linguistic, cognitive, and computational perspectives*. Studies in Nat-
        ural Language Processing. Cambridge: Cambridge University Press.

Bravmann, M. M.

1953   *Studies in Arabic and general syntax*. Cairo: Institut Francais d'Archeologie
        Orientale.

Brockelmann, Carl

1956   *Hebräische Syntax*. Neukirchen-Vluyn: Moers.

Brody, Jill

1984   Some problems with the concept of basic word order. *Ling* 22: 711–36.

Brongers, Hendrik A.
   1981   Some remarks on the biblical particle "hᵃlō." Pp. 177–89 in *Remembering all the way: A collection of Old Testament studies published on the occasion of the fortieth anniversary of the Oudtestamentisch Werkgezelschap in Nederland*, ed. B. Albrekton. OTS 21. Leiden: Brill.
Brown, Gillian, and George Yule
   1983   *Discourse analysis*. Cambridge Textbooks in Linguistics. Cambridge: Cambridge University Press.
Brown, Michael L.
   1987   "Is it not?" or "indeed!": *HL* in Northwest Semitic. *Maarav* 4: 201–19.
Buth, Randall
   1987   *Word order in Aramaic from the perspectives of functional grammar and discourse analysis*. Ph.D. diss. University of California.
   1990   Word order differences between narrative and non-narrative material in Biblical Hebrew. Pp. 9–16 in vol. 1 of *Proceedings of the Tenth World Congress of Jewish Studies, Jerusalem August 16–24 1989*. Jerusalem: World Union of Jewish Studies.
   1992   Topic and focus in Hebrew poetry: Psalm 51. Pp. 83–96 in *Language in context: Essays for Robert E. Longacre*, ed. Shin Ja J. Hwand and William R. Merrifield. SIL and the University of Texas at Arlington Publications in Linguistics 107. Arlington: SIL and the University of Texas at Arlington.
   1994a   Methodological collision between source criticism and discourse analysis. Pp. 138–54 in Bergen 1994.
   1994b   Contextualizing constituent as topic, non-sequential background and dramatic pause: Hebrew and Aramaic evidence. Pp. 215–31 in *Function and expression in functional grammar*, ed. Elisabeth Engberg-Pedersen, Lisbeth F. Jakobsen, and Lone S. Rasmussen. Functional Grammar Series 16. Berlin: de Gruyter.
   1995   Functional Grammar, Hebrew and Aramaic: An integrated, textlinguistic approach to syntax. Pp. 77–102 in Bodine 1995.
   1999   Word order in the verbless clause: A generative-functional approach. Pp. 79–108 in Miller 1999.
Carnie, Andrew, and Guilfoyle, Eithne, eds.
   2000   *The syntax of the verb initial languages*. Oxford Studies in Comparative Syntax. New York: Oxford University Press.
Cassuto, U.
   1961a   A *commentary on the book of Genesis*, part 1: *From Adam to Noah*, trans. Israel Abrahams. Publications of the Perry Foundation for Biblical Research in the Hebrew University of Jerusalem. Jerusalem: Magnes.
   1961b   *The documentary hypothesis and the composition of the Pentateuch: Eight lectures*, trans. Israel Abrahams. Publications of the Perry Foundation for Biblical Research in the Hebrew University of Jerusalem. Jerusalem: Magnes.
Chafe, Wallace
   1976   Givenness, contrastiveness, definiteness, subjects and topics. Pp. 27–55 in Li 1976.

1987   Cognitive constraints on information flow. Pp. 21–51 in *Coherence and grounding in discourse: Outcome of a symposium, Eugene, Oregon, June 1984*, ed. Russell S. Tomlin. TSL 11. Amsterdam: Benjamins.

1994   *Discourse, consciousness and time: The flow and displacement of conscious experience in speaking and writing*. Chicago: University of Chicago Press.

Chatman, Seymour, and Samuel R. Levin, eds.

1967   *Essays on the language of literature*. Boston: Houghton.

Chavel, Chaim Dov, ed.

1966   רבנו בחיי: באור על התורה [*Rabbeinu Baḥye: Commentary on the Pentateuch*]. 3 vols. Jerusalem: Mossad Harav Kook.

1983   פרוש רש״י על התורה על פי דפוס ראשון, כתב־יד אוכספורד ומהדורת ברלינר, עם מבוא, שינויי נוסחאות, ציוני מקורות, מקבילות, הערות וביאורים [Rashi's commentary on the Pentateuch]. Jerusalem: Mossad Harav Kook.

Childs, Brevard S.

1979   *Introduction to the Old Testament as Scripture*. Philadelphia: Fortress.

Chomsky, Noam

1970   Deep structure, surface structure and semantic interpretation. Pp. 52–91 in *Studies in general and Oriental linguistics: Presented to Shiro Hattori on the occasion of his sixtieth birthday*, ed. Roman Jakobson and Shigeo Kawamoto. Tokyo: TEC. Repr., pp. 62–119 in *Studies on semantics in generative grammar*, ed. Noam Chomsky. Janua Linguarum Series Minor 107. Paris: Mouton, 1972.

1977   On Wh-Movement. Pp. 71–132 in *Formal syntax*, ed. Peter W. Culicover, Thomas Wasow, and Adrian Akmajian. New York: Academic Press.

Claassen, Walter T.

1983   Speaker-orientated functions of *kî* in Biblical Hebrew. *JNSL* 11: 29–46.

Clark, Herbert H., and Haviland, Susan E.

1977   Comprehension and the given-new contract. Pp. 1–40 in *Discourse production and comprehension*, ed. Roy O. Freedle. Discourse Processes: Advances in Research and Theory 1. Norwood, NJ: Ablex.

Collins, John C.

1995   The *wayyiqtol* as "pluperfect": When and why. *Tyndale Bulletin* 46: 117–40.

Comrie, Bernard

1989   *Language universals and linguistic typology: Syntax and morphology*. 2nd ed. Oxford: Blackwell.

Cook, John A.

2001   The Hebrew verb: A grammaticalization approach. *ZAH* 14: 117–43.

2004   The semantics of verbal pragmatics: Clarifying the roles of *wayyiqtol* and *weqatal* in Biblical Hebrew prose. *JSS* 49: 247–73.

Coulmas, Florian, ed.

1986   *Direct and indirect speech*. Trends in Linguistics Studies and Monographs 31. Berlin: de Gruyter.

Creider, Chet A.

1979   On the explanation of transformations. Pp. 3–21 in Givón 1979.

Croft, William
2003   *Typology and universals*. 2nd ed. Cambridge Textbooks in Linguistics. Cambridge: Cambridge University Press.

Culicover, Peter W. and Louise McNally, eds.
1998   *The limits of syntax*. Syntax and Semantics 29. San Diego: Academic Press.

Davidson, A. B.
1901   *Hebrew syntax*. 3rd ed. Edinburgh: T. & T. Clark.

Davis, Steven, ed.
1991   *Pragmatics: A reader*. Oxford: Oxford University Press.

Dawson, David A.
1994   *Text-linguistics and Biblical Hebrew*. JSOTSup 177. Sheffield: Sheffield Academic Press.

DeCaen, Vincent
1995   *On the placement and interpretation of the verb in Standard Biblical Hebrew prose*. Ph.D. diss. University of Toronto.
1999   A unified analysis of verbal and verbless clauses within Government-Binding theory. Pp. 109–31 in Miller 1999.

Dempster, Stephen G.
1985   *Linguistic features of Hebrew narrative: a discourse analysis of narrative from the classical period*. Ph.D. diss. University of Toronto.

Dijk, Teun A. van
1977   *Text and context: explorations in the semantics and the pragmatics of discourse*. Longman Linguistics Library 21. London: Longman.
1979   Pragmatic connectives. *JPrag* 3: 447–56.

Dik, Simon C.
1980   *Studies in functional grammar*. London: Academic Press.
1989   *The theory of functional grammar*, part 1: *The structure of the clause*. Functional Grammar Series 9. Dordrecht: Foris.

Dik, Simon; Hoffman, Maria; de Jong, Jan R.; Djiang, Sie I.; Stroomer, Harry; and de Vries, Lourens
1981   On the typology of focus phenomena. Pp. 41–74 in Hoekstra et al. 1981.

Disse, Andreas
1998   *Informationsstruktur im biblischen Hebräisch: Sprachwissenschaftliche Grundlagen und exegetische Konsequenzen einer Korpusuntersuchung zu den Buchern Deuteronomium, Richter und 2 Könige*. 2 vols. Arbeiten zu Text und Sprache im Alten Testament 56. St. Ottilien: EOS.

Downing, Pamela
1995   Word order in discourse: By way of introduction. Pp. 1–28 in Downing and Noonan 1995.

Downing, Pamela, and Noonan, Michael, eds.
1995   *Word order in discourse*. TSL 30. Amsterdam: Benjamins.

Driver, S. R.
1892   *A treatise on the use of the tenses in Hebrew and some other syntactical questions*. 3rd ed. London: Oxford University Press. Repr., Biblical Resource Series. Grand Rapids: Eerdmans, 1998.

1913   *An introduction to the literature of the Old Testament.* 9th ed. Edinburgh: T. & T. Clark.

Dryer, Matthew S.

1995   Frequency and pragmatically unmarked word order. Pp. 105–35 in Downing and Noonan 1995.

1996   Focus, pragmatic presupposition and activated propositions. *JPrag* 26: 475–523.

Dyk, Janet W., and Talstra, Eep

1999   Paradigmatic and syntagmatic features in identifying subject and predicate in nominal clauses. Pp. 133–85 in Miller 1999.

Erteschik-Shir, Nomi

1997   *The dynamics of focus structure.* Cambridge Studies in Linguistics 84. New York: Cambridge University Press.

1998   The syntax-focus structure interface. Pp. 211–40 in Culicover and McNally 1998.

Esh, Shaul

1957   על מלות-פתיחה לפני דיבור ישיר בעברית [On particles introducing direct speech in Hebrew]. *Leš* 22: 48–53.

Eskhult, Mats

1990   *Studies in verbal aspect and narrative technique in Biblical Hebrew prose.* Studia Semitica Upsaliensia 12. Uppsala: Almqvist & Wiksell.

Exter Blokland, A. F. den

1995   *In search of text syntax: Towards a syntactic text-segmentation model for Biblical Hebrew.* Applicatio 14. Amsterdam: VU University Press.

Ewald, Heinrich

1879   *Syntax of the Hebrew language of the Old Testament,* trans. James Kennedy. Edinburgh: T. & T. Clark.

Firbas, Jan

1966a   On defining the theme in functional sentence analysis. *Travaux linguistiques de Prague* 1: 267–80.

1966b   Non-thematic subjects in contemporary English. *Travaux linguistiques de Prague* 2: 239–56.

1992   *Functional sentence perspective in written and spoken communication.* Studies in English Language. Cambridge: Cambridge University Press.

Floor, Sebastian J.

2003   From word order to theme in Biblical Hebrew narrative: Some perspectives from information structure. *JSem* 12: 197–236.

2004   *From information structure, topic and focus, to theme in Biblical Hebrew narrative.* Ph.D. diss. University of Stellenbosch.

2005   Poetic fronting in a wisdom poetry text: The information structure of Proverbs 7. *JNSL* 31: 23-58.

Fokkelman, J. P.

1991   *Narrative art in Genesis: Specimens of stylistic and structural analysis.* 2nd ed. Biblical Seminar 12. Sheffield: JSOT Press.

Follingstad, Carl M.
 1995   Hinnēh and focus function: With application to Tyap. *JTT* 7: 1–24.
 2001   *Deictic viewpoint in Biblical Hebrew text: A syntagmatic and paradigmatic analysis of the particle* כי. Dallas: SIL.
Folmer, M. L.
 1995   *The Aramaic language in the Achaemenid period: A study in linguistic variation.* Orientalia Lovaniensia Analecta 68. Leuven: Peeters.
Fox, Andrew
 1983   Topic continuity in early Biblical Hebrew. Pp. 215–54 in Givón 1983.
Fraser, Bruce
 1990   An approach to discourse markers. *JPrag* 14: 383–95.
 1996   Pragmatic markers. *Prag* 6: 167–90.
Freedman, David N.
 1977   Pottery, poetry and prophecy: An essay on Biblical poetry" *JBL* 96: 5–26.
Friedman, Richard Elliott
 1997   *Who wrote the Bible?* 2nd ed. New York: Harper & Row.
Garr, W. Randall
 2004   הן. *RB* 111: 321–44.
Ginsberg, H. L.
 1942   Aramaic Studies Today. *JAOS* 62: 229–38.
Giora, Rachel
 1982   סדר המלים במשפט ויחסו אל הטקסט: נתוח פונקציונליסטי-פרגמטי של משפטים ממוקדים [The function of topicalization at the sentence and discourse level]. Pp. 301–39 in עיונים בחקר השיח: קובץ מאמרים [*Studies in discourse analysis*], ed. Shoshana Blum-Kulka, Yishai Tobin, and Raphael Nir. Jerusalem: Hebrew University Press.
Givón, Talmy
 1977   The drift from VSO to SVO in Biblical Hebrew: The pragmatics of tense-aspect. Pp. 181–254 in *Mechanisms of syntactic change*, ed. Charles N. Li. Austin: University of Texas Press.
 1979   *Discourse and syntax.* Syntax and Semantics 12. New York: Academic Press.
 1983   *Topic continuity in discourse: A quantitative cross-language study.* TSL 3. Amsterdam: Benjamins.
 1987   Beyond foreground and background. Pp. 175–88 in *Coherence and grounding in discourse: Outcome of a symposium, Eugene, Oregon, June 1984*, ed. Russell S. Tomlin. TSL 11. Amsterdam: Benjamins.
 2001   *Syntax: An introduction.* Rev. ed. 2 vols. Amsterdam: Benjamins.
Glinert, Lewis
 1989   *The grammar of Modern Hebrew.* Cambridge: Cambridge University Press.
Goldenberg, Gideon
 1971   Tautological infinitive. *IOS* 1: 36–85. Repr., pp. 66–115 in Goldenberg 1998b.
 1977   Imperfectly-transformed cleft sentences. Pp. 127–33 in vol. 1 of *Proceedings of the Sixth World Congress of Jewish Studies*. Jerusalem: World Union of Jewish Studies. Repr., pp. 116–22 in Goldenberg 1998b.
 1991   On direct speech and the Hebrew Bible. Pp. 79–96 in Jongeling et al. 1991.

1998a   On verbal structure and the Hebrew verb. Pp. 148–96 in Goldenberg 1998b.
        English translation of על תורת הפועל והפועל העברי. *Language Studies* 1
        (1985): 295–348.
1998b   *Studies in Semitic linguistics: Selected writings.* Jerusalem: Magnes.
Goldfajn, Tal
1998   *Word order and time in Biblical Hebrew narrative.* Oxford Theological
        Monographs. Oxford: Clarendon.
Gómez-González, María A.
2001   *The theme-topic interface: Evidence from English.* Pragmatics and Beyond
        n.s. 71. Philadelphia: Benjamins.
Gordis, Reuben (Robert)
1944   על מבנה השירה העברית הקדמה [On the structure of ancient biblical poetry].
        Sefer Hashanah: The American Hebrew Year Book 7: 136–59.
Goutsos, Dionysis
1997   *Modeling discourse topic: Sequential relations and strategies in expository
        text.* Advances in Discourse Processes 59. Norwood: Ablex.
Graesser, Arthur C.; Wiemer-Hastings, Peter; and Wiemer-Hastings, Katja
2001   Constructing inferences and relations during text comprehension. Pp. 249–71
        in *Text representation: Linguistic and psycholinguistic aspects*, ed. Ted Sand-
        ers, Joost Schilperoord, and Wilbert Spooren. Human Cognitive Processing
        8. Philadelphia: Benjamins.
Greenberg, Joseph H.
1966a   Some universals of grammar with particular reference to the order of mean-
        ingful elements. Pp. 73–113 in *Universals of language.* Cambridge: MIT
        Press.
1966b   *Language universals, with special reference to feature hierarchies.* Janua
        Linguarum Series Minor 59. The Hague: Mouton.
Greenstein, Eliezer (Ed)
2000   הדיבור הישיר וצורת התקבלת [Direct discourse and parallelism]. Pp. 33–40 in
        עיוני מקרא ופרשנות כרך ה: מנחות ידידות והוקרה לאוריאל סימון [*Studies in Bible
        and exegesis*, vol. 5: *Presented to Uriel Simon*], ed. Moshe Garsiel, Shmuel
        Vargon, Amos Frisch, and Jacob Kugel. Ramat Gan: Bar Ilan University
        Press.
Gregory, Michelle L., and Michaelis, Laura A.
2001   Topicalization and left-dislocation: A functional opposition revisited. *JPrag*
        33: 1665–706.
Grimes, Joseph E.
1975   *The thread of discourse.* Janua Linguarum Series Minor 207. The Hague:
        Mouton.
Gross, Walter
1986   Zum problem der Satzgrenzen im Hebräischen: Beobachtungen an Pendens-
        konstruktionen. *BN* 35: 50–72.
1987a   Zur Syntagmen-Folge im hebräischen Verbalsatz: Die Stellung des Subjekts
        in Dtn 1–15. *BN* 40: 63–96.

1987b *Die Pendenskonstruktion im biblischen Hebräisch: Studien zum althebrae-*
       ischen Satz 1. Arbeiten zu Text und Sprache im Alten Testament 27. Mün-
       chener Universitätsschriften. St. Ottilien: EOS.

1988a Der Einfluss der Pronominalisierung auf die Syntagmen-Folge im he-
       bräischen Verbalsatz, untersucht an Dtn 1–25. *BN* 43: 49–69.

1988b Satzgrenzen bei Pendenskonstruktionen: Der Pendenssatz. Pp. 249–58 in
       Text and Context: Old Testament and Semitic Studies for F.C. Fensham, ed.
       W. Claassen. JSOTSup 48. Sheffield: JSOT Press.

1993a Die Position des Subjekts im Hebräischen Verbalsatz, untersucht an den asyn-
       detischen ersten Redesätzen in Gen, Ex 1–19, Jos–2 Kön. *ZAH* 6: 170–87.

1993b Das Vorfeld als strukturell eigenständiger Bereich des hebräischen Verbal-
       satzes. Pp. 1–24 in *Syntax und Text: Beiträge zur 22. Internationalen Öku-*
       menischen Hebräisch-Dozenten-Konferenz 1993 in Bamberg, ed. Hubert
       Irsigler. Münchener Universitätsschriften. Arbeiten zu Text und Sprache im
       Alten Testament 40. St. Ottilien: EOS.

1994   Zur syntaktischen Struktur des Vorfeldes im hebräischen Verbalsatz. *ZAH* 7:
       203–14.

1996   *Die Satzteilfolge im Verbalsatz alttestamentlicher Prosa: Untersucht an den*
       Buchern Dtn, Ri und 2Kon. Forschungen zum alten Testament 17. Tübingen:
       Mohr Seibeck.

1999   Is there really a compound nominal clause in Biblical Hebrew? Pp. 19–49 in
       Miller 1999.

2001a *Doppelt besetztes Vorfeld: Syntaktische, pragmatische und ubersetzung-*
       stechnische Studien zum althebraischen Verbsaltz. Beihefte zur Zeitschrift
       fur die alttestamentliche Wissenschaft 305. Berlin: de Gruyter.

2001b Die Stellung der Zeitangabe in Sätzen mit zwei oder mehr nominalen/pro-
       nominalen Satzteilen vor dem Verbum finitum in alttestamentlicher Poesie.
       Pp. 35–50 in *Sachverhalt und Zeitbezug: Semitistische und alttestamentliche*
       Studien. Adolf Denz zum 65. Geburtstag, ed. Rüdiger Bartelmus and Norbert
       Nebes. Wiesbaden: Harrassowitz.

2004   Satzteilfolge—Aufmerksamkeitsleitung—Gedankenführung. *KUSATU* 5: 33–
       66.

Gundel, Jeanette K.

1977   *The role of topic and comment in linguistic theory.* Bloomington: Indiana
       University Linguistics Club.

1985   Shared knowledge and topicality. *JPrag* 9: 83–107.

1988   Universals of topic-comment structure. Pp. 209–39 in *Studies in syntactic ty-*
       pology, ed. Michael Hammond, Edith Moravcsik, and Jessica Wirth. TSL 17.
       Amsterdam: Benjamins.

1999   On different kinds of focus. Pp. 293–305 in Bosch and Sandt 1999.

Gundel, Jeanette K.; Hedberg, Nancy; and Zacharski, Ron

1993   Cognitive status and the form of referring expressions in discourse. *Lang* 69:
       274–307.

Gussenhoven, Carlos

1999   On the limits of focus projection in English. Pp. 43–55 in Bosch and Sandt
       1999.

Halliday, M. A. K.
1967   Notes on transitivity and theme in English: Part 2. *JLing* 3:199–244.
2004   *An introduction to functional grammar.* 3rd ed. London: Arnold.
Halliday, M. A. K., and Hasan, Ruqaiya
1976   *Cohesion in English.* English Language Series 9. London: Longman.
Hannay, Mike
1991   Pragmatic function assignment and word order variation in a functional grammar of English. *JPrag* 16: 131–55.
Hatav, Galia
1985   Criteria for identifying the foreground. *TheorLing* 12: 265–73.
1997   *The semantics of aspect and modality: Evidence from English and Biblical Hebrew.* Studies in Language Companion Series 34. Amsterdam: Benjamins.
2000a   (Free) direct discourse in Biblical Hebrew. *HS* 41: 7–30.
2000b   תנועת הזמן בסיפור המקראי [Movement of time in biblical narrative]. *BI* 47: 63–84.
Heimerdinger, Jean-Marc
1999   *Topic, focus and foreground in ancient Hebrew narratives.* JSOTSup 295. Sheffield: Sheffield Academic Press.
Heller, Roy L.
2004   *Narrative structure and discourse constellations: An analysis of clause function in Biblical Hebrew prose.* Harvard Semitic Studies 55. Winona Lake, IN: Eisenbrauns.
Hirschberg, Julia L.
1991   *A theory of scalar implicature.* Outstanding Dissertations in Linguistics. New York: Garland.
Hockett, Charles F.
1958   *A course in modern linguistics.* New York: Macmillan.
Hoekstra, Teun; van der Hulst, Harry; and Moortgat, Michael, eds.
1981   *Perspectives on Functional Grammar.* Dordrecht: Foris.
Hoftijzer, Jacob
1973   The nominal clause reconsidered. Review essay on Andersen 1970. *VT* 23: 446–510.
1981   *A search for method: A study in the syntactic use of the h-locale in Classical Hebrew.* SSLL 12. Leiden: Brill.
1985   *The function and use of the imperfect forms with nun paragogicum in Classical Hebrew.* SSN 21. Assen: Van Gorcum.
Holes, Clive
1995   The structure and function of parallelism and repetition in spoken Arabic: A sociolinguistic study. *JSS* 40: 57–81.
Holmstedt, Robert D.
2002   *The relative clause in Biblical Hebrew: A linguistic analysis.* Ph.D. diss. University of Wisconsin.
2003   Adjusting our focus. Review essay on Shimasaki 2002. *HS* 44: 203–15.
2005   Word order in the book of Proverbs. Pp. 135–54 in *Seeking out the wisdom of the ancients: Essays offered to honor Michael V. Fox on the occasion of his*

sixty-fifth birthday, ed. K. G. Friebel, D. R. Magary, and R. L. Troxel. Winona Lake, IN: Eisenbrauns.

Hoop, Raymond de
2003   Genesis 49 revisited: The poetic structure of Jacob's Testament and the ancient Versions. Pp. 1–32 in Korpel and Oesch 2003.

Hopper, Paul J.
1979   Aspect and foregrounding in discourse. Pp. 213–41 in Givón 1979.

Horn, Laurence R.
1989   *A natural history of negation*. Chicago : University of Chicago Press.

Hornkohl, Aaron
2003   *The Pragmatics of the X + Verb Structure in the Hebrew of Genesis*. M.A. thesis. Hebrew University.

Huddleston, Rodney D.
1984   *Introduction to the grammar of English*. Cambridge Textbooks in Linguistics. Cambridge: Cambridge University Press.

Huddleston, Rodney D., and Pullum, Geoffrey K.
2002   *The Cambridge grammar of the English language*. Cambridge: Cambridge University Press.

Huehnergard, John
1985   Asseverative **la* and hypothetical **lu/law* in Semitic. *JAOS* 103: 569–93.

Hurvitz, Avi
1972   בין לשון ללשון: לתולדות לשון המקרא בימי בית שני [*The transition period in Biblical Hebrew: A study in post-exilic Hebrew and its implications for the dating of Psalms*]. Jerusalem: Bialik Insititute.
1982   *A linguistic study of the relationship between the priestly source and the book of Ezekiel: A new approach to an old problem*. Cahiers de la Revue Biblique 20. Paris: Gabalda.

Ilie, Cornelia
1994   *What else can I tell you? A pragmatic study of English rhetorical questions as discursive and argumentative acts*. Stockholm Studies in English 82. Stockholm: Almqvist & Wiksell.

Jackendoff, Ray
1972   *Semantic interpretation in generative grammar*. Studies in Linguistics Series 2. Cambridge: MIT Press.

Jacobs, Louis
1972   The *qal va-ḥomer* argument in the Old Testament. *BSOAS* 35: 221–27.

Jakobsen, Roman
1967   Linguistics and poetics. Pp. 296–322 in Chatman and Levin 1967.

Johnstone, Barbara
1991   *Repetition in Arabic discourse: Paradigms, syntagms, and the ecology of language*. Pragmatics and Beyond n.s. 18. Amsterdam: Benjamins.

Jong, Jan de
1981   On the treatment of focus phenomena in Functional Grammar. Pp. 89–115 in Hoekstra et al. 1981.

Jongeling, Bastiaan
1980   Some remarks on the beginning of Genesis I, 2. *FolOr* 21: 27–32.

Jongeling, K.
1991   On the VSO character of Hebrew. Pp. 103–11 in Jongeling et al. 1991.
Jongeling, K.; Murre-Van den Berg, H. L.; and van Rompay, L., eds.
1991   *Studies in Hebrew and Aramaic syntax: Presented to Professsor J. Hoftijzer on the occasion of his sixty-fifth birthday.* SSLL 17. Leiden: Brill.
Joosten, Jan
1989   The predicative participle in Biblical Hebrew. *ZAH* 2: 128–59.
1992   Biblical Hebrew "wᵉqāṭāl" and Syriac "hwā qāṭel" expressing repetition in the past. *ZAH* 5: 1–14.
2002   Do the finite verbal forms in Biblical Hebrew express aspect? *JANES* 29: 49–70.
Joüon, Paul
1947   *Grammaire de l'hébreu biblique.* 2nd ed. Rome: Pontifical Biblical Institute.
1991   *A grammar of Biblical Hebrew*, trans. and rev. T. Muraoka. 2 vols. Subsidia Biblica 14. Rome: Pontifical Biblical Institute.
Karttunen, Lauri
1974   Presupposition and linguistic context. *TheorLing* 1: 181–94. Repr., pp. 406–15 in Davis 1991.
Keenan, Elinor Ochs, and Schieffelin, Bambi B.
1976   Topic as a discourse notion. Pp. 337–84 in Li 1976.
Khan, Geoffrey
1988   *Studies in Semitic syntax.* London Oriental Series 38. Oxford: Oxford University Press.
Kinberg, Naphtali
1985   Adverbial clauses as topics in Arabic: Adverbial clauses in frontal position separated from their main clauses. *Jerusalem Studies in Arabic and Islam* 6: 353–416.
Kintsch, Walter
1998   *Comprehension: A paradigm for cognition.* Cambridge: Cambridge University Press.
Knott, Alistair
2001   Semantic and pragmatic relations and their intended effects. Pp. 127–51 in Sanders et al. 2001.
Kogut, Simcha
1986   On the meaning and syntactical status of הנה in Biblical Hebrew. Pp. 133–54 in *Studies in Bible 1986*, ed. Sara Japhet. Scripta Hierosolymitana 31. Jerusalem: Magnes.
1996   כיצד – למיעוט 'רק 'טעמי [The excluding biblical רק: Its syntactical usages as reflected in its accentuation]. *Leš* 59: 203–6.
König, Friedrich Eduard
1897   *Historisch-kritischen Lehrgebaudes des hebräischen*, part 3: *Historisch-comparative Syntax der hebräischen Sprache.* Leipzig: Hinrichs.
Korpel, Marjo C. A., and Oesch, Josef M., eds.
2003   *Unit delimitation in Biblical Hebrew and Northwest Semitic.* Pericope: Scripture as Written and Read in Antiquity 4. Assen: Van Gorcum.

Kotzé, Robert J.
1989   The circumstantial sentence—a catch-them-all term? A study in sentence relationships in 1 Samuel 1–12. *JNSL* 15: 109–26.
Kropat, Arno
1909   *Die Syntax des Autors der Chronik verglichen mit der seiner Quellen: Ein Beitrag zur historischen Syntax des Hebraeischen.* Beihefte zur Zeitschrift für die alttestamentliche Wissenschaft 16. Giessen: Alfred Topelmann.
Kugel, James
1981   *The idea of biblical poetry: Parallelism and its history.* New Haven, CT: Yale University Press.
Kuno, Susumu
1972   Functional sentence perspective: A case study from Japanese and English. *LingInq* 3: 269–320.
Kuroda, S.-Y.
1972   The categorical and the thetic judgment: Evidence from Japanese syntax. *Foundations of Language* 9: 153–85.
Kutscher, Edward Yechezkel
1982   *A history of the Hebrew language*, ed. Raphael Kutscher. Jerusalem: Magnes.
Kuzar, Ron
1989   מבנה המסר של המשפט בעברית ישראלית [*Message structure of the sentence in Israeli-Hebrew*]. Ph.D. diss. Hebrew University.
2002   תבנית החג"ם הפשוטה בלשון המיוצגת כמדוברת [The simple impersonal construction in texts represented as colloquial Hebrew]. Pp. 329–52 in מדברים עברית: לחקר הלשון המדוברת והשונות הלשונית בישראל [*Speaking Hebrew: Studies in the spoken language and in linguistic variation in Israel*], ed. Shlomo Izre'el and Margalit Mendelson. Teudah 18. Tel Aviv: Tel Aviv University Press.
Labov, William
1972   *Language in the inner city: Studies in the Black English vernacular.* Philadelphia: University of Pennsylvania Press.
Labuschagne, Casper J.
1966   The emphasizing particle "gam" and its connotations. Pp. 193–203 in *Studia Biblica et Semitica: Theodoro Christiano Vriezen qui munere professoris theologiae per XXV annos functus est, ab amicis, collegis, discipulis dedicata.* Wageningen: Veenman.
1973   The particles הן and הנה. Pp. 1–14 in *Syntax and meaning: Studies in Hebrew syntax and biblical exegesis*, ed. C. J. Labuschagne et al. OTS 18. Leiden: Brill.
Ladd, D. Robert
1980   *The structure of intonational meaning: Evidence from English.* Bloomington: Indiana University Press.
Lambdin, Thomas O.
1971   *Introduction to Biblical Hebrew.* New York: Scribners.

Lambert, Mayer
1972   *Traité de grammaire hébraïque*, ed. Gérard E. Weil. 2nd ed. Publications de l'Institut de Recherche et d'Histoire des Textes: Section Biblique et Massoré-tique: Collection Massorah Series 3. Hildesheim: Gerstenberg.

Lambrecht, Knud
1994   *Information structure and sentence form: Topic, focus, and the mental repre-sentations of discourse referents*. Cambridge Studies in Linguistics 71. Cam-bridge: Cambridge University Press.
2000   When subjects behave like objects: An analysis of the merging of S and O in sentence-focus constructions across languages. *Studies in Language* 24: 611–82.

Lambrecht, Knud, and Michaelis, Laura A.
1998   Sentence accent in information questions: Default and projection. *Linguistics and Philosophy* 21: 477–544.

Lerner, Yoel
1975   עיון מחודש בשאלת ההבחנה בין מושא לתיאור [A reexamination of the question of the distinction between complement and adverbial]. *Leš* 40: 148–51.

Levinsohn, Stephen H.
1987   *Textual connections in Acts*. SBLMS 31. Atlanta: Scholars Press.
1990   Unmarked and marked instances of topicalization in Hebrew. *Work Papers of SIL, University of North Dakota Session* 34: 21–33.

Levinson, Stephen C.
1983   *Pragmatics*. Cambridge Textbooks in Linguistics. Cambridge: Cambridge University Press.

Lewis, David
1979   Scorekeeping in a language game. *Journal of Philosophical Language* 8: 339–59. Repr., pp. 416–27 in Davis 1991.

Li, Charles
1976   *Subject and topic*. New York: Academic Press.
1986   Direct speech and indirect speech: A functional study. Pp. 29–45 in Coulmas 1986.

Li, Charles N., and Thompson, Sandra A.
1976   Subject and topic: A new typology of language. Pp. 459–89 in Li 1976.

Lode, Lars
1984   Postverbal word order in Biblical Hebrew: Structure and function. *Semitics* 9: 113–64.
1988   Postverbal word order in Biblical Hebrew: Structure and function part 2. *Se-mitics* 10: 24–39.

Longacre, Robert E.
1979   The paragraph as a grammatical unit. Pp. 115–34 in Givón 1979.
1982   Discourse typology in relation to language typology. Pp. 457–84 in *Text processing: Text analysis and generation, text typology and attribution. Pro-ceedings of Nobel symposium 51*, ed. Sture Allen. Data Linguistica 16. Stock-holm: Almqvist & Wiksell.
1989   Two hypotheses regarding text generation and analysis. *Discourse Processes* 12: 413–60.

1992   The analysis of preverbal nouns in Biblical Hebrew narrative: Some overriding concerns. *JTT* 5: 208–24.

1994   *Weqatal* forms in Biblical Hebrew prose. Pp. 50–98 in Bergen 1994.

1995   Left shifts in strongly VSO languages. Pp. 331–54 in Downing and Noonan 1995.

2003   *Joseph: A story of divine providence. A text theoretical and textlinguistic analysis of Genesis 37 and 39–48.* 2nd ed. Winona Lake, IN: Eisenbrauns.

Lowery, Kirk E.

1999   Relative definiteness and the verbless clause. Pp. 251–72 in Miller 1999.

Lundbom, Jack R.

1999   *Jeremiah 1–20: A new translation with introduction and commentary.* Anchor Bible 21a. New York: Doubleday.

Lunn, Nicholas P.

2006   *Word-order variation in Biblical Hebrew poetry: Differentiating pragmatics and poetics.* Paternoster Biblical Monographs. Milton Keynes: Paternoster.

Lyons, John

1977   *Semantics.* 2 vols. Cambridge: Cambridge University Press.

Macdonald, J.

1975   Some distinctive characteristics of Israelite spoken Hebrew. *BibOr* 32: 162–75.

Malbim, Meir Loeb ben Jeḥiel Michael

1964   לב מלכים [Heart of Kings]. In נביאים וכתובים: מקראות גדולות עם פירוש מלבים [*The Prophets and Writings*], vol. 3: מלכים [*Kings*]. Jerusalem. Based on the 1897–99 Lublin ed.

1973   אילת השחר [Hind of the dawn]. In חמשה חומשי תורה עם תרגום אונקלוס, פירש״י, שפתי חכמים, בעל הטורים והתורה והמצוה [*The Pentateuch*], vol. 3: ויקרא [*Leviticus*]. Jerusalem. Based on the 1880 Warsaw ed.

Mali, Uziel

1983   לשון השיחה בנביאים ראשונים [*The language of conversation in the former prophets*]. Ph.D. diss. Hebrew University.

Mallinson, Graham, and Blake, Barry J.

1981   *Language typology: Cross-linguistic studies in syntax.* North-Holland Linguistic Series 46. New York: North-Holland.

Martin, W. J.

1968–69   "Dischronologized" narrative in the Old Testament. Pp. 179–86 in *Congress volume: Rome 1968.* VTSup 17. Leiden: Brill.

Mathesius, Vilem

1975   *A functional analysis of present day English on a general linguistic basis*, ed. Josef Vachek. Janua Linguarum Series Practica 208. The Hague: Mouton.

Matthews, P. H.

1981   *Syntax.* Cambridge Textbooks in Linguistics. Cambridge: Cambridge University Press.

McCarthy, Dennis J.

1980   The uses of *wᵉhinnēh* in Biblical Hebrew. *Bib* 61: 330–42.

McCawley, James D.

1970   English as a VSO language. *Lang* 46: 286–99.

McEvenue, Sean E.
1971   *The narrative style of the priestly writer.* Analecta Biblica 50. Rome: Pontifical Biblical Institute.
1974   The style of a building instruction. *Sem* 4:1–9.

McNally, Louise
1998   On the linguistic encoding of information packaging instructions. Pp. 161–83 in Culicover and McNally 1998.

Merwe, Christo H. J. van der
1989   The vague term "emphasis." *JSem* 1: 118–32.
1990   *The old Hebrew particle 'gam': A syntactic-semantic description of gam in Gn–2Kg.* Philosophische Fakultat. Arbeiten zu Text und Sprache im Alten Testament 34. Munchener Universitatsschriften. St. Ottilien: EOS.
1991   The function of word order in Old Hebrew, with special reference to cases where a syntagmeme precedes a verb in Joshua. *JNSL* 17: 129–44.
1999a   The elusive biblical Hebrew term "vayehi": A perspective in terms of its syntax, semantics, and pragmatics in 1 Samuel. *HS* 40: 83–14.
1999b   Explaining fronting in Biblical Hebrew. *JNSL* 25: 173–86.
1999c   Towards a better understanding of Biblical Hebrew word order. Review essay of Gross 1996. *JNSL* 25: 277–300.

Merwe, Christo H. J. van der, and Talstra, Eep
2002–3 Biblical Hebrew word order: The interface of information structure and formal features. *ZAH* 15–16: 68–107.

Merwe, Christo H. J. van der; Naude, Jackie A.; and Kroeze, Jan H.
1999   *A Biblical Hebrew reference grammar.* Biblical Languages: Hebrew 3. Sheffield: Sheffield Academic Press.

Meyer, Rudolph, ed.
1972   *Hebräische Grammatik*, vol 3: *Satzlehre.* 3rd ed. Sammlung Göschen 5765. Berlin: de Gruyter.

Miller, Cynthia L.
2003   *The representation of speech in Biblical Hebrew narrative: A linguistic analysis.* Harvard Semitic Monographs 55. Atlanta: Scholars Press.

Miller, Cynthia L., ed.
1999   *The verbless clause in Biblical Hebrew: Linguistic approaches.* Linguistic Studies in Ancient West Semitic 1. Winona Lake, IN: Eisenbrauns.

Mirsky, Aharon
1977   Stylistic device for conclusion in Hebrew. *Sem* 5: 9–23.
1999   סגנון עברי [*Hebrew style*]. Jerusalem: Bialik Institute.

Mithun, Marianne
1992   Is basic word order universal? Pp. 15–61 in Payne 1992.

Moshavi, Adina
2006   The discourse functions of object/adverbial-fronting in Biblical Hebrew. Pp. 231–45 in *Biblical Hebrew in its northwest Semitic setting: Typological and historical perspectives*, ed. Steven E. Fassberg and Avi Hurvitz. Publication of the Institute for Advanced Studies 1. Jerusalem: Magnes / Winona Lake, IN: Eisenbrauns.

2007a   הטופיקליציה עברית של המקרא [Topicalization in Biblical Hebrew]. *Leš* 69: 7–30.

2007b   הלא as a discourse marker of justification in Biblical Hebrew. *HS* 48: 171–86.

2007c   Syntactic evidence for a clausal adverb הלא in Biblical Hebrew. *JNSL* 33: 51–63.

2009   הקדמת הפוקוס בעברית מקראית [Focus preposing in Biblical Hebrew]. *Leš* 71: 35–55.

forthcoming   Rhetorical question or assertion? The pragmatics of הלא in Biblical Hebrew. *JANES* 32.

Muilenberg, James
1953   A study in Hebrew rhetoric: Repetition and style. Pp. 97–111 in *Congress volume: Copenhagen, 1953*. VTSup 1. Leiden: Brill.

1961   The linguistic and rhetorical usages of the particle כי in the Old Testament. *HUCA* 32: 135–60.

Müller, August
1888   *Outlines of Hebrew syntax*, ed. and trans. James Robertson. Glasgow: Maclehose. [Translation of Part 3 of *Hebräische Schulgrammatik*. Halle: Max Niemeyer. 1878]

Munro, Pamela
1982   On the transitivity of "say" verbs. Pp. 301–18 in *Studies in transitivity*, ed. Paul J. Hopper and Sandra A. Thompson. Syntax and Semantics 15. New York: Academic Press.

Muraoka, T.
1979   On verb complementation in Biblical Hebrew. *VT* 29: 425–35.

1985   *Emphatic words and structures in biblical Hebrew*. Jerusalem: Magnes.

1990   הפסוק השמני בלשון המקרא המאוחרת ובלשון חז״ל [The nominal clause in late Biblical Hebrew and Mishnaic Hebrew]. *Language Studies* 4: 219–52.

1991   The Biblical Hebrew nominal clause with a prepositional phrase. Pp. 143–51 in Jongeling et al. 1991.

Myhill, John
1985   Pragmatic and categorial correlates of VS word order. *Lingua* 66: 177–200.

1992a   Word order and temporal sequencing. Pp. 265–78 in Payne 1992.

1992b   *Typological discourse analysis: Quantitative approaches to the study of linguistic function*. Oxford: Blackwell.

1995   Non-emphatic fronting in Biblical Hebrew. *TheorLing* 21/2–3: 93–144.

Myhill, John, and Xing, Zhiqun
1993   The discourse functions of Patient fronting: A comparative study of Biblical Hebrew and Chinese. *Ling* 31: 25–57.

Naudé, Jacobus A.
1990   A syntactic analysis of dislocations in Biblical Hebrew. *JNSL* 16: 115–30.

1999   Syntactic aspects of co-ordinate subjects with independent personal pronouns. *JNSL* 25: 75–99.

Niccacci, Alviero
1987   A neglected point of Hebrew syntax: Yiqtol and position in the sentence. *Liber Annus* 37: 7–19.

1990   *The syntax of the verb in Classical Hebrew prose*, trans. W. G. E. Watson. JSOTSup 86. Sheffield: JSOT Press.

1994   The Stele of Mesha and the Bible: Verbal system and narrativity. *Or* 63: 226–48.

1997   Basic facts and theory of the Biblical Hebrew verb system in prose. Pp. 167–202 in Wolde 1997.

Nir, Raphal, and Roeh, Itzhak

1984   היבטים רטוריים של מיקוד במשפטי-פתיחה של פריטי חדשות ברדיו [Rhetorical aspects of topicalization in opening sentences of radio news items]. *Balšanut Ivrit Ḥapašit* 22: 25–45.

O'Connor, M.

1980   *Hebrew verse structure*. Winona Lake, IN: Eisenbrauns.

2002   Discourse linguistics and the study of Biblical Hebrew. Pp. 17–42 in *Congress volume: Basel 2001*, ed. A. Lemaire. VTSup 92. Leiden: Brill.

Oosten, Jeanne van

1985   *The nature of subjects, topics and agents: A cognitive explanation*. Bloomington: Indiana University Linguistics Club.

Paran, Meir

1989   דרכי הסגנון הכוהני בתורה: דגמים, שימושי לשון, מבנים [*Forms of the Priestly style in the Pentateuch: Patterns, linguistic usages, syntactic structures*]. Publication of the Perry Foundation for Bbiblical Research in the Hebrew University of Jerusalem. Jerusalem: Magnes.

Partee, Barbara H.

1973   The syntax and semantics of quotation. Pp. 410–18 in *A Festschrift for Morris Halle*, ed. Stephen R. Anderson and Paul Kiparsky. New York: Holt, Rinehart, & Winston.

Payne, Doris L., ed.

1992   *Pragmatics of word order flexibility*. TSL 22. Amsterdam: Benjamins.

Payne, Geoffrey

1991   Functional sentence perspective: Theme in Biblical Hebrew. *JSOT* 1: 62–82.

Peretz, Yitzhak

1967   משפט הזיקה בעברית לכל תקופותיה [*The relative clause*]. Dvir: Tel Aviv.

Polak, Frank H.

1999   The oral and the written: Syntax, stylistics and the development of biblical prose narrative. *JANES* 26: 59–105.

2001   The style of the dialogue in biblical prose narrative. *JANES* 28: 53–95.

2003   Style is more than the person: Sociolinguistics, literary culture and the distinction between written and oral narrative. Pp. 38–103 in Young 2003.

Polinsky, Maria

1999   Review essay on Lambrecht 1994. *Lang* 75: 567–82.

Polzin, Robert

1976   *Late Biblical Hebrew: Toward an historical typology of Biblical Hebrew prose*. Harvard Semitic Monographs 12. Missoula, MT: Scholars Press

Pope, Emily N.

1972   *Questions and answers in English*. Ph.D. diss. Massachusets Institute of Technology.

Postal, Paul M.
  1971   *Cross-over phenomena.* Transatlantic Series in Linguistics. New York: Holt, Rinehart, & Winston.
Prince, Ellen F.
  1981   Toward a taxonomy of given-new information. Pp. 223–55 in *Radical pragmatics*, ed. Peter Cole. New York: Academic Press.
  1985   Fancy syntax and "shared knowledge." *JPrag* 9: 65–81.
  1986   On the syntactic marking of presupposed open propositions. Pp. 208–22 in *Papers from the parasession on pragmatics and grammatical theory, at the twenty-second regional meeting, Chicago Linguistic Society*, ed. Anne M. Farley, Peter T. Farley, and Karl-Erik McCullough. Chicago: Chicago Linguistic Society.
  1988   On pragmatic change: The borrowing of discourse functions. *JPrag* 12: 505–18.
  1992   The ZPG letter: Subjects, definiteness and information-status. Pp. 295–325 in *Discourse description: Diverse linguistic analyses of a fund-raising text*, ed. William C. Mann and Sandra A. Thompson. Pragmatics and Beyond n.s. 16. Amsterdam: Benjamins.
  1998   On the limits of syntax, with reference to left-dislocation and topicalization. Pp. 281–302 in Culicover and McNally 1998.
Qimron, Elisha
  1998   כתובות עבריות חדשות וייחודי לשונן [New Hebrew inscriptions: Their linguistic contribution]. *Leš* 61: 181–85.
Quirk, Randolph; Greenbaum, Sidney; Leech, Geoffrey; and Svartvik, Jan
  1985   *A comprehensive grammar of the English language.* London: Longman.
Ravid, Dorit
  1977   מספר היבטים של בעית סדר המרכיבים בעברית ישראלית מודרנית [Several aspects of the problem of the order of elements in general Israeli Hebrew]. *Balšanut Ivrit Ḥapašit* 11: 1–45.
Reckendorf, H.
  1895–98 *Die syntaktischen Verhaltnisse des Arabischen.* 2 vols. Leiden: Brill.
Redeker, Gisela
  1990   Ideational and pragmatic markers of discourse structure. *JPrag* 14: 367–81.
Regt, L. J. de
  1988   *A parametric model for syntactic studies of a textual corpus, demonstrated on the Hebrew of Deuteronomy 1–30.* SSN 24. Assen: Van Gorcum.
  1991   Word order in different clause types in Deuteronomy 1–30. Pp. 152–71 in Jongeling, Murre-van den Berg, and van Rompay 1991.
  2006   Hebrew syntactic inversions and their literary equivalence in English: Robert Alter's translations of Genesis and 1 and 2 Samuel. *JSOT* 30: 287–314.
Reinhart, Tanya
  1981   Pragmatics and linguistics: An analysis of sentence topics. *Phil* 27: 53–94. Repr., Bloomington: Indiana University Linguistics Club, 1982.
  1984   Principles of gestalt perception in the temporal organization of narrative texts. *Ling* 22: 779–809.

Rendsburg, Gary
1980   Late Biblical Hebrew and the date of P. *JANES* 12: 65–80.
1986   *The redaction of Genesis*. Winona Lake, IN: Eisenbrauns.
1990   *Diglossia in ancient Hebrew*. American Oriental Series 72. New Haven, CT: American Oriental Society.
1991   The strata of Biblical Hebrew. *JNSL* 17: 81–99.

Revell, E. J.
1989a   The conditioning of word order in verbless clauses in Biblical Hebrew. *JSS* 34: 1–24.
1989b   The system of the verb in standard Biblical prose. *HUCA* 60: 1–37.
1992   Masoretic Text. Pp. 598–99 in vol. 4 of *The Anchor Bible dictionary*, ed. David N. Freedman et al. New York: Doubleday.
1999   Thematic continuity and the conditioning of word order in verbless clauses. Pp. 297–319 in Miller 1999.

Rochemont, Michael S.
1986   *Focus in generative grammar*. SIGLA 4. Amsterdam: Benjamins.

Rooker, Mark F.
1990a   Ezekiel and the typology of Biblical Hebrew. *HAR* 12: 133–55.
1990b   *Biblical Hebrew in transition: The language of the book of Ezekiel*. JSOTSup 90. Sheffield: JSOT Press.

Rosén, Haim B.
1965   על משפטים חסרי-פועל בעברית המקראית [On some types of verbless sentences in Biblical Hebrew]. Pp. 167–73 in *Third World Congress of Jewish studies: Jerusalem, 25th July–1st August 1961*. Jerusalem: World Union of Jewish Studies.
1977   *Contemporary Hebrew*. Trends in Linguistics: State-of-the-art Reports 11. The Hague: Mouton.
1982   אספקטים בחקר סדר חלקי המשפט בעברית הישראלית הכתובה [Aspects in the study of sentence order in literary Israeli Hebrew]. Pp. 43–49 in *Proceedings of the eighth world congress of Jewish studies, Jerusalem, August 16–21, 1981*, vol. 4: *Division D: The Hebrew language and languages of the Jews; Jewish folklore and art*. Jerusalem: World Union of Jewish Studies.

Rosenbaum, Michael
1997   *Word-order variation in Isaiah 40–55: A functional perspective*. SSN 35. Assen: Van Gorcum.

Ross, John R.
1967   *Constraints on variables in syntax*. Ph.D. diss. Massachusets Institute of Technology. Repr., Bloomington: Indiana University Linguistics Club, 1968.

Sáenz-Badillos, Angel
1993   *A history of the Hebrew language*, trans. John Elwolde. Cambridge: Cambridge University Press.

Sanders, Ted J.
1997   Semantic and pragmatic sources of coherence: On the categorization of coherence relations in context. *DiscProc* 24: 119–47.

Sanders, Ted J., and Noordman, Leo G.
   2000   The role of coherence relations and their linguistic markers in text processing. *DiscProc* 29: 37–60.
Sanders, Ted; Schilperoord, Joost; and Spooren, Wilbert, eds.
   2001   *Text representation: Linguistic and psycholinguistic aspects.* Human Cognitive Processing 8. Amsterdam: Benjamins.
Sanders, Ted, and Spooren, Wilbert
   2001   Text representation as an interface between language and its users. Pp. 1–25 in Sanders et al. 2001.
Sanders, Ted J; Spooren, Wilbert P.; and Noordman, Leo G.
   1992   Toward a taxonomy of coherence relations. *DiscProc* 15: 1–35.
Sappan, Raphael
   1976   הכיאזם בשירת המקרא [Chiasmus in Biblical poetry]. *Beit Mikra* 21: 534–39.
   1981   הייחוד התחבירי של לשון השירה המקראית [*The typical features of the syntax of biblical poetry in its classical period*]. Jerusalem: Kiryat Sefer.
Sarna, Nahum M.
   1989   *Genesis: The traditional Hebrew text with the new JPS translation.* JPS Torah Commentary. Philadelphia: Jewish Publication Society.
Savran, George W.
   1988   *Telling and retelling: Quotation in Biblical narrative.* Indiana Studies in Biblical Literature. Bloomington: Indiana University Press.
Schiffrin, Deborah
   1987   *Discourse Markers.* Studies in Interactional Sociolinguistics 5. Cambridge: Cambridge University Press.
Schlesinger, K.
   1953   Zur Wortfolge im hebräischen Verbalsatz. *VT* 3: 381–90.
Schmerling, Susan F.
   1976   *Aspects of English sentence.* Austin: University of Texas Press.
Schmidt-Radefeldt, Jürgen
   1977   On so-called "rhetorical" questions. *JPrag* 1: 376–77.
Schoors, Antoon
   1981   The particle "kî." Pp. 240–76 in *Remembering all the way: A collection of Old Testament studies published on the occasion of the fortieth anniversary of the Oudtestamentisch Werkgezelschap in Nederland*, ed. B. Albrektson. OTS 21. Leiden: Brill.
Schourup, Lawrence
   1999   Discourse markers: Tutorial overview. *Lingua* 107: 227–65.
Selkirk, Elisabeth O.
   1995   Sentence prosody: Intonation, stress and phrasing. Pp. 550–69 in *The handbook of phonological theory*, ed. John A. Goldsmith. Blackwell Handbooks in Linguistics 1. Cambridge: Blackwell.
Shimasaki, Katsuomi
   2002   *Focus structure in Biblical Hebrew: A study of word order and information structure.* Bethesda, MD: CDL.

Shopen, Timothy
  1985   *Language typology and syntactic description*. 3 vols. Cambridge: Cambridge
          University Press.
Shulman, Ahouva
  1996   *The use of modal verb forms in Biblical Hebrew prose*. Ph.D. diss. University
          of Toronto.
Siewierska, Anna
  1988   *Word order rules*. Croom Helm Linguistics Series. London: Helm.
  1991   *Functional grammar*. Linguistic Theory Guides. London: Routledge.
Singer, Murray
  1990   *Psychology of language: An introduction to sentence and discourse pro-
          cesses*. Hillsdale: Erlbaum.
Sivan, Daniel, and Schniedewind, William
  1993   Letting your "yes" be "no" in ancient Israel: A study of the asseverative לֹא
          and הֲלֹא. *JSS* 38: 209–26.
Skinner, John
  1930   *A critical and exegetical commentary on Genesis*. 2nd ed. International Criti-
          cal Commentary. Edinburgh: T. & T. Clark.
Snyman, F. P. J.
  2004   *The scope of negative lōʾ in Biblical Hebrew*. Acta Academica Supplemen-
          tum 3. Blomfontein: Acta Academica.
Snyman, F. P. J., and Naudé, J. A.
  2003   Sentence and constituent-negation in Biblical Hebrew. *JSem* 12: 237–67.
Stalnaker, Robert C.
  1974   Pragmatic presuppositions. Pp. 197–213 in *Semantics and philosophy*, ed.
          Milton K. Munitz and Peter K. Unger. New York: New York University Press.
          Repr., pp. 471–81 in Davis 1991.
Stec, D. M.
  1987   The use of *hēn* in conditional sentences. *VT* 37: 478–86.
Steiner, Richard C.
  1979   Review of Blau 1977. *AfroLing* 6: 5–10.
  1992   A colloquialism in Jer. 5:13 from the ancestor of Mishnaic Hebrew. *JSS* 37:
          11–26.
  1997   Ancient Hebrew. Pp. 145–73 in *The Semitic Languages*, ed. Robert Hetzron.
          Routledge Language Family Descriptions. London: Routledge.
  1998   Saadia vs. Rashi: On the shift from meaning-maximalism to meaning-mini-
          malism in medieval biblical lexicology. *JQR* 88: 213–58.
  2000   Does the Biblical Hebrew conjunction -וֹ have many meanings, one meaning,
          or no meaning at all? *JBL* 119: 249–67.
Sweetser, Eve
  1990   *From etymology to pragmatics: Metaphorical and cultural aspects of seman-
          tic structure*. Cambridge Studies in Linguistics 54. Cambridge: Cambridge
          University Press.
Taglicht, Josef
  1984   *Message and emphasis: On focus and scope in English*. English Language
          Series 15. London: Longman.

Tannen, Deborah
1986   Introducting constructed dialogue in Greek and American conversational and
        literary narrative. Pp. 311–32 in Coulmas 1986.
Thompson, Sandra A.
1978   Modern English from a typological point of view: Some implications of the
        function of word order. *LingBer* 54: 19–35.
Tov, Emanuel
1992   *Textual criticism of the Hebrew Bible*. Minneapolis: Fortress. [Revised and
        enlarged edition of ביקורת נוסח המקרא: פרק מבוא. The Biblical Encyclopedia
        Library 4. Jerusalem: Bialik Institute, 1989]
Ulrich, Eugene
2003   Impressions and intuition: Sense divisions in ancient manuscripts of Isaiah.
        Pp. 279–307 in Korpel and Oesch 2003.
Vallduví, Enric
1992   *The informational component*. Outstanding Dissertations in Linguistics. New
        York: Garland.
Vallduví, Enric, and Engdahl, Elisabet
1996   The linguistic realization of information packaging. *Ling* 34: 459–519.
Vallduví, Enric, and Vilkuna, Maria
1998   On rheme and contrast. Pp. 79–108 in Culicover and McNally 1998.
Walker, Marilyn A.; Joshi, Aravind K.; and Prince, Ellen F.
1998a   Centering in naturally occurring discourse: An overview. Pp. 1–28 in Walker,
        Joshi, and Prince 1998b.
1998b   *Centering Theory in Discourse*. Oxford: Clarendon.
Waltke, Bruce K., and O'Connor, M.
1990   *An introduction to Biblical Hebrew syntax*. Winona Lake, IN: Eisenbrauns.
Ward, Gregory L., and Prince, Ellen F.
1991   On the topicalization of indefinite NPs. *JPrag* 16: 167–77.
Watson, Wilfred G. E.
1984   *Classical Hebrew poetry: A guide to its techniques*. JSOTSup 26. Sheffield:
        JSOT Press.
Williams, Ronald J.
1976   *Hebrew syntax: An outline*. 2nd ed. Toronto: University of Toronto Press.
Wimsatt, W. K.
1967   Style as meaning. Pp. 362–73 in Chatman and Levin 1967.
Winther-Nielsen, Nicolai
1992   "In the beginning" of Biblical Hebrew discourse: Genesis 1:1 and the fronted
        time expression. Pp. 67–80 in *Language in context: Essays for Robert E.
        Longacre*, ed. Shin ja J. Hwang and William R. Merrifield. SIL and the Uni-
        versity of Texas at Arlington Publications in Linguistics 107. Arlington: SIL
        and the University of Texas at Arlington.
Wolde, Ellen van
1997a   Linguistic motivation and Biblical exegesis. Pp. 21–50 in Wolde 1997b.
1997b   *Narrative syntax and the Hebrew Bible: Papers of the Tilburg conference
        1996*. Biblical Interpretation Series 29. Leiden: Brill.

Young, Ian, ed.
2003   *Biblical Hebrew: Studies in chronology and typology.* JSOTSup 369. New York: Continuum.
Zatelli, Ida
1994   Analysis of lexemes from a conversational prose text: "hnh" as signal of a performative utterance in 1 Sam. 25:41 *ZAH* 7: 5–11.
Zevit, Ziony
1982   Converging lines of evidence bearing on the date of P. *ZAW* 94: 481–511.
1998   *The anterior construction in classical Hebrew.* SBLMS 50. Atlanta: Scholars Press.
Zewi, Tamar
1992   ההסבות התחביריות הכרוכות במבנה הפונקציונלי של המשפט בעברית מקראית [*Syntactical modifications reflecting the functional structure of the sentence in Biblical Hebrew*]. Ph.D. diss. Hebrew University.
1994   The nominal sentence in Biblical Hebrew. Pp. 145–67 in *Semitic and Cushitic Studies*, ed. Gideon Goldenberg and Shlomo Raz. Weisbaden: Harrassowitz.
1996   The particles הנה and והנה in Biblical Hebrew. *HS* 37: 21–37.
1997   On similar syntactical roles of *inūma* in El Amarna and והנה, הנה, and הן in Biblical Hebrew. *JANES* 25: 71–86.
1999   Interrupted syntactical structures in Biblical Hebrew. *ZAH* 12: 83–95.
2004   Review of Heller 2004. *HS* 45: 298–302.
Ziv, Yael
1988   Word order in children's literature: FSP and markedness. Pp. 123–44 in *The Prague School and its legacy in linguistics, literature, semiotics, folklore, and the arts*, ed. Yishai Tobin. Linguistic and Literary Studies in Eastern Europe 27. Amsterdam: Benjamins.
1996a   Discourse grounding: A constraint on preposing. Pp. 168–93 in *IATL 3: The proceedings of the eleventh annual Conference, Tel Aviv University 1995 and of the Workshop on Discourse, the Technion 1996*, ed. Edit Doron and Shuly Wintner. N.p.
1996b   Review of Lambrecht 1994. *JPrag* 26: 699–710.

Index of Authors

Index of Scripture

CPSIA information can be obtained
at www.ICGtesting.com
Printed in the USA
LVHW111648271220
675126LV00004B/87